ANDEAN CULTURE HISTORY

American Museum Science Books are published for The American Museum of Natural History by The Natural History Press. Directed by a joint editorial board made up of members of the staff of the Museum and Doubleday, this series is an extension of the Museum's scientific and educational activities, making available to the student and general reader inexpensive, up-to-date, and reliable books in the life and earth sciences, including anthropology and astronomy. The Natural History Press is a division of Doubleday and Company, Inc., and has its editorial offices at The American Museum of Natural History, Central Park West at 79th Street, New York 24, New York, and its business offices at 501 Franklin Avenue, Garden City, New York.

WENDELL CLARK BENNETT was born in Marion, Indiana, on August 17, 1905. He graduated from the University of Chicago in 1927, receiving his M.A. and Ph.D. from this same institution. While still at the University of Chicago, Dr. Bennett went to Hawaii and did the first field work on the archaeology of Kauai. In 1930 and 1931 he worked in northern Mexico and spent much of the next fifteen years in the field in South America.

He taught at the University of Wisconsin and at Yale University where he was chairman of the Department of Anthropology until the time of his death in 1953.

Dr. Bennett was the author of many books and articles including *Ancient Art of the Andes*; he contributed several chapters to the *Handbook of South American Indians* published by the Bureau of American Ethnology. He was a Research Associate of the Peabody Museum, a Fellow of Pierson College, and during World War II was the secretary of the Joint Committee on Latin American Anthropology. Dr. Bennett was of constant service to the American Anthropological Association and was its chairman in 1952.

JUNIUS BOUTON BIRD, Curator of Archaeology at The American Museum of Natural History, was born in Rye, New York, on September 21, 1907. He entered Columbia University in 1926, but soon after he left college in favor of an opportunity to join an archaeological expedition.

A member of the staff of The American Museum of Natural History since 1933, he began serving in 1928 on American Museum expeditions. In 1939 he was appointed Assistant Curator of Anthropology; in 1946,

Associate Curator of Archaeology; in 1957, Curator of Archaeology. He has done field-work in various places in the Arctic, Canada, the United States, Middle America, and South America, specializing in the early phases of human occupation in Chile and Peru.

Among Dr. Bird's published works are *Archaeology of the Hopedale Area, Labrador; Excavations in Northern Chile;* and *Paracas Fabrics and Nazca Needlework, Third Century B.C. to Third Century A.D.*

He is Consultant for the Museum of Primitive Art, and Trustee of the Textile Museum, Washington, D.C. In 1958, he was given the honorary degree of D.Sc. by Wesleyan University.

ANDEAN CULTURE
HISTORY

Wendell C. Bennett
and
Junius B. Bird

SECOND AND REVISED EDITION

Originally published as an
Anthropological Handbook for
The American Museum of Natural History

AMERICAN MUSEUM SCIENCE BOOKS
Published for
The American Museum of Natural History

The Natural History Press
GARDEN CITY, NEW YORK

The line illustrations for this book were prepared by the Graphic Arts Division of The American Museum of Natural History. The photographs were supplied by The American Museum of Natural History unless otherwise acknowledged.

Andean Culture History was originally published by The American Museum of Natural History in 1949. The American Museum Science Books edition is published by arrangement with The American Museum of Natural History.

The 1960 hardcover edition of *Andean Culture History* published by The American Museum of Natural History is available through The Natural History Press.

American Museum Science Books edition: 1964

PREFACE TO SECOND EDITION

Any brief summation of an involved and imperfectly known subject has inevitable weaknesses. Yet, despite its shortcomings, this small volume has found some favor and a continued demand makes reprinting necessary. Unfortunately, the death of the senior author, a deep sadness to all who knew him, deprives us of his guidance and good judgment in this task.

In the few years since the first printing various archaeological projects have been reported on and others undertaken, all bringing new data, clarifying old problems, or posing new ones. Bennett, himself, visited the great site of Wari and secured a record of ceramic changes there. John H. Rowe, Chávez Ballón, and others did the same for sites in the Cuzco Basin. Further south, Alfred Kidder, II, William Coe, and Alan Sawyer excavated at Chiripa, Pucará, and other sites. W. Duncan Strong and his associates worked in the Nazca-Ica Area in an effort to re-define Nazca culture. In connection with Victor von Hagen's survey of the Inca road system, Dorothy Menzel and Francis A. Riddell together studied Inca and post-conquest communities on the Southern Coast. In the Cajamarca Area, Henri Reichlen and H. D. Disselhoff have been concerned with cultural sequence and Coastal-Highland relationship; in the Jequetepeque-Chicama region, H. U. Doering returned for further work. Under the auspices of the University of Trujillo, Richard Schaedel uncovered the remarkable adobe relief of the Huaca del Dragón, a structure desecrated by the Spaniards at the time of the Conquest. At the site of

Chavín de Huántar, Jorge Muelle's program to free the ruins of debris carried in by disastrous flooding brought to light remarkable and important new finds. Near the mouth of the Casma valley, Donald Collier has checked the cultural record and, in the northern valleys, a survey has been undertaken by James A. Ford.

On the Central Coast, at Ancón, Peruvian archaeologists working for Rebecca Carrión and the Museo de Antropología y Arqueología de Magdalena Vieja, in advance of building and real estate development, have recovered a vast amount of material. Nearby at Playa Grande, Louis Stumer, has recovered important material; to the south of Lima, Frédéric Engel and Edward Lanning tested a Chavín horizon deposit near San Bartolo and have found similar and preceramic sites at many of the suitable locations along the coast. More recently the University of San Marcos, with the support of the Fulbright Commission instituted a three-year program with various North American archaeologists working with Peruvians in different parts of the coast. The personnel included: David Kelly, Dorothy Menzel, Louis Stumer, Paul Tolstoy, Dwight Wallace, Gary Vescelius. Far to the north sites with early ceramics have been found and studied; in Colombia by Reichel-Dolmatoff, in Lowland Ecuador by Emilio Estrada, Clifford Evans and Betty Meggers. Earlier the Evans-Meggers team did intensive work at the mouth of the Amazon and in British Guiana. Other Amazonian sites near Pucallpa were studied by Donald Lathrap.

This brief and incomplete listing of archaeological investigations undertaken since the first edition indicates how much has been done. Some reports have been published but as others have not we have mentioned the individuals involved in each case.

Among publications on field-work completed prior to the appearance of the first edition one should note:

Jijón y Caamaño's "Maranga", A. L. Kroeber's "Proto-Lima, a Middle Period Culture of Peru", R. Larco's "Cronología Arqueologíca del Norte del Peru", and various reports on the Viru Valley survey by Bennett, Collier, Ford, Strong, Evans, and Willey; also the Ancón report of Willey and Corbett with its most important section on textiles by the late Lila O'Neale.

Last, but not least, is the development of a method for measuring age by counting the radioactivity of the Carbon 14 isotope present in organic materials. Nothing seemed to promise more valuable aid in clearing the fog from Peruvian chronology than this method developed by W. F. Libby, J. R. Arnold, and associates. However, the number of age measurements of Peruvian material is still inadequate and the dates derived are puzzling in certain details. A brief comment on the results will be found on pages 223–228.

The incorporation of new data and the elimination of some errors is here attempted within the format of the original edition. Errors and omissions in the section on ceramics have been corrected by Robert Sonin and a needed revision of the section on metalwork has been done by Dudley Easby. Both John H. Rowe and Clifford Evans suggested changes or additions which have been incorporated. Such help, freely and generously given, cannot be adequately acknowledged.

When the first edition appeared, Rowe published the most detailed and conscientious review.[1] One of his major criticisms, and a valid one, concerns the simplified chronological framework here applied to the whole Central Andean Area. Such broadly descriptive period designations as "Formative" and "Expansionist" and others were first proposed by Rafael Larco Hoyle as a substitute for and an improvement on the use of an

[1] *American Antiquity* (Vol. 16, No. 2, pp. 170–172, October, 1950).

ever-increasing and overlapping list of pottery type and
cultural horizon designations. It had become fashionable, not only to propose names for newly recognized
pottery types or ceramic complexes and use them as
culture period designations, but to re-name well-
known material. Thus, in publications of the past ten
years we can find "Early Chimu", "Mochica", and
"Huancaco" used synonymously. Early Chimu is a survival of earlier terminology, Mochica is generally accepted and well understood, while Huancaco was
proposed for Mochica material from the Viru Valley,
most of which cannot be distinguished from contemporary products used fifteen miles away in the Moche
Valley. Similarly we have the "Gallinazo", "Negative",
and "Viru" cultures, as well as various others. The
meanings are not always clear even to those actively
engaged in ceramic classification, for there is some disa-
greement among the specialists.

Larco contended that a broader frame of reference
was needed. The speedy adoption of his proposal
which was even extended to the Middle American field,
testifies to the need for some such system. Its weakness
is that only the very broadest terms apply to any extensive geographical area, and when so extended they
lose some of their value.

Objections can be raised to virtually all such period
designations as used in this volume. It may help the
reader if they are mentioned briefly here and kept in
mind when using the text and the chart in Fig. 19.

To begin with the oldest division, the "Hunters",
the finds from the San Pedro-Chicama Area may be
associated with the mastodon and possibly other extinct animals, but the sites are all open and eroded. The
material might conceivably date back nine or ten
thousand years, but until intact deposits are discovered
and carefully excavated, we do not know. It is inevitable that the period designation "Hunters" will ulti-

mately be subdivided into three units; first, those early migrants who dealt with big game; second, their followers who presumably depended on the wild ancestors of the llama and alpaca and smaller game; and, third, those who lived mainly on birds, marine mammals, and fish. However, this will not preclude the use of the broad period designation.

The second major division, "Early Farmers", seemingly a safe designation, applies to the pre-ceramic, premaize farmers of the Chicama and Viru valleys on the North Coast, but includes the pre-ceramic maize growers of Aspero, on the Central Coast, and Arica, in northern Chile. The questions raised are: one, should such culturally unrelated groups be bracketed together, and, second, where should the "Early Farmers" division be terminated—with the introduction of ceramics or with the introduction of maize? The two are not coeval throughout the Andean Area.

The term "Cultists" is also relatively broad. Its use was prompted by such obvious evidence of religious organization as the Chavín de Huántar ruins. Possibly the term "Early Cultists" is preferable, for religious activities continued throughout all subsequent periods.

Similarly there are objections to the concept of the two subsequent divisions, the "Experimenter" and "Mastercraftsman". What we may now interpret as diversity resulting from local experimentation can prove to be intrusive influences displacing, disrupting, or fusing with local development. So, too, features on which a Master Craftsmen period is based may prove so varied in age and distribution as to make it impossible to fix a dividing line between it and the Experimenters.

Far less criticism can be focussed on the Expansionist concept. We may and do lack agreement on its dates, source, motivation, and course. We can agree that it marks the second time in the Andean Area when a single culture influence spread over regions which at other times maintained more marked local distinctions. It may have been just as Imperialistic in nature as the Inca expansion, but the answers did not survive in legend and they remain a challenge to archaeology.

Over and above the problems mentioned, we have a more serious criticism, that not all of these designations apply to exactly the same area. Beyond certain limits we can only suggest what we believe to be contemporaneous. In doing this, and even in indicating the sequence of the cultural phases, there will always be errors of interpretation as long as we lack exact dates.

Junius B. Bird

June, 1959

PREFACE TO FIRST EDITION

Collections from the indigenous Indian cultures, both past and present, from the whole continent of South America are exhibited in the South American hall in the American Museum of Natural History. In other words, this exhibition unit includes both ethnography, materials from contemporary Indian cultures, and archaeology, materials from past cultures and civilizations. By far the largest and most varied collections are from the pre-Spanish civilizations of Peru and Bolivia. This reflects the fact that the Central Andes was the most outstanding center of high civilization in South America for many centuries.

The present volume, although issued in the Handbook series of the Museum, is not intended to be a guide to the exhibits in the South American hall. Instead, it is a reconstructed history of pre-Spanish Peru, a summary of Indian cultures elsewhere in South America, and a general treatment of some outstanding techniques. Nonetheless in preparing this book the collections in the Museum have been kept in mind, so that the exhibits might serve as illustrations, and the Handbook might be used in a broad way for general information about them. Illustrations, unless otherwise noted, are of specimens in the Museum's collection or from Museum field-work.

As mentioned, the emphasis in this volume is on Peruvian prehistory. Consequently all other regions and materials are treated in less detail and their relationship to Peru is stressed. The first part, The Setting, presents a brief review of the geography, the area cultural patterns, and the archaeology of South America outside of Peru, but simultaneously stresses the cultural and environmental distinctness of the Peruvian unit. In other words, this part summarizes the physical and cultural setting of Peru in the total South American picture.

The second part is devoted principally to the history of Peruvian cultural development in pre-Spanish times, to which is appended a brief statement on Indian culture in the Spanish Colonial era and at present. The archaeological materials are arranged in an over-all historical sequence, from their earliest known beginnings to the Spanish conquest. This approach is valid because the cultural past of Peru forms a unit, even though there are many regional differences. In spite of the range and quantity of excavation carried out in Peru, there are still many gaps in our knowledge and many unrelated time sequences. Consequently certain liberties of interpretation have been taken, although every attempt has been made to keep speculation within reasonable bounds. Most archaeologists agree on the major trends, although each one varies somewhat in his interpretation of the precise time and space divisions.

The third part deals with ceramics, metallurgy, and textiles, from a technical rather than an historical view. These techniques were well advanced in ancient Peru and are of interest in themselves.

This Handbook was originally projected as a joint account by the senior author, once Assistant Curator of South American Archaeology, and Mr. Junius Bird, now Associate Curator of Archaeology in the American Museum of Natural History. However, Mr. Bird became so engaged in enlarging the archaeological history of Peru through extended field excavation, that the plan for joint authorship was abandoned. Consequently, Dr. Bennett prepared the first two parts, Mr.

Bird the third. Both authors have reviewed the total text and selected the illustrations. Mr. Fred Scherer has prepared all maps, charts, and figures. Dr. Harry L. Shapiro, Chairman of the Department of Anthropology, likewise encouraged and directed this report. Señor Rafael Larco Hoyle, Director of the Museo Larco Herrera at Chiclín, Peru, not only furnished many excellent illustrations from his superb collections, but also provided many stimulating ideas for the interpretation of Peruvian prehistory. Many other archaeologists, both in this country and in South America, should also receive credit for ideas and materials. Their principal publications are listed in the bibliography, but this expresses only a fraction of the debt due them. Finally, Miss Bella Weitzner, Associate Curator of Ethnology, has once again provided her skillful editing and stimulating ideas of the production of this volume.

Wendell C. Bennett
YALE UNIVERSITY

Junius B. Bird
AMERICAN MUSEUM OF
NATURAL HISTORY

July, 1947

CONTENTS

PART 3: TECHNIQUES
(*by Junius B. Bird*)

LIST OF ILLUSTRATIONS

PART 1: THE SETTING

THE SOUTH AMERICAN ENVIRONMENT

The region designated as the Central Andes includes the Peruvian coast and highlands and most of the Bolivian highlands, particularly the high plateau around Lake Titicaca. The abundant archaeological remains in the Central Andes have long been intensively studied because this area, in spite of its striking environmental contrasts and its remarkable diversity of materials, presents a unit of cultural development unmatched in intensity in South American prehistory. Here centered the Inca culture which, at its peak, maintained an empire that extended from Colombia in the north to Argentina and Chile in the south. The Spaniards described the Inca Empire as they found it flourishing in the early sixteenth century. The archaeologist projects the story backward from that date and can demonstrate that the basic components of the Inca culture were developed in the Central Andes many centuries before the Spanish conquest.

The major purpose of this account is to reconstruct the story of cultural development in the Central Andes from its earliest known manifestations to historic times. However, it seems profitable to begin with the South American scene as a whole and to describe the total physical and cultural environment within which the Central Andean cultures played so distinctive a role. It has long been recognized that topography and other features of the geographic environment may affect migration, trade, transportation, and expansion; that the

natural resources present or absent in an area may influence cultural growth; and that culture and geographic environment are linked in many ways. The
cultural environment is equally important. This involves knowledge of the size of a population, its technology, specialization, divisions of authority and
over-all pattern. Likewise, it is hard to understand one
group without a knowledge of its neighbors.

Topographically, the South American continent is
divisible into three major zones: the Andes along the
Pacific Coast, the tropical and temperate plains, and
the highlands of east Brazil and the Guianas (Fig. 1).
These major zones extend from north to south, a topo-
graphical factor that has long influenced migrations
and cultural diffusions. Even the briefest examination
reveals that there are many contrasting environments
in South America. The rugged Andes rise in marked
contrast to the flat plains of the Argentine Pampas.
Northern Chile is an extreme desert; the Amazon and
its tributaries flow through one of the greatest known
stretches of tropical rain forest. However, in spite of
size and environmental variety, in terms of pre-Spanish subsistence patterns large sections of South America
could not be effectively utilized. Some of the richest
agricultural areas, like the Argentine Pampas, were of
little use to Indians who had no knowledge of the plow
or other means of eradicating the deep-rooted grasses.
The extensive grazing lands now in use had an insig-
nificant value before the introduction of European
domesticated animals.

The rugged Andes dominate western South America, extending from the Caribbean coast of Venezuela
and Colombia, along the entire Pacific Coast to Cape
Horn. Only in Bolivia do the Andes expand to much
over one hundred miles in width. They vary from section to section. Three parallel ranges in Colombia re-
duce to two in Ecuador, break up into short diagonal

FIG. 1. Environmental regions of South America.

chains in Peru, expand again to a pair in Bolivia, and
narrow to a single range in Chile. Temperatures in the
Andes are more or less consistent, reflecting altitude
rather than latitude, so that most sections are cool to
cold during the whole year, although freezing temperatures are rare in the habitable areas. Although trees
grow in some sections, much of the region is unfor-

ested and may be classed either as grassland, bushland, or desert.

The geographers recognize a northern, central, and southern division of the Andes and these are important in cultural considerations. The Northern Andes, which include Colombia, Ecuador, and a small part of Peru, are characterized by a double rainy season which supports wet rain forest in areas of high altitude between 10,000 feet and the snow line. Such highland areas are unfavorable for grazing llamas and alpacas, so that the two most important domesticated animals of pre-Spanish America were not permanently acquired by the people who occupied this northern region. The Central Andes have a contrasting rainy and dry season, resulting in a highland covered by a bunch grass, ideal for grazing, which makes the region environmentally distinct from the Northern Andes. From Bolivia southward, the Southern Andes are separated from the Central Andes by a desert strip which extends from north Chile to the Patagonian plateau. The limited habitable areas are not unlike those of the Central Andes.

The Andes everywhere present formidable mountain barriers with numerous peaks over twenty thousand feet in altitude and few passes under twelve thousand feet. The habitable sections are the intermont basins, high plateaus, and valley flats of the rivers that drain into the Amazon. These basins and flats, however, have well watered, fertile soil, and many resources contributing to cultural development, such as stone and clay usable for building materials, and easily mined copper, silver, gold, and tin. Many regions are extensive enough to support a reasonably large population, and distant enough from each other to permit easy defense without excessive isolation. In today's terms the Andes present difficult transportation problems, but in pre-Spanish times when travel was essentially on foot, the mountains did not constitute a great obstacle. Today wild food plant and animal life are limited in the Andes, due in part to the fact that intensive agriculturists have occupied the region for over two thousand years. However, since many domesticated plants and at least two domesticated animals appear to be indigenous to this region, it seems reasonable to assume that wild forms were abundant at one time.

Although not very extensive, the plains along the Pacific Coast present a considerable contrast in environment. In Ecuador and Colombia, where they are widest, they lie within the tropics, with characteristic high temperatures, excessive rainfall, and jungle forest coverage. In Colombia, therefore, the environmental contrast between the plains and the highlands prevented much cultural interchange. The narrow coastal plains of southern Ecuador, Peru, and northern Chile form the west coast desert. This climatic change is attributed to the effect of the cold Humboldt current which cools the air of the on-shore winds sufficiently so that there is no precipitation over the hot coastal land and desert conditions result. The aridity increases in intensity from north to south, reaching its maximum in the Atacama desert of north Chile. The habitable portions of the west coast, except for small fishing sites, are limited to the valleys of the rivers that have their source in the mountains and flow rapidly to the Pacific.

In terms of gross environment, the contrast between the desert coast and the high Andes seems enormous; but in terms of Indian subsistence patterns it is not very significant. In fact, the coastal valleys and highland basins share such favorable features as rich, easily cultivated soils, an absence of deep-rooted grasses or forest coverage, a relatively genial climate, and sufficient water supply to permit controlled irrigation. The

Central Valley of Chile is an alluvium-filled trough lying between the main Andes and a low coastal range. Here the climate is classed as Mediterranean; the soils are rich and the rains abundant. Following the introduction of European plants and animals, the Central Valley became the garden spot of Chile. The long southern archipelago of Chile is a continuation of the coastal mountain range. The climate is cold and wet; the coverage, wet rain forest. This region was inhabited by small groups of fishermen who spent most of their lives in canoes.

East of the Southern Andes are the high semi-desert table-lands of Patagonia where the winds blow constantly. The soil is shallow and not very fertile, trees are rare, and most of the area is classed as grassland. North of Patagonia are the Argentine Pampas with their rich soil, low elevation, and temperate climate. The Pampas are the finest grasslands in South America, famed today for their cereals and beef. In the past, however, grasslands were not favorable to native digging-stick cultivation, so that the distinction between the Pampas and Patagonia was not of special significance. Instead, this region was occupied by hunters who pursued such wild fauna as the guanaco and the rhea, or ostrich, and gatherers who collected seeds and roots.

The transition from the temperate to the tropical lowlands is illustrated by that great area known as the Gran Chaco which includes parts of Argentina, Paraguay, and Bolivia. This uninterrupted flat plain is characterized by a concentrated rainy season and an exceedingly contrasting dry season which results in a greatly varied vegetal coverage. It includes sections of grassland, parkland, bushland, and, along the rivers, tropical forest. The rivers are full of fish and some game hunting is possible, but, on the whole, this area was never very attractive either to hunters or agriculturists.

The Amazon lowlands lie in the true tropics. The region is mostly below a thousand feet elevation. The rainfall is excessive, temperatures are consistently high, and tropical forest is characteristic. The Amazon River with its numerous tributaries forms a network over the whole area so that with any form of watercraft, transportation is no problem. There is a reasonable amount of wild animal life, abundant fish in the rivers, and some wild edible roots and fruits. However, these tropical forests were probably never very enticing to simple hunters and certainly they were not extensively occupied until suitable plants had been domesticated. Even for agriculturists the region offers no great attraction since the soils are thin and poor, clearing a field is an arduous task, and the protection of a village is difficult.

The llanos or flats of the Orinoco River in Venezuela are in some ways similar to the Amazonian lowlands, but irregularities in the distribution of rainfall produce a coverage of grass and scattered trees, rather than dense tropical forest. In cultural terms, however, the two regions do not contrast markedly. This is also true of the highlands which cover most of the Guianas and parts of Brazil and Venezuela. These are old, badly eroded mountains, completely surrounded by tropical forest. The higher sections, however, are not very favorable for agriculture, so that the contrast between highlands and tropical lowlands never became culturally important.

The east Brazil highlands cover an enormous area and present a number of internal divisions. Grasslands and scattered trees are typical and the variety of plant life is great. The climate is subtropical with ample rainfall and little variation in temperature throughout the year. In the past, game and wild life were apparently sufficiently abundant to attract land hunters and gatherers.

South America can, then, be divided into a dozen major environmental zones, which can be further subdivided with ease. However, from the point of view of this historical summary, such detailed subdivision is unnecessary because, by the time of the European conquest, the whole continent was dominated by three basic cultural patterns: the Southern Hunters, the Tropical Agriculturists, and the Andean Farmers. Furthermore, this broad review demonstrates that despite some of its internal contrasts, the Central Andes forms a distinctive environmental zone, a uniqueness even more marked when the contrasting cultural factors are considered.

EARLY MIGRANTS

South America was first populated by nomadic hunters, fishermen, and gatherers with no knowledge of agriculture, metals, or pottery. All the known evidence indicates that the Isthmus of Panama was the migration route of these land nomads to the South American continent. The only alternative possibility is by way of the chain of Caribbean islands, a route which presupposes a knowledge of watercraft. In spite of the important development of water travel in the Amazon area and the Chilean archipelago, we still lack proof that these early nomadic people had such knowledge.

Land hunters and gatherers who migrated to South America via Panama could easily enter the Andean highlands by way of the Cauca and Magdalena rivers, both of which flow from south to north. Some groups may have migrated eastward into Venezuela, but further expansion in that direction was probably blocked by the Amazon jungle where there is, as yet, no evidence for the antiquity of a hunting-gathering culture pattern. The same line of reasoning applies to the Pacific Coast of Colombia and Ecuador which is also a tropical jungle. The highlands would, however, offer a reasonable quantity of game and wild food sufficient to support a hunting and gathering people. Furthermore, once adjustment had been made to the Andean environment, there would be no major barriers to a continued southward migration. Small groups may have moved to favorable fishing sites on the arid Pacific Coast, but these minor movements would not affect the main direction of migration. Once Argentina had been reached, a rapid spread throughout the Pampas and Patagonia, even to distant Tierra del Fuego, probably occurred since this great expanse of grassland presented many favorable possibilities for hunters and gatherers. From northern Argentina it would be easy to enter the open park country of the east Brazil highlands. The fishing potentials of the Chilean archipelago were probably exploited as soon as water travel was perfected.

This reconstruction of the probable migration routes of the early hunting people is based partially on geographic logic, but it is confirmed by the meager archaeological and historical evidence. The earliest remains of man yet found are in the Andean highlands, the east Brazil highlands, and in southern Patagonia. Furthermore, at the time of the European conquest hunting and gathering peoples still occupied the east Brazil highlands, the Pampas, Patagonia, and the Chilean archipelago.

The archaeological evidence for these early migrations consists of human skeletal remains found in association with extinct fauna and cultural remains excavated in the camping and fishing sites. In 1835 the Danish naturalist, T. W. Lund, explored some eight hundred caves in the Lagoa Santa region of Minas

Geraes in the east Brazil highlands. These caves contained not only the bones of extinct Pleistocene fauna,
but assorted human remains some of which represented
physical types distinct from those of the modern Indians. A recent excavation of the Confins Cave in the
same region has confirmed the results of the earlier
work. The mouth of this cave was completely sealed by
fallen debris. Excavations in the alluvial deposits on
the cave floor encountered at about two meters depth
the skull of a fossil horse, the molars and bones of a
young mastodon, and a human skeleton which, although in extended position, was not an intrusive
burial. The skull is long-headed, similar to the Lagoa
Santa type. At Punín, Ecuador, another skull of this
type, again without artifacts, was found in volcanic ash.
Association with extinct horse, mastodon, sloth, deer,
and camel was implied by geology. Probably contemporary with this fauna are projectile points, identical
with the oldest from South Chile (Fig. 2), found in
1959 on a hilltop near Quito, Ecuador.

At about 10 degrees south latitude, near Lake
Lauricocha in the center of the Peruvian Highlands,
cave deposits, at an elevation of 13,000 feet, show early
and continued occupation. This discovery, by Augusto
Cardich, is remarkable both for the antiquity of the
first occupation, 7566 B.C. ±250 from radiocarbon,
and the altitude, which is near the upper limits for
habitable sites. A comparable date, 6013 B.C. ±100,
was obtained for similar remains found by A. R.
Gonzalez in the lower strata of Intihuasi Cave, 70 kilometers north of San Luis, Cordoba, Argentina, again
with modern fauna. The oldest artifacts at both sites
are stone projectile points of related forms; later levels
yield some pottery.

Many finds of fossil man and early campsites have
been reported for Patagonia, but few of these are based
on scientific excavations. The best evidence comes

from the extreme southern part of Patagonia near the Straits of Magellan. Here two caves, Palli Aike and Fell's, excavated by Junius Bird, contained stratified remains of five distinct periods of habitation. Both caves were below lava outcrops on the semi-desert plains. The two caves furnish evidence for an historical reconstruction.

Their first occupants used stemmed projectile points, many rough scrapers, lava cylinders, and a variety of bone flaking tools (Plate 1). Bones of guanaco and of the extinct ground sloth and native American horse in the same level show that these animals were eaten in abundance. In several contemporary human burials the bodies had all been cremated. One skull, patiently reconstructed, is long headed and somewhat resembles the Lagoa Santa type. A sterile level formed of slabs which had fallen from the roof of the cave isolated the remains of this first period of occupation. In the second period of occupation the fossil animals were not present, but fox and bird bones were common. The artifacts were limited to a few chipped flakes and scrapers, crude bone points, and polished bone awls. The third period of occupation marked the appearance of stemless stone points and the first use of bolas, mostly small ones for hunting birds. The graves contained several skeletons covered with red paint. In the fourth occupational period, small arrowheads were present, thus demonstrating that the bow and arrow was later here than the bolas. Shell and bone beads, some incised, were used for ornaments. The final occupants made small stemmed arrowpoints, bone beads, combs, spatulas, pressure flaking tooks and other artifacts, all similar to those of the Ona Indians of Tierra del Fuego. Thus these caves present a sequence of occupation from the early hunters up to the historic Ona.

Bird's excavations of shell middens on the shores of Beagle Channel also proved a relative antiquity for some of the fishing groups in southern Tierra del Fuego and the archipelago. The earliest occupants used mussel shell knives, single barbed harpoon points, bird bone beads, whetstones, notched pebble fishline sinkers, and rough stone choppers or hand axes. The technique of pressure flaking stone artifacts was completely lacking. This is surprising for apparently bolas and the idea of using the small hafted endscrapers or flensing tools were obtained from contacts with the inland peoples at a time which would correspond roughly to the fourth period of occupation of Fell's Cave.

On the extreme north coast of Chile, Bird found additional evidence of early fishing cultures in stratified shell middens near Arica, Pisagua, and Taltal. This showed that long prior to the introduction of agriculture people had been able to survive on this desert coast by depending on the sea for food. Two distinct periods of occupation were determined. The first, designated as the Shell Fishhook culture after the most distinctive artifact, contained composite fishhooks with stone weights and bone barbs, harpoons with detachable forepieces, bone barbs, stone points, small lava bowls, and a variety of scrapers (Plate 2). The occupants of the second period used bone fish harpoons, thorn fishhooks instead of the earlier shell hooks, sinkers, bolas, chipped stone points, and spear-throwers. In spite of the suggestion of some writers these north Chilean coastal cultures are unrelated to those of Patagonia.

The association of extinct fauna with the oldest artifacts in the region of Magellan Straits implies considerable antiquity for the human record there. Carbon, derived from charred horse and sloth bones found in Palli Aike Cave, has given a C14 date of 6689 B.C. ±450 years. A similar measurement, using plant material from dried sloth manure secured without cultural

association in another cave 125 miles away, indicated
8882 B.C. ±400 as the most probable date for that
sample. A test of Fell's Cave charcoal, (USGS laboratory sample W-915,) yielded the date 8760 B.C. ±300
for the artifacts shown on Plate 1. This suggests that
the figure obtained from Palli Aike bones is conservative. As yet no tests have been made of North Chilean
material.

There is little direct information about succeeding
migrations, although small groups presumably continued to enter South America over a long period of
time. The earliest fossil finds correspond to the long-
headed physical type. However, the higher civilizations
in both Middle and South America are represented by
a short, round-headed physical type, implying more recent migrations. Likewise the wide spread of food
plants and other elements common to the higher civilization throughout large parts of the Americas, as well
as the known penetration of Arawaks and Caribs into
the West Indies from South America, all indicate that
migrations in one direction or another were a continu-
ing pattern.

PLANT DOMESTICATION

The hunting-gathering culture pattern persisted in
southern South America up to historic times, but the
other two major South American patterns were dependent upon the domestication of plants and the
development of agriculture. The plants domesticated
in the New World, except for the gourd, and perhaps
cotton, are for the most part seemingly indigenous
species not related to those utilized in Asia or other
parts of the Old World. This then poses the problem
of determining the New World center or centers in
which various plants were domesticated, a problem

which involves the technical knowledge of the botanists and the archaeologists. Formerly, it was believed that three of the more important New World plants, maize, beans, and squash, were first domesticated in Mexico and spread as a unit from that center. Present evidence fails to confirm this theory for squashes and beans were cultivated in Peru centuries before maize. Obviously, as knowledge of plant cultivation spread, new plants were exploited when and where available. Plants like beans and squash, represented by several distinct species, may have been independently developed in several localities.

This is far less likely for food plants classed as single species, like maize or sweet potatoes, unless the ancestral forms were widely distributed. A South American origin for maize was proposed and favored for some years, but new evidence now points to Central America or Mexico.

Cotton, like maize, has been intensively studied. Unlike maize, two linted species are present and a center of variability is known for each. These are interpreted as foci of diffusion, but their relation to the cultural record is not clear. The first is located in northern Peru, the second in southern Mexico and Guatemala. As a fiber-producing plant the motive for domestication was a need for yarn, not food. Geneticists agree that these linted American cottons are related to an Old World species, but differ on whether this relationship was established before or after cultivation. If the latter is true, it would mean that contrary to current belief some knowledge of agriculture and at least one plant, a species now extinct in America, was introduced from Asia. This implication should not yet be accepted as fact nor dismissed summarily.

This pattern of shifting controversial opinions will probably be repeated as other comparable studies are made. Fortunately Peruvian coastal middens will yield a complete record of the plants utilized there. In addition to the botanical data, the sequence, relative distribution, and instances where two or more genera first appear simultaneously will go far to indicate areas of origins and dispersal routes.

Estimated dates for the first domestication of plants are very vague. Botanists point out that the process of domestication could have been accomplished in a few thousand years. Carbon 14 measurements seem to bear this out with third millennium B.C. figures for maize in New Mexico and various plants in Peru.

Table 1 lists the principal pre-Colombian domesticated plants in Andean South America. Some are particularly suited to the warmer lowlands, others grow best in the highlands or in the sandy desert regions. Most of these plants were cultivated in the Central Andes wherever the local environment was favorable. The range of local environments, plus a systematic exchange of food products, provided the ancient inhabitants of the Central Andes with a wider variety of domesticated food plants than were available to any other peoples of South America.

TABLE I

PRINCIPAL PRE-COLOMBIAN DOMESTICATED PLANTS
IN THE ANDEAN AREA[1]

Seed Crops

Common Name	Botanical Name	Occurrence
Maize	*Zea mays*	All areas
Lupine	*Lupinus tauris*	Highlands
Quinoa	*Chenopodium quinoa*	Highlands
Cañahua	*Chenopodium pallidicaule*	Highlands
Amaranth	*Amaranthus sp.*	Highlands

[1] Based on Table 1, Handbook of South American Indians, Volume 2, The Andean Civilization. Bureau of American Ethnology, Bulletin 143, Washington, 1946.

TABLE I—*Continued*

Beans

Common Name	Botanical Name	Occurrence
Kidney	*Phaseolus vulgaris*	General
Scarlet runner or ayecote	*Phaseolus multiflorus* (or *coccineus*)	Cauca River
Lima	*Phaseolus lunatus*	Coast
Jack	*Canavalia ensiformis*	Coast

Fruits

Avocado	*Persea Americana*	Tropical
Lucumo	*Lucuma obovata*	Temperate valleys
Pacai, guaba	*Inga edulis*	Tropical
Pineapple	*Ananas sativus*	Tropical
Soursop	*Annona muricata*	Lowlands
Pepino	*Solanum mauricatum*	Temperate

Roots

Potato	*Solanum tuberosum*	Chile Coast
Potato	*Solanum andigenum*	Highlands
Oca	*Oxalis tuberosa*	Highlands
Ulluco	*Ullucus tuberosus*	Highlands
Mashua	*Tropaeolum tuberosum*	Highlands
Achira	*Canna edulis*	Coast; temperate valleys
Arracacha	*Arracacia xanthorrhiza* (or *esculenta*)	Temperate valleys
Yacon	*Polymnia edulis*	Temperate valleys
Sweet manioc	*Manihot utilissima*	Tropical lowlands
Peanut	*Arachis hypogaea*	Lowlands
Sweet potato	*Ipomoea batatas*	Tropical lowlands

Miscellaneous

Gourd	*Lagenaria*	General
Squash	*Cucurbita maxima*	General
Peppers, ají	*Capsicum annum*	Medium climates
Cacao, chocolate bean	*Theobroma cacao*	Low valleys
Cotton	*Gossypium hirsutum* (var. *marie-galante*)	Tropical Coast
Cotton	*Gossypium barbadense*	General

Narcotics

Tobacco	*Nicotiana tabacum*	General
Tobacco	*Nicotiana rustica*	Highlands
Coca	*Erythroxylon coca*	Warm valleys

DOMESTICATED ANIMALS

Domesticated animals, with the exception of the dog, were unknown in most parts of South America. The guinea pig had a wide Andean distribution, but was not of major importance. In the Central Andes, however, two animals, the llama and the alpaca, were domesticated at an early date, presumably from wild forms related to the guanaco and the vicuña. The llama and the alpaca contributed greatly to the Central Andean economy since they grazed on the high grasslands which could not be used for agriculture. Both animals were not only useful for transportation but also furnished wool, meat, hides, fertilizer, fuel, sinews, and even bones for making tools. Unlike many domesticated plants that are adaptable to different environments, the llama and the alpaca were largely restricted to the terrain of the high dry grasslands which include the Central Andes and parts of Northwest Argentina.

SOUTHERN HUNTERS

Roughly in the year 1500 all of southern South America and most of the east Brazil highlands were occupied by Indians who were basically dependent on hunting, fishing, or gathering for their subsistence. Among the better known tribes are the Alacaluf and Yahgan of the Chilean archipelago, the Ona of Tierra del Fuego, the Tehuelche of Patagonia, the Puelche and Querandí of the Pampas, the Charrua of Uruguay, and the numerous Gê-speaking peoples of east Brazil (Fig. 2). As the archaeological records demonstrate, the

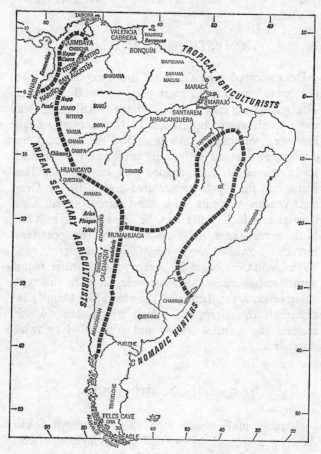

Fig. 2. South American cultural divisions.

culture pattern of all of these groups reflects, in part, a survival from the first nomadic hunters in the region. However, in spite of a common history and a similar subsistence pattern, the component tribes present considerable cultural variation. An immediate contrast is apparent between the "Canoe" Indians who lived in the archipelago region and depended largely upon marine products and the "Foot" Indians of Tierra del Fuego and the mainland who hunted the land animals. The isolated Ona and the Yahgan are among the most primitive people of the New World, while the Gê-speaking tribes of east Brazil, in contrast to their simple economy and technology, have an elaborate ceremonial and social organization.

The emphasis on hunting, fishing, or gathering varied not only seasonally but in terms of the specific environment. The Canoe Indians fished, hunted seals, sea-otters, and other sea mammals, and gathered shellfish and certain wild plants. The hunters of the open plains pursued guanaco and ostrich and collected starchy roots and wild grass seed. Deer, tapirs, and monkeys were hunted in the forests of east Brazil, and a variety of roots and edible vines were gathered. Hunting was invariably a male occupation, while the women were responsible for the collecting activities. The east Brazil tribes made underground ovens, but elsewhere meat was cooked on a wooden spit or directly in the ashes.

The weapons reflect the nature of the hunting. The marine hunters used spears, harpoons, slings, snares, clubs, and nets. The land hunters preferred bows and arrows, clubs, and bolas. This last weapon consists of two or more stone balls attached to the ends of thongs. It was thrown so as to entangle the legs of an ostrich or guanaco. Some of these weapons also served in the occasional disputes between groups, although, by and large, conflicts of a magnitude which can be termed warfare were decidedly uncommon. However, in east Brazil closer contact with Amazonian neighbors sometimes led to more extensive combat in which sharp-bladed wooden clubs were the weapons.

Since these hunters were constantly traveling, their shelters were necessarily temporary or easily transportable. The Ona used a simple skin windbreak consisting of several guanaco hides sewn together and supported by upright sticks set to form an open semicircle. When they moved, the skin covers of the shelter were rolled up and carried by the women. The Alacaluf, who were able to transport larger skin coverings for their dwellings in their canoes, made an elliptical, dome-shaped house frame of arched saplings which was abandoned when shifting camp. The Patagonians are reported to have built a large rectangular skin shelter partitioned into rooms, but it is doubtful that these were transportable before the introduction of the Spanish horse. Today the east Brazil natives erect a gabled frame house, but their earlier shelters were of the simple domed type consisting of a frame of arched saplings covered with bark or grass. All the groups erected larger and somewhat more durable shelters for their rare ceremonial gatherings. Difficulty of transportation accounts for the simplicity of the dwellings. All land travel and transportation was by foot and their scant household equipment and house covering had to be carried on their backs. With the introduction of the horse, houses became more elaborate. Canoes, used only in the archipelago, were constructed of three cigar-shaped pieces of beech bark sewn together and held taut by split saplings which served as thwarts and gunwales. Sod and earth fireplaces were built in the bottom of the canoe. The women propelled the canoes with wooden paddles.

Despite the rigors of the climate, the Southern Hunters wore very simple clothing. The Ona male costume consisted of a cape, moccasins, and rarely, leggings; all of which were made from guanaco skins. A headband was worn for decoration rather than warmth. The Canoe Indians made similar clothing of sealskin, but their capes were much shorter than those of the Ona, so that they could be worn in the canoes. Both groups greased their bodies for protection against the cold and sometimes added simple painted designs for ornamentation. In east Brazil, where the climate was more genial, no clothing was worn, but considerable attention was paid to body painting, to lip- and ear-plugs, and innumerable varieties of feather ornaments.

The material equipment of all of these nomads was limited to utensils and implements easily transportable or easily manufactured; their handicrafts can in no sense be called elaborate. Fire was made with a hand drill, except by the Ona and the Yahgan, who were unique in South America in using flint and pyrites. They also used simple stick fire tongs for moving hot stones, hammerstones, and a stone on which animal bones were broken so that the grease would coagulate. The Canoe Indians made bark bailing buckets, dip nets for fishing, and five types of baskets. Their principal tools were bone bark removers, bone awls, stone knives and scrapers, and weighted shell hand adzes. The Ona seldom made baskets, but used skin bags to carry water, for storage, and to transport necessary equipment. They also used hafted stone knives, fleshers, wood scrapers, awls, pressure flakers, and polishers. Virtually all of these tools were needed to make their bows and arrows. The latter were beautifully finished, tapering at each end, and were perhaps the finest arrows made by any group in America. The equipment of the Patagonians was equally simple, although they had, in addition, stone mortars for grinding seeds, and may have made wooden bowls, cups, and spoons. Even in east Brazil, where the life was less nomadic, material equipment was meager. The neighboring Amazonian tribes made hammocks, mats, wooden stools, cloth, and pottery, but none of these penetrated into east Brazil. Instead, the people of this area made simple mortars and vessels of wood and bamboo, bark bags and nets, and one type of waterproof basket.

In Patagonia and extreme southern South America, social organization was based on family units that were loosely organized into territorial bands. The Yahgan recognized five districts, not politically organized but differing slightly in dialect. Large assemblages of people for any purpose were rare because of the limited food supplies, and territorial chiefs, if recognized at all, were of secondary importance. The life crises of birth, marriage, and death were family affairs surrounded by extremely simple ritual. Only the puberty initiation involved a number of families. The Ona restricted this ceremony to boys, combining it with initiation into the men's secret society. The most elaborate Yahgan ceremonies were puberty rites for both boys and girls and those connected with the men's secret society which they borrowed from the Ona. A distinctive lodge was constructed for these occasions. The novices were isolated, given special instruction, and subjected to specific ordeals to test their fitness for the transition from childhood to adulthood. The older men dressed in skin and bark costumes decorated to represent chosen spirits that were supposed to terrify the women.

Recent studies in east Brazil report a more elaborate type of social organization today, although its antiquity is still unknown. Modern villages, of circular or U-shaped plan, have as many as three hundred inhabitants, but inter-village organization is weak or non-existent. Within the village the members are assigned to different halves, or moieties, for the purposes of regulating marriage, performing ceremonies, and competing in games. The divisions differ for each purpose. For example, the Canella Indians have one division for regulating marriage. A child belongs to his mother's group and must marry someone from the opposite moiety. Another dual division for ceremonies functions during the rainy season. All boys go through a prolonged initiation ceremony which takes about ten years for completion. Each group of initiates belongs throughout life to his age class and the various classes are assigned to one of two groups for competition in games. There are also six men's societies, semi-secret in nature, again arranged in two sets of three each. All of these divisions and societies perform seasonal ceremonies, own property, and compete in various ways. The village recognizes one or more chiefs, but the chieftaincy is a position of prestige rather than real power.

The ceremonies of east Brazil are intimately associated with religious rituals and concepts. Elsewhere the religious beliefs and practices of the Southern Hunters were simpler. Most tribes recognized a supreme god and numerous lesser deities such as the spirits of the forest and ancestral ghosts. Medicinemen and sorcerers, men who had received special inspiration as well as formal training, were important. They cured the sick, cast evil spells, and predicted weather changes, employing special paraphernalia and such devices as going into a trance, singing, fasting, and posturing to achieve their goals.

Contact with European civilization caused profound changes in these hunting groups, eliminating some, strengthening others. The horse was introduced to the Indians of Patagonia sometime before 1700, increasing their mobility and effectiveness in hunting and permitting larger numbers to assemble. Warlike tendencies emerged and leadership became important. Foreign equipment, including such trappings as saddles, bits, spurs, and stirrups, was also introduced; new techniques of working metal were learned; and many other new items hitherto unknown. After the introduction of horse transportation, the simple skin houses were enlarged so that as many as forty or fifty guanaco hides formed the cover. The size of camps increased to include two or three thousand inhabitants. Ceremonies, particularly those surrounding birth, puberty, marriage, and death, became far more elaborate. The tribes now engaged in stealing cattle and raiding border settlements. The history of Indian wars in Argentina is similar to the history of warfare on the plains of the United States, and the Indian threat was not eliminated finally until 1880.

TROPICAL AGRICULTURISTS

The culture pattern of the Tropical Agriculturists is characterized by semi-nomadism, the slash and burn method of clearing fields, the psychological importance of hunting, fishing, and warfare, a weak political structure based on band organization, and a number of distinctive crafts. By 1500 this basic pattern was widely distributed over most of the tropical forest, which includes the tropics of Brazil, eastern Bolivia, Peru, Ecuador, and Colombia; the llanos of Venezuela; most of the Guiana Highlands; part of the east Brazil highlands; the West Indies; and the Caribbean and Pacific coasts of Colombia. A few tribes in the tropics do not conform to this pattern which suggests, although by no means proves, that it may not have been the earliest in the area. Some of these simple "underlying" tribes are the Maku on the Japurá River, the Warrau on the delta of the Orinoco, the Sirionó of eastern Bolivia, and the Shiriana on the Venezuelan-Brazilian border.

The complex network of tropical rivers permitted a great mobility for canoe travelers and consequently a wide cultural diffusion, but, in spite of this, too much cultural uniformity would not be expected in so vast an area. Some of the differences are due to diversity of cultural origins; others are based on linguistic, geographic, and cultural factors. For example, there are three widespread linguistic stocks—Carib, north of the Amazon; Tupí-Guaraní, south of the Amazon; and Arawak, peripheral; but along the eastern margin of the Andes are a large number of small linguistic stocks which suggest that before the spread of the major ones the linguistic picture was complicated indeed.

The basic culture pattern of the Tropical Agriculturists, irrespective of subdivisions, contrasts with that of the Southern Hunters and the Andean Farmers. Consequently, a generalized picture is presented here, allowing for regional variation where necessary. Because of their great number, the selection of specific tribes for illustration is difficult. However, the following have been chosen for special emphasis: the Wapisiana, Macusi, and the Barama River Caribs of the Guianas; the Goajiro of Venezuela; the Tupinamba, Tapirapé, and other Guaraní groups of Brazil; and the Bora, Witoto, Campa, Yagua, Jívaro, and Chama of the upper Amazon.

From an objective point of view, agriculture was the principal economic basis for life in the tropical forest, but the Indians themselves placed greater emphasis on hunting. Except for the heavy labor of clearing the fields, agricultural work was left to the women. Religious and magical practices surrounded hunting rather than planting. As a consequence, agricultural techniques were not too advanced and because of the wasteful methods, fields were utilized for a few seasons only. The villages were moved at regular intervals, although this practice was motivated by the diminishing of the game supply rather than by the exhaustion of the fields. The fields were cleared by the slash and burn technique. The larger trees were cut down and the underbrush burned. Then the seeds were planted, using a simple digging-stick which also served as hoe, shovel, and rake. Manioc was the principal crop, but corn, sweet potatoes, yams, peppers, peanuts, beans, and cotton were also important. Little effort was expended on cultivation, so that harvesting was the next major activity.

The bitter or poison manioc, or cassava, common throughout Brazil, contains hydrocyanic acid which has the advantage of supplying the plant with its own insecticide, but this must be removed before eating. The process and equipment for preparing bitter manioc are similar wherever it is grown. The tubers are soaked in water, peeled with shell scrapers, and grated on a special curved board with projecting points of wood or stone. The grated pulp is then placed in a long narrow cylindrical basket with a loop handle at each end. One loop is hooked over a branch of a tree, the pulp squeezed by means of a log lever in the lower loop, and the poisonous juice drained into a jar. Later, it is boiled until the poison has evaporated and the residue, now in the form of tapioca, is served as a sauce. The dried pulp is taken from the squeezer, mixed with water to form a batter, and cooked on a large cylindrical clay platter into cassava pancakes. Corn and some other foods are placed in large log mortars and ground with extremely long wooden pestles. In eastern Bolivia, food was ground with a wooden rocker in a hollowed-out trough mortar of wood.

Hunting, as previously stated, was perhaps of greater psychological than economic importance, but it consumed a major part of the men's time and attention and brought considerable prestige. The principal animals, none too abundant, were deer, tapirs, peccaries, monkeys, birds, and several local rodents. The hunting weapons were a long bow, arrows with specialized points for different game, wooden paddle clubs with sharpened edges, spears, and blowguns. The Guiana blowgun was made of a section of bamboo tubing covered with pitch and bound tightly. The upper Amazon blowgun consisted of two pieces of chonta palm, grooved on the inside for the bore, and bound together with bast. The mouthpiece was of carved bone. The blowguns were about eight feet long. The standard equipment for the blowgun included a bamboo quiver for the supply of split palm darts; a gourd full of tree cotton to be used as a wadding on one end of the dart; the jaw of a piranha fish, the teeth of which are sharp enough to cut a groove near the point of the dart; and a clay jar of curare poison. Only specialists trained in the proper magical ritual were permitted to prepare the curare poison which was an important article of trade. The strychnine element in curare produces a paralyzing effect on the game but does not permanently poison the meat. Traps were also used in hunting and included spring bows, spring nooses, deadfalls, pitfalls, and nets. Dogs, the only domesticated animals, were specially trained for hunting.

The rivers of the tropics abound in fish; these were shot with bow and arrows, harpooned, or speared. Weirs were constructed and many kinds of basketry traps were known and some groups used dip nets. The most widely used technique was to dam a stream and poison the fish. Many varieties of effective poisonous plants were known. Wild plants supplemented the food supply: over twenty-two plants and edible fruits, of which palm cabbages and nuts were most important, were collected by the women who also gathered honey, birds' eggs, and shellfish where available.

Fish and meat were grilled over the fire, but the basic dish was the pepper pot, a stew of the available meat and vegetables. Some foods were dried or smoked, but in general little attention was paid to preserving for storage, due in part to the scarcity of salt, itself an important article of trade. The firedrill and basketry fire fan were part of the standard equipment. Most forest tribes prepared mildly intoxicating drinks from fermented cassava bread or from the local fruits and also used several narcotics. Tobacco, the most important of these, was rolled into cigars, chewed with lime, taken as snuff, or, in liquid form, snuffed up the nose through tubes. Most of the tobacco was used in connection with ceremonies, particularly those of initiation.

Although the tribes changed locale from time to time, a village might be occupied for two or three years and the houses were correspondingly durable. All houses were constructed of log frames covered with thatch, and, in spite of considerable variation in detail, conformed generally to two types. One, the round house, had an outer circle of upright wall posts connected to a tall center pole by crossbeams. The conical roof thus formed was thatched with grass or palm leaves. This type of house was common south of the Amazon and in the Guianas. The second type, the *maloca*, had a rectangular groundplan outlined with short wall posts, a central ridgepole, and a gabled roof. The ends might be bowed outward to form an oval groundplan. The roof extended almost to the ground and was closely thatched as a protection against rain and wind. House walls might be left open or filled in with bamboo splints, bark, or poles covered with wattle. In some regions the houses were sealed tight to guard against mosquitoes. The floor was of packed clay. Each house had an entrance at either end, one for the women, one for the men and their guests. Some houses were large, others small, the size depending in part on the type of village. Three main village plans were followed: the barnyard type, consisting of a number of small houses without special alignment; the Guaraní type, with regular streets flanked by large houses; and the upper Amazon type in which the village consisted of one large house. Some of the last-mentioned houses had a groundplan one hundred fifteen by seventy-five feet and a height of thirty feet.

The hammock, a common article of household equipment, was made of palm fiber or cotton, either woven on a true loom, or netted. Some tribes of the upper Amazon built platform beds of split palm poles set on a frame raised from the floor. Wooden stools, with either two or four legs, which might be carved in animal form were used everywhere. Other household equipment was part of the craft tradition. Many types of palm leaf baskets were woven, including openwork carrying baskets, telescope storage baskets, work baskets of various shapes, and square baskets with fitted covers. Palm leaves and reeds were also used in plaiting manioc squeezers and sieves, fire fans, fish traps, and crowns for feather headdresses. Fish nets, net bags, and hair nets were made of bast fibers, twisted on the thigh. Pottery, used everywhere, was either painted in geometric designs or decorated with modeled lugs. The main forms were plates, bowls, cooking pots, big platters, storage jars, and large burial urns. Weaving had a wide distribution although it was not always of major importance. Both cotton and palm fibers were spun on a supported spindle or rolled on the thigh. A frame loom was used to weave hammocks, bolts of cloth for clothing, headbands, bags, and similar articles. The techniques were competent, but not unusually complex. In eastern Bolivia and elsewhere, bark cloth was made from the inner bark of certain trees, soaked and pounded with wooden clubs or flat stones. The bark cloth was painted and used for dance masks and ceremonial costumes. Many artifacts, mortars, pestles, stools, drums, clubs, bows, platters, and bowls were made from wood; bark vessels were common; and bones and teeth were used to make a number of implements. Stone tools were rare, metals infrequent, and dressed skin work unusual.

The manufacture of many of these articles was usually a village specialty. In a limited area the people in one village made pottery, in another they prepared calabashes, another basketry, another blowguns, another poisons, etc. The finished products were then traded by private informal barter or gift exchange, but this practice did not result in regular markets, middlemen, mediums of exchange, or formal trade. Still, this exchange system provided each village with a reasonably wide selection of craft products. The quality and versatility of craftsmanship was relatively high, but it led neither to the formation of craft guilds nor to any particular emphasis on the individual artist. Likewise, wealth and property concepts remained undeveloped.

Boat building was also a village or tribal specialty. Of course, all groups made simple rafts by lashing logs together, and some authorities consider these the oldest form of water transportation in the area. The log dugouts, the most widespread type of watercraft, required exceptional skill in manufacture, especially those used for ocean travel which were up to sixty feet long and capable of carrying from thirty to sixty men. Large trees were felled by fire and ax, chopped and trimmed to the desired size, and the interior burned out with controlled fire. Both the outer and inner sides were then scraped to the proper thickness and thwarts inserted. The paddles were of wood with a crutch handle and a long thin blade. Bark canoes were also widely used. A large piece of bark was cut from a tree in the shape required. The ends were turned up and the ribs and thwarts inserted. Some bark canoes were forty feet long and could hold thirty persons. In contrast, land transportation was of minor importance. Paths were cut through the forest and log or twisted cable bridges were built for crossing small streams.

In most parts of the tropics, clothing was restricted to the simplest genital covering. An exception to this rule was found in the upper Amazon where, due to Andean influence, loin cloths, belts, and slit neck shirts were worn. Everywhere, however, ceremonial costumes were more elaborate than the ordinary dress. The use of ornaments and body decoration compensated in part for the paucity of clothing. Ligatures were bound tightly around the upper arms and the ankles, giving a distorted appearance to the limbs. This practice was followed for magical increase of strength rather than for beauty. Heads were deformed by means of tightly wrapped boards in the upper Amazon area. Most groups tattooed their faces and arms, and some filed or blackened their teeth. Lip plugs, earplugs, and noseplugs were made from stone, shell, and wood. Grease paint was used on the body, not only for decoration on ceremonial occasions but also for protection from insects. Each tribe had a distinctive style of hairdress; all used combs made of palm splints bound between two wooden bars. There were many types of feather ornaments. Feathers were attached to basketry hats and sewn on woven bands for back hangings, arm pendants, and aprons. Capes had a net base to which feathers were attached. The Tupí glued feathers on their bodies with honey. Beadwork aprons were common, and necklaces were made of jaguar teeth and claws, stones, shells, seeds, beetle wings, human teeth, and bird bones. Quite apart from their aesthetic value, these ornaments indicated distinctions of sex, age, and position, designated tribal affiliations, and furnished magical protection for the wearers.

Subsistence activities and material culture were more or less uniform throughout. There were, to be sure, some differences in details and emphases, but no startling contrasts. The social, religious, and political organization, on the other hand, was far more variable. The village was the basic social unit, and its members were usually loosely united by kinship ties. The villages varied greatly in population, but the maximum figure was probably around the six hundred reported for the Tupí. It is difficult to establish the minimum because of the common practice of a larger village absorbing one that became too small to function. Most villages were composed of several enlarged families, with relationship traced through either the mother or the father. These enlarged families occupied a single house within which each of the component families had its own fireplace and sleeping quarters. However, many activities, such as house building and group hunting, required the cooperation of all the village members.

Each village had a chief who sometimes acquired considerable power through his ability as a war leader. However, permanent political organization rarely extended beyond the village itself. Even though many members of two villages might be related, kinship did not outlaw internecine fighting. Common language helped to unite a number of villages, but the unity was informal. Several Jívaro villages might unite for a time under a single chief, but they had no name for this larger political group. Everywhere a powerful village might dominate a weaker one, but such fitful unity lasted only until strength was regained by the subject people.

Perhaps as a reflection of the intimacy of the village life and the numerous social and kinship relationships, events in the individual life cycle were treated as public affairs. Birth was an occasion for public celebration. The whole village saw to it that the parents observed the proper taboos, particularly the widespread custom of the couvade, in which the father, not the mother, goes into confinement and receives the visits of his neighbors. Soon after birth the child was named, an important event supervised by the magician or medicineman. At puberty, girls were isolated for several days, forced to observe special food taboos, and instructed by the older women. A change in style of hairdress or facial tattooing signified that they had completed the ceremony. Boys were subjected to certain tests before being admitted to full adult tribal status. In one of the more drastic of these ordeals reported for the Guianas, a wickerwork frame which contained many wasps was placed on a boy's bare back. When simultaneously stung by these insects, he was expected to show no sign of pain. Marriage was not celebrated with great ceremony since it was usually prearranged by the parents, according to standard rules of the village. Death, on the other hand, was an occasion of grave concern for all the community since the ghosts might return, a circumstance avoided by abandoning the house, performing wild dances, mutilating the corpse, building fires on the grave, and participating in complex purification rites.

Warfare, one of the curses of Amazonia, played an important role in the activities of many groups. Motives for aggression were numerous, including plunder, revenge, and individual prestige for the warrior. Some groups sought trophy heads, others wanted prisoners for their cannibalistic practices. Even the non-aggressive tribes were forced to take measures in their own defense. The weapons for warfare and hunting were interchangeable, except for the blowgun, which apparently was ineffective in fighting. Protection was a major consideration. Consequently, many villages were situated well back from the rivers, were approached by hidden paths, and might be further protected with palisades, reinforced outer walls, sentry boxes, and watch towers. Pitfalls with poisoned stakes and spring traps were placed along the open approaches. In northern Amazonia, log signal drums were used to summon aid and warn friendly neighbors. The war spirit was drilled into the boys from early childhood, not only through specific instruction in fighting, but also through tales of the honor and prestige to be gained by becoming a full-fledged warrior.

As mentioned before, some warfare was inspired by the desire for trophy heads which not only brought great prestige to the taker, but also transferred the ghost power of the victim. Carefully preserved and decorated trophy skulls were commonly collected, but the Jívaro Indian *tsantsas*, the shrunken heads, are probably the best known trophies. The Jívaro warrior tried to obtain his enemy's head so that it could later be skinned and shrunk for a trophy. Only heads taken in formal warfare with established enemies were recognized. The residents of neighboring villages who frequently were actually relatives were often the traditional enemies. It was a violation of custom to allow the head of a blood relative to be shrunk, but the killer was permitted to substitute a sloth or monkey head. The heads were prepared before the war party returned to its home village. The process took about twenty hours. A slit from the top of the head to the base of the neck facilitated the removal of the skin from the skull. The slit, the eyes, and the mouth were sewn so that the skin formed a bag which was then simmered but not boiled in a vine juice solution that contained some tannin. Next, round stones were heated and rolled inside the skin bag, and hot sand was poured in at intervals. The outside was ironed with hot stones. This repeated scorching process reduced the skin to about the size of a doubled fist. A ring was then sewn around the neck and a suspension cord inserted through the top. Finally the trophy was smoked over a smudge for final curing. When the warriors returned to their village, they were received in a triumphal entry which was succeeded by elaborate ceremonies, intended to purify the killer and to transfer the power of his trophy head to him. Later, the slayer himself gave a victory feast at which the purification rites were repeated and the transfer of enemy power completed.

Not all tropical forest tribes were cannibals. However, some, like the Witoto and Bora of the upper Amazon and the Tupinamba of the Brazilian coast, were ardent practitioners. Tupinamba cannibalism has been recorded in some detail. In every battle the warriors attempted to take prisoners alive in order to bring them back as slaves until the time arrived for their sacrifice. The prisoners were forced to do menial tasks and were frequently insulted verbally, but otherwise they were well treated and even permitted to intermarry with their captors. Dressed like other Tupinamba, they were distinguished only by a cotton rope around the neck or by a string of beads representing the number of months preceding the day of sacrifice. Prisoners never attempted to escape, even though they were not closely guarded, since it would be a great disgrace for them to return to their own villages. A ceremony of several days' duration preceded the execution. The prisoner was painted black, decorated with feathers, and was even forced to escape and be recaptured, thus giving prestige to still another warrior. Finally, the victim was led around the village, secured by a rope around his waist, but otherwise free to repel attacks, until, still fighting, he was killed by a selected executioner. The orgy of eating his barbequed flesh was enjoyed by men, women, and children alike. The skull was cleaned and placed on a pike set on the village stockade. The executioner went through a long period of purification.

The Tropical Agriculturists had numerous ceremonies, but these were not calendrical, reflecting their lack of interest in the agricultural seasons. Instead, ceremonies were coincidental with such irregular occasions as baptism, house-warming, death, or the return of a war party. All such celebrations presented a mixture of social and religious elements, but in general they were gay affairs, involving beer drinking, singing, animated dancing, and distinctive costumes and ornaments. The music was furnished by split log or skin-headed drums, flutes, panpipes, trumpets, and rattles.

As suggested by the social nature of the ceremonies, the religious practices were not very formalized. The Indians were strongly animistic, with a belief in many nature demons, ghosts, and good and evil spirits, but none of these was arranged into a complex hierarchy. Cults were rare although some groups had secret religious societies, but none of these was led by formal priests. The medicineman, however, was prominent both as a curer of sickness and a sorcerer. He was carefully schooled by older members of the profession and taught a knowledge of herbs, ventriloquism, and the methods of attaining a state of trance. This last ability involved taking strong narcotics, such as tobacco juice, which induced visions and, according to belief, allowed the spirits to speak through the medium.

Centuries of European contact have changed these tropical forest Indians. Some have been eliminated, others have been driven from their original territory, none has escaped modification of culture principally through the acquisition of European trade goods. A few have maintained their independent culture patterns by the simple device of retiring still deeper into the vast Amazonian jungle.

LOWLAND ARCHAEOLOGY

It is difficult to do more than speculate on the antiquity of tropical agriculture. The region involved is so vast, the number of tested sites and areas so small, that we do not have adequate data. Nor do we know, as is assumed, that pottery marks the initial spread of the Tropical Agriculturists. In this region, as in the

Andean, agriculture may have had an early stage among people not yet familiar with pottery. The most pertinent data on age comes from a study of Venezuelan chronology and radiocarbon dates. This implies that agriculture, as marked by the presence of pottery, was established on the lower Orinoco at the beginning of the first millennium B.C.

Prior to this there were two unrelated preceramic phases, the oldest, an Early Hunter stage known from chipped stone artifacts, is designated El Jobo complex. No extinct faunal remains have been found in association. Other sites without pottery, shell deposits presumably left by canoe-using fishermen, occur on the coast and islands. These are under three meters in thickness, on what may be a subsiding shoreline. Carbon from the bottom of one site indicates an age of over 4000 years. Culturally there are similarities with comparable Caribbean deposits but none with the sometimes huge preceramic middens of the Atlantic coast of Brazil.

The subsequent record in Venezuela has been divided by Cruxent and Rouse into four periods within which three basic ceramic traditions form or give rise to six classes or series of ceramics. These are not all sequential as they overlap to some extent in time and distribution. The oldest, the Saladoid, from the lower Orinoco, has flat-based, flaring bowls with vertical strap handles and white on red painting, a ware which ultimately spread via Lake Valencia to the north coast, Trinidad, the Lesser Antilles and Puerto Rico. Later, starting in the same area, the Barancoid wares have annular bases, incised flange rims, and modeled and incised lug ornaments. These spread, via Lake Valencia, to the north coast, Trinidad, perhaps the Guianas, and influenced Antillean potters. The third ware, Tocuyanoid, which may have spread eastward from Colombia, brought three and four-legged bowls, broad line incision, and red and black curved designs on white ground.

Existing archaeological collections from the Amazon come mainly from three widely separated localities. The ceramics forming the bulk of the material are distinctive, yet the three complexes share the trait of anthropomorphic burial urns decorated with relief, modeling, polychrome painting, and broad line incision. We may assume that a broadly similar cultural pattern prevailed but the relationships are still undefined. Systematic field-work on the island of Marajó, at the mouth of the Amazon, shows that the Marajoara culture is intrusive in this area. More than one hundred cemetery and habitation mounds have been reported, the former containing abundant, elaborately decorated pottery. The basic decorative techniques are incision, excision of background adjacent to the design, painting, and modeling. These were used with red and white slips covering the vessel surface or applied to incised or excised areas, producing a complex, varied, and impressive ceramic art (Plate 3). These elaborate styles disappeared before the beginning of the historic period and only the more simple forms survived.

The second site area, Mirakanguéra, is on the middle Amazon at the mouth of the Madeira River. Here bowls and effigy urns have been found. The head of the effigy figure is on the cover of the urn; the limbs are represented in low relief; and the urns are further decorated by incised and painted rectilinear designs. The final site, on the Río Napo in eastern Ecuador, again has bowls and anthropomorphic urns. The urns have relief features, but the limbs are modeled as separate appendages and are banded in a fashion suggesting ligatures (Plate 26). The decoration combines broad incisions with black, red, and white polychrome painting to form patterns of alternating broad and narrow lines. In brief, these three Amazonian sites all have effigy urns with covers decorated in somewhat similar patterns in relief, modeling, polychrome painting, and broad line incision.

At Santarem, at the junction of the Tapajoz and the Amazon, the style of ceramics is quite different. There are many variations on the basic shapes of open bowls, open mouth jars, and constricted neck vessels. Many ceramics are painted; another type is so elaborated with modeled lugs and other appended elements that it can be called the most bizarre pottery of South America (Fig. 3). A few, possibly older pieces, more simply modeled are geometrically painted, either black on red, red on buff or black and red on white. Most of the material seems to be more recent than the effigy urn group described above. Anthropomorphic urns continued to be made well into the historic period, as illustrated by those found with glass bead bracelets at the site of Maracá in the Brazilian Guianas. At Mojos, in the eastern Bolivian tropics, stratified habitation mounds have been excavated. The earlier levels contain polychrome painted ceramics, but no urns; tripod urns painted in a manner suggestive of the Amazon effigy urn group are found in the later levels.

These ceramic features suggest that the older cultures were more highly developed in that regard than are the Modern Agriculturists. At the mouth of the Amazon the elaborately decorated Marajoara material (Plate 3) is intrusive. It appears suddenly, fully developed and ends abruptly. Beneath it are types of simple ceramics and traits which imply that the culture of the Modern Agriculturists derives from this older stock and not from the Marajoara or the Tapajo. The latter has not been fully investigated.

This raises the questions of the origin and fate of the intrusive elements. The area is so vast, the problems of recovery so difficult that the answers may not all be found for some time. The marked stylistic connection

FIG. 3. Santarem vessels and figure urn from Maracá. *Courtesy of Belem Museum (Santarem) and Museo Nacional, Rio de Janeiro.*

between the Marajoara and Río Napo material led to field-work in the latter region. This showed a strong, direct connection even though the areas are eighteen hundred miles apart. Certain Marajoara elements are lacking and are assumed to have developed at some intermediate point within the Amazon basin.

Sites near Pucallpa on the Ucayali yield evidence of occupation of some depth. In a succession of changes in the ceramic sequence the strongest connections are with early material found at Valdivia in the Province of Guayas, Ecuador, and to a much lesser degree with Marajoara. These similarities occur in the second Ucayali horizon.

ANDEAN FARMERS

The third major South American culture pattern was based on intensive sedentary agriculture. The pattern was distributed throughout most parts of the Andes, or, in terms of modern political divisions, the highlands of Colombia, Ecuador, Peru, and Bolivia; the coast of Ecuador and Peru; northwest Argentina; and north and central Chile. All of this area, except Colombia, formed part of the Inca Empire when it was conquered by the Spaniards in 1532, which accounts for some of the cultural uniformity. However, the Inca held this region only a short time and there is considerable evidence that the basic Andean pattern had prevailed long before.

In many countries, the names of outstanding pre-Inca tribes were recorded. The Chibcha, the most advanced tribe in Colombia, were limited in distribution to the Departments of Cundinamarca and Boyacá, roughly around modern Bogotá. Elsewhere the Colombian highlands were occupied by many small tribes, of which the best known were the Tairona of the Santa

Marta Mountains and the Quimbaya, Lile, and Coco-
nuco of the Cauca Valley. Each major basin of the Ecuadorian highlands was dominated by a single tribe,
named, from north to south, Pasto, Cara, Panzaleo,
Puruhá, Cañari, and Palta. The Esmeralda, Manta, and
Puná occupied the coastal plains. The pre-Inca cultures
in Peru and Bolivia will be discussed in detail, in terms
of their archaeological remains, in the second section
of this volume. North Chile was held by the Atacameño, while Northwest Argentina was divided between
the Humahuaca and the Diaguita. The Araucanians
once occupied the whole Central Valley of Chile, but
were forced southward by the Inca invaders. The Araucanians deviated considerably from the Andean Farmers pattern and were in many ways equally close to the
Southern Hunters.

The Andean Farmers based their subsistence on intensive agriculture; hunting, fishing, and gathering
were definitely secondary activities. Agriculture was
both a male and female occupation. The major religious ceremonies and rituals concerned the agricultural
cycle. The principal domesticated plants were distributed to their full climatic limits within the area wherever they could possibly be grown. Most important
were maize, beans, squash, potatoes, quinoa, sweet potatoes, manioc, peanuts, cotton, peppers, tobacco, and
coca. The agricultural implements were simple: a digging-stick, with or without a metal point, a hoe, and a
club with a stone head for breaking up clods. In spite
of these simple tools, technical knowledge of planting
and cultivating was well advanced. Fields were systematically irrigated; most groups not only used fertilizers,
but understood the virtues of crop rotation and allowing land to lie fallow. Terraces were built to utilize
hillsides and to prevent erosion. This agricultural
knowledge was shared by the total population and was
not the property of a few specialists.

Everywhere food preservation and storage were important. Drying and freezing were the principal methods of preservation, and special granaries were built for storage. Foods were prepared by boiling, toasting, roasting, and baking in underground ovens. Corn was fermented for a mild beer called *chicha*. In areas where the narcotic coca was chewed with lime, tobacco was of secondary importance and was used more like a medicine. Elsewhere it was smoked in pipes or taken through nose tubes as snuff. In the Central Andes, Northwest Argentina, and northern Chile, herding was second only to agriculture in importance. The domesticated llama and alpaca added greatly to the total economy of these people.

The crafts were advanced. The potters made utilitarian cooking jars, bowls, plates, and water jars for daily use, as well as elaborately decorated vessels for ceremonials and burial. Both men and women shared the work of weaving their garments on simple looms. Both cotton and wool were employed. A distinction was maintained between clothing for common wear and the superlative cloth woven for ceremonial and mortuary purposes. Utilitarian tools and fine ornaments were made of gold, silver, copper, and tin as well as combinations of these metals in a variety of techniques, such as hollow casting, soldering, filigree, and gilding. Other craft skills were devoted to basketry, woodwork, the decoration of calabashes, and the manufacture of numerous artifacts of stone, shell, and bone. In general, each family produced its own utilitarian articles, but more skilled craft work was in the hands of specialists. Villages as well as individuals might specialize and exchange the products of their skills. In some places, fixed markets were established.

All clothing was loom woven. The standard male costume consisted of a breechclout, belt, slit neck shirt, shawl, and headband. The women wore a wrap-around garment secured at the waist by a belt, a headband, and a shoulder shawl. Woven bags with carrying straps were a constant part of the costume. More elaborate costumes were made for religious and ceremonial occasions and for interment. Body painting, tattooing, skull deformation, earplugs, noseplugs, necklaces, and many other types of ornaments were elaborated and often distinguished people of different rank, profession, or tribe.

On the whole, water transportation was only slightly developed. Simple rafts and reed balsas were used on Lake Titicaca and on the coast of Peru; more elaborate rafts were built on the north coast of Ecuador. The Araucanians were exceptions, and made large dugouts and plank canoes. Elsewhere, more attention was paid to land travel, on foot, and with llamas and alpacas as transport animals. The widespread Inca Empire was united by a network of roads, bridges, and wayside inns for the traveler.

Intensive agriculture resulted in a relatively stabilized food economy and the consequent support of large permanent populations. Houses were built accordingly. In the Central Andes the commonest building materials were sunbaked adobe and stone. The tribes of Ecuador and Colombia constructed round frame houses with conical thatched roofs. The side walls were either of stone or lined with clay. Plank houses were built by the Araucanians in Chile. The village which consisted of a number of houses formed an important social and cooperative labor unit and often held title to the real property. Each village had a chief or headman, and usually its own religious cult. The households represented several closely related families who were united as a village by affiliations of residence alone. The Andean Farmers pattern was characterized by political organization of the village units. The complexity of this political superstructure varied: in many places it assumed the form of a confederacy and among the Inca it became a true state or empire. Both within the village and in the political superstructure class distinctions were marked, were based on wealth and leadership, and tended to crystallize into true caste systems.

Warfare was well organized. The military leaders were also political figures, and the warriors constituted a specialized class. The spear-thrower, spear, club, sling, and shield were basic weapons; the bow and arrows and the bolas were of secondary importance. The war tactics involved the use of spies, blockades, storming, and formation fighting. Many villages were fortified and special forts and places of refuge were built.

Events in the life crises of the individual, birth, puberty, and marriage, were usually family affairs with little public ceremony. Death, however, involved considerable public ritual in the preparation of the corpse, the tomb, and the grave equipment. In part this was associated with the widespread practice of ancestor worship. Other public ceremonials were correlated with the calendrical agricultural cycle and were conducted by specialized priests. Medicinemen, as distinguished from priests, confined their practices to individuals and did not participate in the great public ceremonials. The priests were the interpreters of the formalized religion and the leaders of specialized cults. Religious centers and temples were constructed. The gods were arranged in a hierarchy and surrounded with specific ceremonies. The Araucanians were the exception to this formalized religious pattern; among them animistic beliefs, sorcerers, and medicinemen were of paramount importance.

This basic pattern existed throughout the Andean area, although in varying degrees of elaboration, since its intensity depended in large part on the availability of large areas suitable for wide scale agriculture. The European conquest initiated profound changes, eliminating, displacing, or absorbing some groups, radically modifying the cultures of all others. The modern Indian population, judged culturally as well as physically, is concentrated in certain areas. The Quechua-speaking Indians, descendants of the Inca, live in the highlands of Ecuador, Peru, and eastern Bolivia. Around Lake Titicaca are the Aymara, who successfully resisted both Inca and Spanish absorption. The Araucanians survive in the extreme southern part of the Central Chile Valley. Elsewhere the Indian cultures have been largely eliminated, although a few small groups of minor significance are still extant. The Indian of the past is rapidly becoming the Mestizo of today, mixed both in blood and in culture.

The Andean Farmers pattern is demonstrably old in the Central Andes, where sufficient archaeological work has been done to furnish the data for an historical reconstruction of development from its earliest beginnings to its culmination in the Inca Empire. Outside of the Central Andes the evidence for antiquity is less satisfactory, due in part to the limited amount of recorded excavation. The Central Andean cultures seem to have been united for many centuries. Elsewhere, there was apparently greater cultural diversity. This may be clarified in a brief review of the outstanding archaeological finds beyond the boundaries of the Central Andean region. These archaeological finds are presented in terms of the major geographical divisions: the Northern Andes, which covers Colombia and Ecuador; and the Southern Andes, which includes Northwest Argentina and Chile.

NORTHERN ANDEAN ARCHAEOLOGY

COLOMBIA

Although the western mountainous section of Colombia is extensive, it contains only a few regions suitable for the intensive development of the Andean Farmers pattern. The best terrain with cultivable soil and adequate rainfall is the high plateau of the Departments of Cundinamarca and Boyacá where the Chibcha achieved their significant cultural development. Elsewhere appropriate flat lands and intermont basins are relatively small, with the exception of the Cauca Valley flats which in early times were too swampy or too grass-covered to be utilized by Indian farmers. The archaeological records demonstrate that the full Andean pattern crystallized late and principally in the Chibcha region. The small mountain areas developed local cultures which were comparatively isolated and had little influence on each other. At least we have no evidence for widespread organization or for any great cultural overlap from one region to another.

The Colombian cultures are in some ways similar to those of the Tropical Agriculturists. Slash and burn clearing was practiced; the circular houses were of frame construction; secondary burial in effigy urns was widespread; leg ligatures were worn; and four-legged wooden stools were used. However, the Colombian cultures are distinguishable from those of the Amazon in their great emphasis on agriculture and in their craft skills in metallurgy, ceramics, and weaving (Plate 4). Moreover, in view of the extremely limited amount of scientific archaeological work, it is premature to draw conclusions. Many areas have never been investigated and others are known only through undocumented collections. Consequently, the archaeology must still be described in terms of the major geographic zones which present distinctive local styles. The evidence for arranging these zones and styles in any chronological order is largely conjectural.

The Chibcha civilization, in its advanced development, is frequently classified with the Inca and Aztec. Its builders occupied the most favorable plateau in Colombia. It is in this area, then, that one would anticipate discovering the most elaborate archaeological remains and the best evidence for the antiquity of the pattern. As yet, however, the archaeology is disappointing. Large village sites have not been discovered, although there are some circles of upright stones outlining the foundations of conical houses. Chibcha burials are in simple pits, either with or without stone slab covers, or in dry caves. The ceramics are not very well made. The principal shapes are ollas, pedestal bowls, and jars with either short or tall collars decorated with painted or relief faces and figures. However, most of the vessels are decorated with simple geometric designs executed by painting, incision, punch, appliqué, and, more rarely, relief. There are also elaborately decorated clay figurines, incised whorls, effigy ocarinas, clay pipes, and carved stamps. A few pieces of cotton shawls with painted and some warp pattern designs have been found in dry caves. These have loom widths in excess of fifty inches and show a curious multiple bobbin handling of the weft. The goldwork, to which the style term "Muisca" is now applied, has a rough surface unlike most other Colombian gold. Seemingly made of sheet metal, with soldered wire details, it is actually all cast reproduction of wax originals. Two examples of such work are shown (Plate 5, top row, right). The collections also contain many utilitarian artifacts, such as stone axes, celts, and grindstones as well as wooden stools, lances, and spear-throwers. Although all of this

material is pre-Spanish, it does not imply any great antiquity for the Chibcha culture.

The isolated mountain range of Santa Marta in
northeastern Colombia was the center of the Tairona
culture. This region is the best known scientifically,
but the large collections have not been temporally subdivided although they are all believed to be pre-Spanish. Some of the Tairona sites are large villages with a
great deal of above-ground stone construction. The
stone masonry includes both rough stone and carefully
dressed and fitted blocks. Ring house platforms lined
with single or double rows of stone are typical. The
houses have two entrances approached by stone slab
steps. Other stone building features are faced terraces,
long stairways, paved roads, slab bridges, and lined reservoir pits. A village consists of a number of ring houses
surrounded by paths, terraces, stairs, and reservoirs.
Most burials were in simple pits or in large urns, but a
few were in stone-lined boxes or in dressed stone burial
vaults. There are two major types of ceramics; thick
redware plates, bowls, and jars with appliquéd design;
thin incised blackware annular base open bowls, cups,
double spout vessels, tetrapod jars, stirrup spouts, and
modeled effigy vessels. Tall cylindrical "treasure" jars
with fitted clay covers are also characteristic. Rarely do
these have polychrome painted designs. Tairona collections abound in small artifacts. These include clay
toys, rattles, cylindrical stamps, ocarinas, whistles, and
small modeled figures, but, interestingly, no spindle
whorls. Among the numerous stone artifacts are utilitarian metates, manos, mortars, and pestles, as well as
better finished polished axes, incised batons, winged
pendants, and many types of beads. Jade was used to
some extent. Incised and carved objects of bone and
shell are also characteristic. Beads, rings, and pendants
were also made of gold, copper, and tumbaga. The
Tairona culture had certainly achieved a reasonable

complexity, but again evidence for antiquity is lacking.

The hills on both sides of the Upper Cauca Valley, roughly between Cali and Popayán, are dotted with small scattered house sites, again dated as pre-Spanish. The house platforms are simple cut-out earth terraces with a thin refuse deposit, indicating only a brief occupation. Graves are found in or near the houses. A typical grave has a square or round shaft about one meter in diameter and some two meters deep, and a hollow side chamber entered through a slab-covered window door. Several extended burials and as many as two hundred pots may be found in a single grave. The pots, mainly open bowls, pedestal jars, ollas, and constricted mouth vessels with conical bases, seem to have been made especially for burial. They have a red slip, but no painted designs. Decoration is by incision, punch, crude scoring, and simple appliqué. Other associated artifacts are clay spindle whorls and gold noseplugs.

The Chibcha and Tairona cultures present some evidence of complexity. Other Late period sites are similar to those of the Upper Cauca, without evidence of concentrated population, large settlements, or great complexity. Because of certain stylistic analogies with Ecuador and Peru, the Nariño and Quimbaya cultures seem to be slightly earlier in time than the Late period cultures described above. In gross comparative terms these cultures may be classed as Middle period in Colombia.

The Nariño sites are in the Nariño Department along the Ecuadorian border at the headwaters of the Cauca River. No surface ruins are known, but there are both short and deep shaft graves that contain both direct and crude urn burials. The main ceramic shapes are variants of ollas, plates, and annular base bowls, all decorated in two-color positive, or, commonly, in resist negative decoration. Positive designs were applied directly before firing. Negative ones were formed after firing by using a resistant coat of liquid clay to protect certain areas from a subsequent over-all deposit of carbon. Most designs are carelessly applied broad line geometric figures, but there are some animal motifs. Among the typical associated artifacts are clay ocarinas, spindle whorls, and whistles; stone chisels, celts, T-shaped axes, pounders, and grindstones; and some simple gold discs and plaques.

The Quimbaya sites are located in the Departments of Antioquia and Caldas in the Central Cauca Valley. The large Quimbaya ceramic collections include a great variety of materials which may eventually be temporally subdivided. The most typical pottery shapes are double jars, modeled containers, double spout vessels, whistling jars, tripod and tetrapod vessels, annular base bowls, tall shoulder jars, and many open bowls and ollas. These vessels are decorated in fired red and white positive painting, resist negative decoration, and may also have modeling, incision, and excision in which the background is cut away to produce a relief design. The designs are generally simple geometric patterns. Seated and standing clay figurines, incised whorls, and a variety of decorated clay stamps are also common. Stonework is abundantly represented by celts, T-shaped axes, beads, and grindstones. The Quimbaya culture is best known for its metal work in gold and tumbaga, a combination of gold and copper. The objects demonstrate great technical skill in solid and hollow casting, cast filigree, cutouts, and repoussé. Most of the gold was worked into ornaments, such as nose rings, breast plates, bells, and bracelets, but this metal was also fashioned into hollow jars, bottles, and figurines (Plate 5). There are gold masks for burials, and solid scepters, decorated by bands of metal of different composition. Although distinctive in many details, both the Quimbaya and Nariño cultures share such features as deep shaft and chamber graves, annular base vessels, and particularly two and three-color resist negative painting. These features also serve to link them with the middle periods of Ecuador.

Between the Upper Cauca and Magdalena rivers lie sites of the Tierradentro culture which is also classed with the Middle periods, although it may be slightly earlier than the Quimbaya and Nariño. Tierradentro culture is distinguished by elaborate painted subterranean tombs excavated directly into the soft rock of the area. A spiral stairway enters the main arched chamber which may have one or more central columns and a series of cut-out side niches. The walls and ceiling are decorated with high relief figures and with an over-all black, white, red painted geometric design. Broken pottery covers the floors but, nevertheless, the chambers seem to have been intended for burial rather than habitation. The ceramic fragments represent several styles: blackware, black-on-red painted, and incised red. Most distinctive, however, are fragments of large vessels with relief serpentine bands decorated with deep incised lines and punctations filled with a white paste. Some of these serpent-like bands end in high relief snake heads. Two crude statues were found in one of these tombs; otherwise the stone artifacts are limited to polished axes, chisels, grindstones, and beads. Gold is the only metal yet found.

The rolling forest-covered hills at the headwaters of the Magdalena River do not appear to be a favorable region either for the support of a large population or for the development of an advanced culture. Yet here are found the San Agustín stone carvings and temples that represent the earliest known remains in Colombia. San Agustín is a general designation for a series of sites in this rather extensive area. Some of the sites consist of large artificial mounds containing stone-lined and covered temples and carved idols. The slabs are not well dressed; some are painted in geometric design. Other sites have isolated, slab-lined tombs, some of which contain monolithic coffins. All structures seem to have been of a religious nature. San Agustín is famed for its stone carvings of which over three hundred have been found. These include bas reliefs on large boulders, cylindrical stones with sculptured heads, carved animal figures, elaborately carved base rock in stream beds, and many statues, some human and some anthropomorphic (Plate 6). The carved figures are depicted as wearing headbands, ornaments, simple clothing, and holding some object in the hands. The sculpture is well executed and highly varied, especially in details. Some carvings are found in the temples; others in isolated spots were possibly intended as grave markers. Grave accompaniment is limited. The ceramics are simple clay bowls, plates, pedestal jars, and tripod vessels, characterized by body angularity and great rim variation. Most vessels are monochrome, but on a few, geometric designs are executed in positive and resist painting, incision, and punch. Other artifacts include plain spindle whorls, simple gold ornaments, stone axes, mortars, pestles, and stone cutting tools.

In spite of the carvings, there is scant evidence in Colombia for any great elaboration of the Andean Farmers pattern until relatively late times. The local cultures of each region show little relationship to those of neighboring regions.

ECUADOR

Ecuador has been investigated more thoroughly than Colombia, although there are still many untouched areas. The evidence thus far assembled indicates that the Andean Farmers pattern was well established in both the highlands and the coast and also that it has a respectable antiquity in some sections. The highlands are dominated by two parallel mountain ranges, between which lie ten large intermont basins with sufficiently rich soils and adequate rainfall for the support of intensive agriculture. The coastal plains vary from

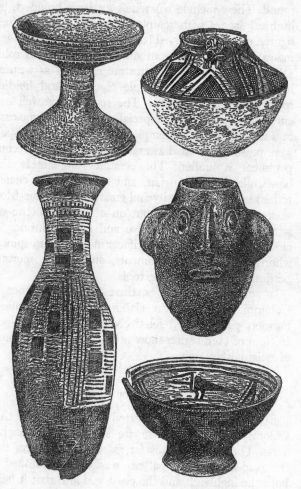

Fig. 4. Types of Ecuadorean pottery.

tropics in the north to desert in the south, but all sections present remains of higher civilization, at least from the immediate pre-Spanish periods. However, significant period names have not been established, except in a few places, and it is still impossible to set up comparable sequences for the whole country. Consequently, a review must follow the major geographic divisions.

A Far North Highlands unit is represented in the basin of Tulcán in Carchi Province, actually the southern extension of Nariño, Colombia. Most of the archaeological finds are virtually identical with those previously described for the Nariño culture, although some Inca materials are known in this basin. The similarities occur in ceramic shapes and design, in gold work, and even in the deep shaft type of tomb. In Ecuador, as in Colombia, there is no evidence of any great antiquity for these finds. Apart from the graves and their contents, there are also circular house foundations with thick earth walls, arranged in village clusters. The roofs were probably of the conical frame and thatch type.

The basins of Ibarra and Quito in the provinces of Imbabura and Pichincha are closely united physically and culturally as a North Highlands unit distinguished by large earthen mounds. Some of these were for burials, others were foundations for houses or temples. The three commonest shapes are circular, elliptical, and squared pyramidal. The mounds contain pottery and fragments in considerable quantity, but none is particularly distinctive. Local archaeologists recognize three major culture periods: the first with burial mounds; the second lacking mounds, but with burial in direct pits; and the third with habitation and temple mounds.

The Central Highlands unit includes the basins of Riobamba and Alausí in the provinces of Chimborazo, Tungurahua, and Alausí. Here seven periods have been established, the longest known sequence for Ecuador.

The Early period, which includes Proto-Panzaleo I and II, has house foundations built of rough stones set in mud, circular pit graves, and simple bowls, jars, pedestal base and tripod vessels. Ceramic designs are geometric and executed by incision, red and black positive, and two-color negative painting. A knowledge of agriculture is demonstrated by finds of maize, stone metates and manos. Llama bones are also associated. The Middle period, called Tuncahuán, is characterized by pedestal bowls and other shapes decorated in three-color negative painting similar to the Far North Highlands and Nariño in Colombia. The Late periods, called collectively, Puruhá, have three subdivisions, namely Guano, Elen Pata, and Huavalac, and are again associated with stone house foundations. The ceramics continue the traditions of the Early period, particularly the emphasis on incision and two-color negative painting. Appliqué design, however, is far more common in this period. Large face collar jars with textile-like patterns in two-color negative are characteristic. Metal work in gold and copper is found. Finally, the Inca Period terminates the sequence. This Central Highland chronology is a key series for Ecuador. With the exception of the Tuncahuán interruption, it seems to represent a continuous development, although possibly not of too extensive a time duration.

The large Cuenca basin covers the provinces of Cañar and Azuay and forms the South Highland unit. All the important surface ruins have been assigned to the Inca Period. An earlier occupation is, however, represented by many small habitation sites, and some remarkable grave finds with hammered gold plaques and ceremonial weapons, not clearly assignable to any period. The pre-Inca habitation refuse represents two major periods, Early and Late Cerro Narrío, and it seems likely that both of these will be subdivided when additional data are available. The Early Cerro Narrío is characterized by red-on-buff painted wares and by polished redwares with engraving and low relief. The late period is, in part, a continuation of the early period, but is associated with various intrusive styles, including painted clay drums. Again, great antiquity has not been established for this sequence.

Although Esmeraldas Province on the tropical north coast of Ecuador does not seem environmentally favorable to higher cultures, numerous earth mounds containing ceremonial artifacts have been reported. No time sequence has been established, nor can the materials be accurately placed in any comparative chronology. Treasure hunters have systematically looted the mounds, searching for the amazingly fine and technically varied miniature gold objects. Copper discs or gongs with high relief, socketed axes, and hollow bells have also been found. Esmeraldas is noted for its small beautifully modeled figurines with detailed appliqué and incised designs and elaborate headdresses. Also common are clay roller stamps with carved curvilinear designs. No stone statues were made, but many axes, ring stones, polishers, and grinders have been found. The ceramic shapes include many types of ollas, wide-mouthed open bowls, and a variety of miniature vessels. Some are plain; others are covered with red slips or decorated by incision, modeling, and appliqué. One modeled vessel represents a frame house with a sway-backed thatched roof.

Manabí Province marks the coastal transition zone between tropics and desert. Surface ruins of stone-faced platform mounds and clusters of house walls are numerous. However, Manabí is most famed for its stonework, including unique U-shaped stone seats (Fig. 5) which rest on crouching human or animal figures, flat slabs with low relief, stone columns, and crude stone statues. Urn burial is also a feature. The ceramic forms comprise ollas, open bowls with annular bases, tripod vessels, double-spout jars, and many others. The designs are varied, ranging from rough and fine line geometric incision, negative decoration on plain and two-color ware, red-on-buff and three-color polychrome, appliqué, to modeled lugs. Clay figurines are numerous and beautifully modeled. Flat carved stamps and incised whorls are also common. The varied

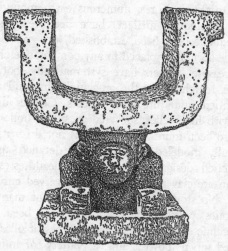

Fig. 5. Stone seat from Manabí, Ecuador.

ceramic collection suggests more than one time period, but, as yet, significant subdivisions have not been established.

Archaeological work elsewhere in Ecuador is in its infancy. The total picture is one of local complexities and certain antiquity, but still quite distinct from the Central Andes. Some pre-Inca influences from Peru can be traced, but these are generalized rather than specific; there are an equal number of parallels with Colombia. Considered in its entirety the archaeology of Ecuador appears diversified rather than unified; on the basis of present evidence an over-all developmental sequence cannot be established.

SOUTHERN ANDEAN ARCHAEOLOGY

The Southern Andes include Northwest Argentina on the east and Chile on the west. That this area, like Ecuador in the north, was ultimately incorporated in the expanding Inca Empire is readily confirmed by numerous archaeological remains. Two main branches of the Inca road system are known, one through Northwest Argentina, the other along the Pacific coast. In Argentina the roads are outlined by rows of stones, and, at regular intervals, clusters of small stone rooms and corrals represent the old rest houses which served the traveler. Large forts are identified as Inca through the associated ceramics. The fortified sites have rough stone room divisions with such typical Inca features as corbeled arches and wall niches. More frequent are mixed sites, such as La Paya in Salta Province, in which local styles are combined with Inca derived designs. Other common Inca artifacts are lacquered wooden keros, bronze knives, stellate stone maces, and slit bells. Many finds of the pre-Inca periods parallel, in a sense, the developments in the Central Andes, but with a distinctive orientation. Again, in spite of the extensive archaeological investigation, a great antiquity has not been established.

NORTHWEST ARGENTINA

Many sites in the Argentine Department of Jujuy reveal Inca influence; as many again are slightly pre-Inca. Among the former, particularly in the high puna which marks the Chilean border, the Inca, and even Colonial materials, are associated with a complex of wooden artifacts identified as the residue of the Atacameño culture. Characteristic types are wooden bells, toggles, knives, whorls, bows, arrows, tubes, and carved snuff tablets. However, the remains of an extensive pre-Inca culture, the Humahuaca, are found in the larger basins and valleys. Stone-faced agricultural terraces are numerous; villages are large and often dominated by fortresses on the higher peaks. The houses are rectangular, with stone walls but without niches. The roofs were made of perishable materials. There are also carefully built subterranean granaries. The burials in unlined pits or in stone-lined tombs contain prepared trophy skulls as well as many artifacts. Ceramics are represented by open bowls, goblets, cups, and ollas painted in black-on-red geometric designs. A few vessels have slight modeling or appliqué features. Gold, copper, and wooden artifacts are also common. The remains of the Humahuaca culture are widespread in this area, but do not extend farther south, nor, for that matter, are there any remains of the southern Calchaquí culture in Jujuy. A few finds seem to antedate Humahuaca somewhat, but none of these is sufficiently well identified to be designated as a separate period.

The other inhabitable basins of Northwest Argentina are found in the Departments of Salta, Tucumán, Catamarca, La Rioja, and San Juan. Here the first major pre-Inca period, called Calchaquí (or Diaguita), presents remains of large populations, extensive irrigation systems, stone-lined agricultural terraces, and sizable villages. The buildings have rough stone walls, rectangular or circular groundplans, and roofs of perishable materials. Clusters of such rooms are arranged irregularly along narrow streets. Some rooms contain geometrically carved stone columns, which, although not statues, seem to mark religious centers. A fort is generally found on some high point near the village.

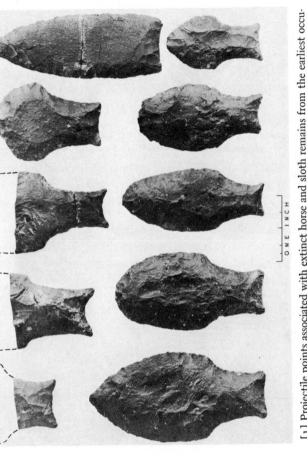

[1] Projectile points associated with extinct horse and sloth remains from the earliest occupation level of Fell's Cave, southern Chile. Age between ten and eleven thousand years.

ONE INCH

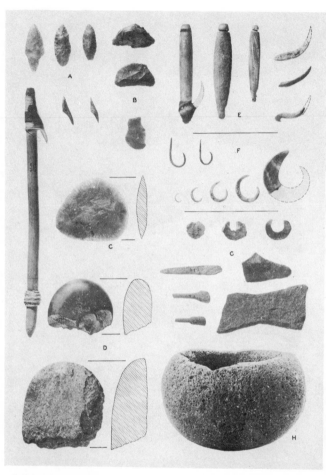

[2] Artifacts of oldest known coastal culture from northern Chile. A, harpoon forepiece, points, and barbs; B, stone scraping tools; C, stone knife; D, choppers (?); E, stone, bone, and shell composite fishhooks and barbs; F, thorn and shell hooks; G, stages in making shell hooks and the tools used; H, stone bowl.

[3] Marajó pottery showing painted, excised, and incised decoration.

[4] Prehistoric ceramics from Colombia. A, B, D, G, Quimbaya; E, Santa Marta; F, Sinu; C, mosquito effigy urn.

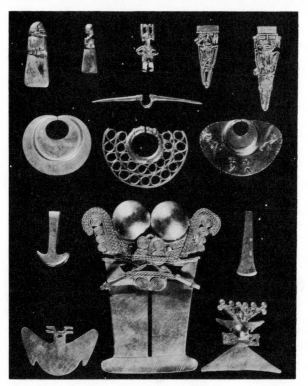

[5] Goldwork from Colombia, various styles.

[6] San Agustín stone carving.

[7] American Museum excavation in a preceramic agricultural community midden, Huaca Prieta, Chicama Valley. The midden is 45 feet thick and was occupied from approximately 2500-1200 B.C.

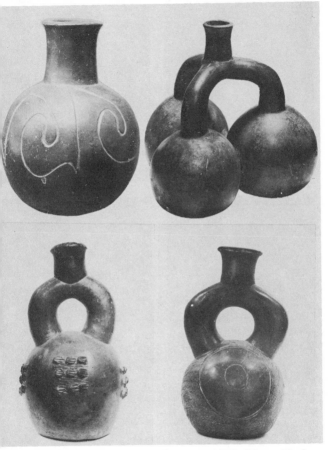

[8] Cultist Period ceramic types. Courtesy of Rafael Larco Hoyle, except upper right.

[9] Cultist Period ceramic types. Courtesy of Rafael Larco Hoyle.

[10] Cultist Period goldwork from Chongoyape and bone artifacts from Chicama. *Courtesy of Museum of the American Indian, Heye Foundation; bone, Courtesy of Rafael Larco Hoyle.*

[11] Building and carving of the Cultist Period. Upper left, modeled clay, Moxeke, *Courtesy of Donald Collier*; lower left, Cerro Sechín; others, Chavín de Huántar.

[12] Chiripa ceramics and house site, Experimenter Period.

[13] Salinar ceramics of the Experimenter Period. Courtesy of
Rafael Larco Hoyle, except upper left.

[14] Resin painted and incised ceramics, Ica-Paracas wares. B, F, I show strong Chavín influence; A, C, D show less pronounced Chavín influence; E, G, H, Paracas Cavernas types.

[15] Pucara style stone carving of the Mastercraftsman Period. Courtesy of Museo Nacional, Lima.

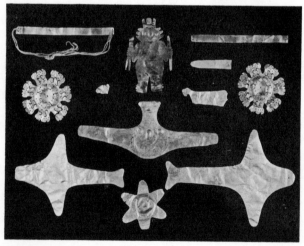

[16] Gold objects from a Paracas mummy bundle of the Mastercraftsman Period.

[17] Varieties of Mochica pottery of the Mastercraftsman Period.

[18] Nazca style ceramics of the Mastercraftsman Period.

The Calchaquí adult burials are in oval or round stone-lined and covered graves, but infants and children are more generally buried in urns. In fact, child urn cemeteries are a characteristic feature of this culture. Large painted urns are the most typical ceramic form. The commonest is in the Santa María style, so named after the type site. It has a short body with two horizontal handles, a wide neck, and a flaring rim. The exterior is painted in black and red on a white or yellowish slip base. The collar is decorated with a face, arms are painted on the body, and the rest of the vessel is covered with geometric steps, scrolls, or serrated lines, or with designs of ostriches, toads, jaguars, birds, and snakes. Several variants of this Santa María urn type, such as the Belém and San José types, have a different geographical distribution suggesting local cultures. Additional Calchaquí ceramic shapes are shoe-shaped vessels, ollas, and open bowls, called *pucos*. These vessels may be plain or painted in the animal or geometric designs found on the urns. Copper, bronze, and gold are represented by decorated breast plates, relief plaques, curved knives, daggers, and knuckle dusters. The stone artifacts are not very numerous; the few preserved wooden pieces resemble the Atacameño examples.

The Calchaquí culture seems to correspond roughly to the Tiahuanaco time horizon in the Central Andes. Several earlier cultures have been found in Northwest Argentina; of these, Barreales is outstanding. In this culture, houses are built of adobe or of rough stone and the burials are in unlined pit graves. The associated ceramics present two contrasting styles: a black or brown monochrome incised series of one-handled cups, pitchers, and vases, decorated with geometric, human, and animal figures; and a polychrome group in black, maroon, and violet, in which semi-globular vessels, goblets, and cups are decorated with a stylized curvilinear jaguar. The name "Draconian" given this style refers to the jaguar or dragon. Other distinctive artifacts of the Barreales culture are stone arrowpoints, mortars, pestles, and particularly carved stone bowls; clay pipes with relief modeled faces and hollow clay figurines; gold and copper objects; and bone flutes, spatulas, and whorls. The Barreales culture is found largely in the Departments of Catamarca, La Rioja, and San Juan. North of this area it is replaced by La Candelaria culture, which is thus far represented by large, conical plain urns, a few polychrome pots, and some black incised vessels not very different from the Barreales style. Although the Northwest Argentine cultures have often been compared with those of Peru, the parallels are general, not specific. At present it is advisable to consider Northwest Argentina as a distinct culture area which reflects the Central Andean development, but is not a part of it.

CHILE

On the western slopes of the Andes, Chile can also be culturally separated into a northern and central region. The northern region, the Atacama desert, one of the driest in the world, has always had a limited occupation. Small fishing groups existed on the coast, but in the interior the only sizable habitable oasis is Calama on the Río Loa. This oasis was the center of the Atacameño culture which is characterized by simplicity and by an emphasis on llama herding as a supplement to agriculture. The villages consisted of clusters of rough stone rectangular houses arranged along irregular streets. Mummies are well preserved in this dry climate and are found in cylindrical crypts. The ceramics are characterized by open bowls, shoe-shaped vessels, ollas, one-handled pitchers, and containers with truncated conical bases, constricted necks, and two side handles. Most of the vessels are plain, but some are painted in black-on-red, or black, red-on-white simple geometric designs. Wooden artifacts are abundant. The inventory includes carved tubes and tablets for snuff (Fig. 6), crude wooden knives, shov-

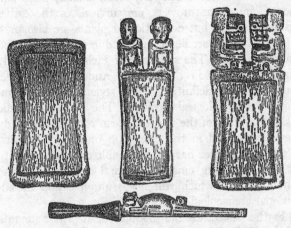

FIG. 6. Tablets and tube for mixing and inhaling snuff, Atacameño, North Chile.

els, bells, whorls, boxes, toggles, spoons, and goblets. Leather was used for making bags and armor. There are also coiled baskets, decorated calabashes, rather good weaving, and copper and gold objects. The Atacameño culture compares favorably with the Central Andean development, but its extreme simplicity, as well as the absence of scientific reports, makes it difficult to identify precise parallels. Furthermore, not only its subdivisions but the time range of Atacameño culture is yet to be established. For example, Tiahuanaco type burials have been found in Calama, but whether these represent a distinct cultural occupation or whether they are contemporary with or earlier than Atacameño has not yet been determined.

At Pichalo on the North Coast, a pre-Atacameño culture has been isolated. It is characterized by simple, thick rimmed open bowls in monochrome black, brown, or red. Coiled baskets, rush mats, feather fans, and a variety of textiles are also associated. Many of the artifacts, such as stone scrapers, drills, sinkers, bone harpoons, and spear-throwers, are survivals of the earlier fishing pattern, but domesticated plants are also present. The burials are flexed, wrapped in mats, and placed in direct graves. The similarity of Pichalo to the Early Farmer cultures in the Central Andes is noticeable, but it lacks the definitive Chavín style and a truly comparable chronological position. The two preceramic fishing cultures of the north Chilean coast have already been mentioned in the discussion of Early Migrants. Certainly this area has a considerable cultural antiquity as well as a long range of cultural development, the importance of which still needs amplification by additional archaeological work.

Farther south, around Coquimbo, are the remnants of the Chilean-Diaguita culture, a local parallel to the Calchaquí of Argentina. The ceramics are superior to those of Argentina and the vessels are generally smaller. This culture is too little known to permit a lengthy discussion. Still farther south, in the Central Chile Valley, the Inca expansion encountered the Araucanians, but it seems likely that these peoples had adopted many of the basic features of the Andean cultural pattern long before this time. The archaeological work which would confirm or deny this is yet to be done.

The Central Andean pattern seems, in many ways, more closely allied to that of the Southern than to that of the Northern Andes. This in part reflects the closer affinity of northern patterns to the Amazonian cultures, an alternative source of influence not available in the south.

This general picture of the South American setting

shows that the Central Andean area forms a distinct unit, distinguishable geographically and culturally from the rest of the continent. This seems more than a mere reflection of differential quantity of archaeological work. The Central Andean pattern is old and its gross history of development is well outlined. A detailed examination of this history is to be found in the following section.

Fig. 7. Principal valleys and major cultural divisions of the Central Andes.

PART 2: THE CENTRAL ANDES

DIVISIONS

The term Central Andes is here used to include the mountains and desert coast of Peru and the mountains of Bolivia. In the first part of this account it was demonstrated that this area can be isolated as a cultural and geographical unit. The Central Andean culture pattern contrasts markedly with that of the Southern Hunters and the Tropical Agriculturists. While it is not so sharply distinguishable from the Northern and Southern Andes, the differences are sufficiently marked to justify separate treatment. The Central Andes also presents an environmental unity when compared with other areas of South America. At first glance, the contrast between the desert Pacific Coast and the formidable highlands seems marked, but when considered in cultural terms the differences diminish in significance. For maximum development, a subsistence economy based on intensive agriculture with simple digging-stick cultivation requires rich soils, a genial climate, an adequate water supply, and an absence of vegetal coverage such as forest or deep-rooted grass which are difficult to eradicate. In this sense the Peruvian coastal valleys and mountain basins have much in common. Except for certain altitude limitations, there were no major physical barriers to the spread of the basic cultural pattern throughout all the large basins and valleys of the Central Andes. Its extension was sharply curtailed, however, by the eastern tropics where the dense forest coverage presented a serious obstacle to highland agricultural techniques. Cultural expansion into the Northern Andes was blocked by a shift in the rainfall pattern which made it difficult to graze the llamas and alpacas, the basic animals in the Central Andean economy. The Southern Andes are separated from the Central by a desert strip; but the principal barrier to great cultural interchange seems to have been gross distance rather than environment.

The Central Andes, despite certain over-all cultural unity, includes numerous regional subdivisions that are not only isolated geographically, but also have local cultural traditions. Considering the size of the area, its inhabited parts are decidedly limited. An examination of these requires more geographical detail. An airplane view of the Peruvian coast reveals a long strip of desert cut across at irregular intervals by mountain streams which drain into the Pacific. Some twenty-five principal rivers are separated not only by barren areas but by sharp mountain spurs. In the past communication between these valleys was always difficult and major intervals between them usually marked significant cultural divisions. The close relation between cultural development and river valleys, while obvious, cannot be overstressed. Although small fishing groups can have existed along the coast, no major advancement of culture was possible until the valley flats were utilized. With the domestication of plants and controlled irrigation, the fertile flats became important agricultural centers capable of supporting large populations. Their size depended, in large part, on the size of the valley itself. It is interesting to observe that the most extensive valleys and those with the most permanent streams are on the North Coast. More intensive desert conditions prevail in the South Coast valleys, and the flats are restricted in area by a low mountain range that skirts the Pacific shore line. It is not surprising, then, that as technology advanced, the northern valleys became the more important centers of cultural development.

In the mountains, surrounded by high snow-covered peaks, are puna grasslands, some plateaus and inter-mountain basins, and numerous rivers, most of which cut their way into the Amazon. Although many small pockets along the rivers can support some population, only six areas are of sufficient size for any elaboration of pre-Colombian development. From north to south these are: the large basins around Cajamarca, the Callejón de Huaylas along the upper Santa River, the basins along the Río Mantaro, the various valleys and flats around Cuzco, the basin of Puno in southern Peru, and the Bolivian plateau south of Lake Titicaca. All these areas have extensive regions of well-watered fertile soils and are surrounded by high punas ideal for grazing. Each of these six areas was a major cultural center in the past, isolated from its neighbors both by distance and by mountains, but not to the extent of blocking some intercommunication.

Each major highland basin and each coastal valley might be treated as a distinct cultural unit, but there is insufficient archaeological evidence to support such consideration even if it were practical. It spite of the numerous archaeological investigations in the Central Andes, perhaps more than in any other part of South America, much still remains to be accomplished and many sections are still unknown. Only a few of the many investigators have been trained archaeologists and only a small percentage of the numerous publications are scientific reports on excavations. Other ac-counts, some of great merit, have been written by travelers, by artists, or by folklorists interested in inter-preting symbolism in design. Even the professional excavators have rarely done more than sample the numerous sites. For practical purposes of presentation, then, the valleys and basins are arranged in six groups, three on the coast and three in the highlands. Each of these groups corresponds to a major geographical division, each has been subjected to a reasonable amount of scientific investigation, and each, as will be explained below, seems to have some historical validity. The groups, with simple geographic designations, are:

1. North Coast. Geographically, the North Coast includes all the valleys from Piura to Casma. Four subdivisions are suggested by the archaeological finds, namely, Piura in the north; Lambayeque; Chicama, Moche, and Viru; and Santa, Chimbote, Nepeña, and Casma. Adequate archaeological data, however, are available only for the third subdivision, Chicama, Moche, and Viru; consequently all references to the North Coast will be so limited unless otherwise stated.

2. Central Coast. The Central Coast extends from Huarmey to Lurín. All of these valleys seem to present a fairly compact unit with the exception of Huarmey which is well isolated geographically and probably forms a subdivision in itself. Since the best information is limited to the valleys of Chancay, Supe, Ancón, Rimac, and Lurín, these are here considered typical of the group.

3. South Coast. In total, the South Coast extends from the Río Mala to the Río Lomas, but it has some major subdivisions, such as Cañete and Chincha in contrast to Ica and Nazca. On the basis of our present knowledge only Pisco, Ica, and Río Grande (Nazca) can be considered here. A series of small valleys in extreme southern Peru are as yet not well enough known to be included in this over-all account.

4. North Highlands. This division extends from Huánuco to the Ecuadorian border, but archaeological records are available only for the Callejón de Huaylas, Chavín de Huántar, and Huamachuco.

5. Central Highlands. The central zone is the exten-

sive stretch from Huánuco to Cuzco. The Inca remains of Cuzco are well known. Elsewhere there are only scattered accounts for important sites in the Río Mantaro basin, east of Lima.

6. South Highlands. Southern Peru and Bolivia are grouped together because of an extensive plateau, the altiplano, which includes Lake Titicaca. Archaeological exploration has largely been limited to sites around the lake. The eastern cordillera of Bolivia is excluded not only because of lack of information but because it is effectively beyond the limits of the Central Andean culture area.

These regional subdivisions are not mere conveniences for describing a region as extensive as the Central Andes, but actually represent significant segments of cultural development. The valleys that are grouped together present similar archaeological materials and sequences. Furthermore, each major division is characterized by certain cultural traditions which persist throughout many of the cultural time periods and stylistic changes. For example, the North Coast ceramics over a long and varied span of cultural history are still united by an emphasis on incised decoration, modeling, pictorial style, mold-made vessels, and the stirrup-spout. The design styles change, but these features persist. The South Coast is distinguished by polychrome ceramic painting and elaboration of weaving. Exceptional climatic conditions have favored the preservation of textiles on the South Coast, but other evidence indicates that so much emphasis was placed on weaving that other aspects of culture were not equally elaborated. In the North Highlands there is a traditional emphasis on stone carving. Likewise the buildings are constructed of rough or dressed stones and commonly utilize such features as galleries, multi-storied floors, and subterranean chambers. Quite apart from these long persisting traditions, the cultural development in each major area was sufficiently distinct to differentiate it from the others at any particular point in the chronological history. In one area that has been intensively studied there is every indication of a basic population continuum through many cultural and political changes. This would account for the regional traditions.

Although the regional subdivisions are important, the Central Andes as a whole was closely united throughout most of its cultural history. Certainly at the time of the Spanish conquest, the Central Andes was a cultural area, that is, a region in which the component tribes shared a significant percentage of their cultural traits. There is also considerable evidence for the antiquity of this common cultural pattern. Some of its distinguishing features are intensive agriculture, based on such plants as maize, beans, squash, potatoes, manioc, oca, and others; digging-stick cultivation; techniques of irrigation, fertilizers, and terracing; the use of narcotic coca instead of tobacco; domesticated cotton; and domesticated llamas and alpacas. Buildings were constructed with adobe, stone and other durable materials. Weaving, metallurgy, basketry, ceramics, and other crafts were highly developed; furthermore, many specific techniques and designs in these crafts were widely employed. A social and political superstructure controlled the village units, and there were distinctions of rank, class, specialized priests, and craftsmen long before the Inca formulated their political empire. In brief, the archaeological record demonstrates that the cultural pattern established at an early date in the Central Andes persisted with more or less uniform modifications to the time of the Spanish conquest.

The concept of a Central Andean cultural block with considerable time depth has been recognized by most archaeologists. This concept not only permits the consideration of the Central Andes as a unit, but also a comparison of its cultural developments and achievements with those of other parts of the world. Moreover, it makes feasible a generalized descriptive account of the cultural development in a chronological sequence. One of the basic assumptions in such an approach is that a major invention or advancement in one part of the Central Andes would soon spread to all the area. In so large a territory with so many well-isolated subdivisions, there is always the possibility that the cultural development in one region might lag seriously behind the others, but it is significant that thus far archaeological investigation has failed to reveal such a lag. This does not signify that the Central Andean culture was everywhere uniform. By definition, a culture area does not imply such uniformity. In fact, it is possible to demonstrate for any specific time horizon that the cultural pattern of each subdivision differed in many respects.

The Central Andes presents, then, a basic cultural pattern established at an early date, and one which advanced everywhere at a more or less uniform rate. This makes feasible a history of the Central Andes which starts at the earliest known beginnings and traces the development through major periods to a culmination in the Inca Empire. This procedure is followed in the succeeding chapter. For each major time period, the general characteristics of the total Central Andes will first be considered, followed by a discussion of local variants, specialized developments, and significant regional differences.

This approach, although valid historically, has certain limitations. For example, the same conditions of preservation do not prevail in all sections. On the coast preservation is generally excellent, even for the most delicate textiles, but the South Coast is more favorable than the North. In the highlands the heavy rains prevent the preservation of all but the most durable materials. Another limitation has its source in the nature of most of the archaeological work. The excavators, primarily interested in establishing time sequence, have directed their techniques towards this end. Thus the greatest emphasis is placed on ceramics, not only because pots and sherds are valuable cultural diagnostics, but also because they are preserved everywhere in house sites, refuse heaps, and other positions favorable for sequence interpretations. Consequently, many field reports include excellent interpretations of the time relations of ceramic styles, but add little or no information on the total cultural content of a period. Finally, an historical approach of this kind demands more than an inventory of the materials preserved for each period. Social implications based on archaeological material are somewhat hazardous even under the best of conditions. Many suggestions are to be found in the realistically painted ceramic designs, the house types, the size and construction patterns of buildings, the extent of territory occupied, and the like, but their interpretation is always in the nature of inferences without final factual proof. All of these limitations are recognized in this history and every attempt has been made to keep the inferences as sound as possible.

In this introductory section the major regional and cultural subdivisions of the Central Andes have been sketched. Before initiating the descriptive historical account, the time divisions must be considered. It seems pertinent to mention briefly the dating techniques employed, the resulting relative chronology, and the major time periods here selected to present the history of cultural development of the Central Andes.

CHRONOLOGY

The Central Andes was occupied by sedentary agriculturists for many generations, so that the archaeologist has an enormous quantity of materials to consider. For example, during recent work in Viru, one of the smaller valleys on the North Coast, the Institute of Andean Research mapped the location of over three hundred sites which were estimated to be about a one-quarter sample. Furthermore, the units designated as sites varied from simple house refuse accumulations to mammoth ceremonial village constructions. Few valleys have been as thoroughly explored, but there is every indication that an enormous number of sites will be found in each valley investigated in the same detail. Several major categories of materials are available for classification and study. The first may be termed "surface ruins." These include habitation refuse, houses, villages, cities, temples, forts, irrigation systems, agricultural terraces, and other constructions. The second, "cemeteries," includes graves of many types, varying from simple pits to stone-lined burial vaults. The graves may include only a skeleton or two, but more frequently they contain cloth-wrapped mummy bundles and a reasonable quantity of grave furniture. The "stone carvings," such as decorated lintels, sculptured heads, and statues, are here treated as a third category although they are technically a subdivision of the first. The utilitarian and ceremonial artifacts found in the habitation sites and in the graves are classified, on the basis of the material employed, as ceramics, cloth, metalwork, basketry, gourd, wood, stone, and shellwork.

The first problem for the Andean archaeologist is to arrange this great variety of materials into periods and their chronological sequence. Which features identify a single culture? Is that culture earlier, contemporaneous with, or later than others in the same area? To accomplish both of these tasks the archaeologist is dependent almost exclusively on his special techniques. The Spanish conquerors described the Inca culture and recorded certain oral accounts of the traditional history. These furnish a few, though not very reliable, dates for the relatively recent times. Neither a form of phonetic writing nor a recorded calendar was known in the Central Andes in pre-European times, in spite of the fact that the early agriculturists must have had some calendrical knowledge. The dating technique based on the annual ring growth of trees, so successfully used in the United States Southwest, has so far not been applicable to the Central Andean woods. Consequently, except for the application of radiocarbon measurements, all dating is based on excavations and their interpretation and has been relative, not absolute. The archaeologist endeavors first to establish relative sequences at the specific sites excavated and then extends these to the valley or basin in which the sites are located, then to adjacent valleys or basins, and finally, on broader comparative grounds, to the entire area.

The dating techniques employed are relatively simple and standardized. Stratigraphy, the superimposition of one type of material over another, is the most reliable and has been the most extensively used. Stratigraphy may refer to various periods of building in a single structure; to one type of building which overlies another; to a building over a grave; or, in reverse, to a grave intrusive in a building. It may also refer to the superimposition of one habitation room over another or to the relative position of graves. The determination of the latter is particularly difficult, since it is the mouth of the grave which is important and not its absolute depth. By far the best stratigraphic records are found at sites where successive inhabitants have built up refuse accumulations. Such sites are common on the coast of Peru; some are nearly fourteen meters deep. The archaeologist cuts through these, level by level, in order to obtain a cross-sectional picture of the history of occupation. In all cases superposition is most meaningful when occupational remains change from one level to the next. The important sites are those with materials from several periods since their stratigraphic positions furnish the basis for relative dating.

Surface sampling is another common technique. Unselected sample collections, usually potsherds, are made from the surfaces of many sites, classified, and arranged in a hypothetical sequence which may ultimately be verified by stratigraphic excavation. Sampling pits, instead of surface collections, may be excavated in a number of sites and the excavated materials classified and compared. Unit sites, that is, those occupied during a single period only, are important for isolating the styles and content of that period, but their relative dating depends on other types of evidence. Grave collections can be analyzed if a record is kept of every piece found in each grave. On the assumption that all materials found in a grave are contemporaneous and that graves of transitional time periods will contain mixed materials, a sequence can be built up by isolation and association of styles. The direction of such a sequence can be fixed only when one end is identified, as for example, by the presence of known Inca material. Seriation might be mentioned as still another technique in which art sequences, technological developments, and similar trends serve as a basis for relative chronological dating.

The valley and inter-valley chronologies depend on the interrelationships of the site sequences. The materials from two adjacent valleys are occasionally so closely identical that there is no question of their common period classification. For example, it is almost impossible to distinguish the Nazca materials in Ica from those in Nazca itself, or the Mochica materials from Chicama, Moche, and Viru valleys. Trade pieces are also important in linking areas. When a typical North Highland negative-painted vessel is found in the top levels of a Gallinazo site in Viru Valley, the sequences in these two regions can be adjusted to each other.

The establishment of a relative chronology for the total Central Andes is a further extension of this matching process. The procedure is aided by the presence of a number of so-called "horizon" styles, each widely distributed. Features which establish or mark an horizon may consist of a single distinctive element such as negative decoration on pottery, while others may consist of combinations of several traits and might better be designated as horizon complexes. To be most usable, the diagnostic elements of the horizon style should be clearly definable and readily identified. Its relative position in the local series must be known. In other words, the horizons are established by relative dating techniques, but once confirmed they are useful for dating new finds and interrelating regions. The particular cultures linked in time by the horizon style may be quite diverse, that is, the horizon style itself may be the result of simple diffusion, a dominating religion, or political conquest. However, the presence of a number of horizon styles in the Central Andes furnishes additional evidence of its cultural unity over a long time period.

At present six important horizon styles are recognized in the Central Andes, although most of them do not extend over the entire area. These are briefly defined below and may be found on the chronological charts in their relative time positions. The order is arranged from the earliest to the latest.

1. Chavín Horizon. The Chavín horizon is charac-

terized by a highly stylized feline design. The full figure feline is represented in profile, or the head alone is presented in front view, top view, or profile, the latter position having the widest distribution. The profile head has a wide U-shaped mouth band that curves outward at the corners, two crossed fangs, and squared teeth. The nose is a circle surmounted by a scroll; the banded eye is oval with a cut-out circle at the top. Other appendages and details are equally distinctive so that the Chavín feline is recognizable by its claws, tail, and other details. The design is executed in a carved technique in curvilinear style. The feline motif is most highly elaborated in the flat stone carving at the highland site of Chavín de Huántar. Elsewhere it appears as a dominant design element in stonework, bonework, ceramics, textiles, and metalwork. The Chavín horizon, the earliest known horizon in the Central Andes, is found in the North Highlands and on the South, Central, and North Coasts.

2. White-on-Red Horizon. The White-on-Red horizon is basically a technique of positive brush painting of ceramics in white on a red clay base. The clumsily executed white designs are composed of simple elements such as bands, plain lines, wavy lines, and triangles filled with dots. This horizon style is difficult to identify because of its simplicity. Some ceramic shapes may be associated, but these associations are not sufficiently varied to constitute a complex. It is distributed on the Central and North Coasts, and in the North Highlands. In time position the White-on-Red always succeeds Chavín and precedes Tiahuanaco.

3. Negative Horizon. This horizon is most clearly marked, as the name implies, by a technique of negative decoration of ceramics. This is, however, such a simple procedure that it requires no special training, equipment, or materials and could have been diffused among potters by word of mouth. One can argue that

it might have been independently developed at different times and places, but no supporting evidence is at hand. To create negative decoration one forms a positive design or figure on a red or light-colored, unglazed ceramic surface using an inert substance which protects the covered areas from subsequent application of carbon (see page 187). This technique is found on the South, Central, and North Coasts, and in the North Highlands where it survives as a tradition into later periods.

4. Tiahuanaco Horizon. The previous horizons are characterized by single styles or techniques, but the Tiahuanaco horizon is composed of a number of elements which form a complex. The dominant style is best represented by the relief carved "Gateway of the Sun" at Tiahuanaco in Bolivia. One design is the profile running figure. Another is a front view figure with stiffly outlined body, rectilinear head, squared eyes with tear bands, and a mouth with squared teeth, but no crossed fangs. Other typical designs are stylized puma, condor, and snake heads. These designs occur in stone carving, tapestry, weaving, wood carving, ceramic painting, and other media. In addition to the characteristic style, the horizon complex is distinguished by polychrome ceramic painting in black, white, yellow, and gray, on a red base; by well executed textiles, particularly tapestries; and by two common vessel shapes, namely, a tall goblet and a flaring-sided squat cup. The Tiahuanaco horizon is truly pan-Central Andean.

5. Black-White-Red Horizon. On the Coast of Peru the Tiahuanaco horizon is followed by a breakdown into a black-white-red geometric style of ceramic painting with design units consisting of small steps, squares, checkerwork, and dots. A flask shape as well as other forms and ceramic details are usually associated. The horizon is present on all the coast and in the North Highlands.

6. Inca Horizon. Like the Tiahuanaco, the Inca horizon is a complex, not a single style. The ceramic design style is call the Cuzco Polychrome after the type site. It is characterized by well applied polychrome designs composed of small geometric elements. The typical and distinctive vessel shapes are a conical base aryballoid, a shallow plate with a bird handle, a pedestal beaker, and a pitcher with a wide ribbon loop handle. Many other features are associated in this horizon complex, but these can best be described in a later chapter. The Inca horizon has a pan-Central Andean distribution corresponding to the total extent of the Inca Empire at the time of the Conquest.

The accompanying chart presents a graphic picture of the distribution and relative time position of the three horizons which appear to have the strongest internal unity and broadest application, the Chavín, Tiahuanaco, and Inca. Only the latter can be assigned dates based on historic data. These have been taken from Dr. John H. Rowe's outstanding study and appraisal of Colonial Spanish documents relative to Inca chronology.

This chart (Fig. 8), like all such attempts to present the chronology of the Andean Area in diagram form is an exercise in compromise and interpretation. It is admittedly inadequate in terms of recent work and like others will be quickly outdated by new discoveries, better understanding of old data, and by additional Carbon 14 dates. The 2000 A.D. point on the time scale does not imply optimism that it will be useful that long. Northern Chile is included as we have data on the chronology there which is pertinent to the rest of the Andean Area. In north Chile there is little evidence of the forces at work during the three major horizons. Physical remains of the presence of Inca culture are extremely scanty. Tiahuanaco material is proportionately more abundant, yet its influence on the local record is not strong. Perhaps more significant is the evidence of a rather direct connection with Tiahuanaco styles of Bolivia rather than the Tiahuanaco-Wari, Wari-to-the-coast relationship which seems to have been the case in Peru. As yet no Chavín material nor clear signs of its influence have been found, so what we have is a marginal situation affected only by certain events occurring elsewhere in the Andean region, an area where some traits persisted long after they had disappeared

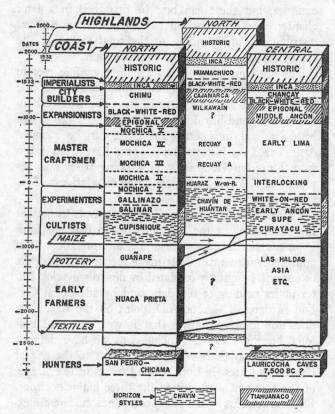

nearer the great cultural centers. One should note that contrary to the situation in northern Peru we find that in north Chile there was only a slight time difference between the appearance of textiles and the first use of maize. Also, that both were present before ceramics. Obviously there was a difference in the rate of dispersal for the three features. Maize, a new food plant, spread more rapidly than the use of ceramics, as indicated on the chart. This suggests that some phase of

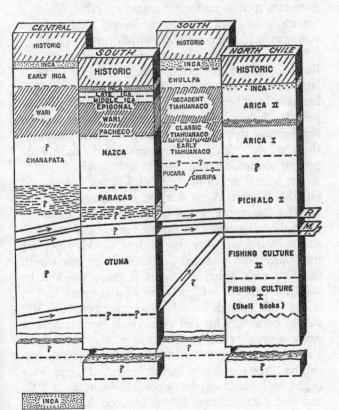

FIG. 8. Chronological chart for the Central Andes with diffusion pattern of textiles, pottery, and maize indicated.

the Early Farmer agriculture was already established
this far south.

We do not yet have any Carbon 14 dates for north
Chile so, except for the Inca material, we are dealing
with guess-dates controlled only slightly by broad cor-
relations. The time allotted the subdivisions is based
in each case on the proportional amounts of occupation refuse. This can be extremely misleading except
where the record can be tied in with some natural phe-
nomenon such as uniformly aggrading valley fill, or if
we are dealing with sites where limited food and fuel
resources held the population within certain limits.

The Highland sequences shown on the chart are,
like the north Chile record, largely dated by guess. A
large series of carbon samples from Chiripa and Tiahuanaco have been processed but the results have not
yet been fully interpreted. Elsewhere we must rely on
the horizon styles and traits and the relationship of
these to local cultural development in order to indicate
general connections and implied time levels.

The coastal record has been worked out in more detail than shown. Again horizon complexes provide a
unifying framework against which Carbon 14 dates can
be applied. The dates by themselves are still an insufficient basis for constructing a chart of this type, but
most have been accepted and used. Even when large
series of such figures are available there will still be
need for personal interpretation of the data. As this
will provide grounds for debate all other pertinent data
should be sought for and considered. For example, a
study of deep, twenty-one feet, soil profiles in the Viru
Valley matched against refuse deposits led to the conclusion that the Early Farmer incipient agriculture
might well have been introduced there by 3000 B.C.
and that ceramics were in use by 1000 B.C. In contrast, Carbon 14 measurements indicate that ceramics
appeared around 1200 B.C. and that the preceramic

pattern of agriculture was established before 2000 B.C. and perhaps as early as 2500 B.C.

The terminology used on the chart for the various periods and sub-periods may seem somewhat complex. It is a common practice among archaeologists to name

FIG. 9. Preceramic sites: On the coast north of Paracas mostly early farmer. South of Paracas principally fishing cultures. Interior sites, including Pampa de Paijan and sites near Ancon nomadic hunters.

new pottery styles after local sites and to use the names to designate cultural periods. This has the advantage of being specific but presents difficulties for those who would prepare a small-sized chart for so large and diverse an area. Some simplification is attained by using the cultural horizons as period markers yet any detailed discussion involves the local terminology.

In the following account the known chronology is divided into seven major periods, somewhat arbitrarily chosen. The descriptive names indicate some trend or characteristic applicable at least in part to each period, and suggest significant steps in the course of Andean Culture. They will be discussed starting with the oldest.

EARLY FARMERS

(*ca.* 2500–1200 B.C.)

The ultimate origins and even the earliest manifestations of culture in the Central Andes are still shrouded in mystery. Some sites represent a simple cultural level with no ceramics, but these are located on the Pacific Coast and were quite possibly marginal to the true centers of development. The early and widespread Cultist Period sites present evidence of a sophisticated and complex culture but the simple coastal cultures, although known to be older, do not seem sufficient in themselves to account for such a development. Future work in the highlands may uncover important centers of early development, but it is equally possible, and in some ways probable, that the initial centers lie outside of the Central Andes, perhaps in the tropics, perhaps in other parts of the Andes.

The evidence for early migrations into South America has previously been presented. On the basis of this evidence it seems logical that man first entered South America via the Isthmus of Panama and moved southward through the Andes. These earliest migrants were hunters and gatherers with relatively simple cultural equipment. In the Central Andes they probably found the highland basins more attractive than the coastal valleys. Presumably snow line was then at a lower elevation resulting in a larger precipitation zone, more vegetation and more game. The known sites occupied by hunters are few in number: two caves or rock-shelters near Lake Lauricocha and possibly several others near Huancayo in the Central Highlands and some isolated workshops between Chicama and Pacasmayo. It is not yet known whether these early hunting peoples remained in the Central Andes or moved on to the south, but in any case, it seems unlikely that they were directly responsible for the higher civilizations which developed later. This is strongly supported by the fact that the technique of pressure flaking stone artifacts was commonly used by the hunters but was not used at all by the preceramic farmers.

The coast, in spite of its limitations for hunters, might well have been attractive to early fishermen. Campsites of ancient fishing groups have been found in Chile as described in Part One. Similar sites should be located at suitable situations in Peru. Burials, with radiocarbon date of 3060 B.C., found at Paracas by Frédéric Engel, appear to be of this phase. They resemble Chilean fishermen burials in that the bodies, extended in the sand, are wrapped in fur robes. With them are chipped stone points, bone needles, a shell bead necklace, gourds, twined "bast" fabrics and other goods. A more meaningful comparison must await detailed information, but the presence of the gourds could indicate contact and cultural overlap with the Early Farmers.

The gourd, considered an Old World plant, has not

been studied sufficiently to establish its record in America. George Carter reported tests showing that seeds of gourds floating in sea water remain vital long enough for intercontinental dispersal by ocean currents and that man need not be involved in such movement. However, in Peru and Chile present data point to human dispersal and a north to south movement. If so, did gourds first appear in company with several other possibly cultivated plants as an initial stage of agriculture?

One plant which might have been part of such a complex is cotton. Genetic studies show that Old and New World cultivated cottons are related and that the oldest diffusion center in America was North Peru. While human intervention was suggested as the most logical explanation the evidence is as yet inconclusive. A study of the oldest available Early Farmer cotton led to the conclusion that it was an early form of the American species, *barbadense*. If an Old World species was brought by man it certainly was at some stage of the agricultural record earlier than what has already been found in Peru. For such reasons data on the Early Farmers are of more than local interest and must be worked out accurately and in detail.

Large sections of Early Farmer middens have been destroyed by sea erosion during a period of relatively static land-sea levels and were saved by a subsequent shift or uplift. Other deposits have been destroyed by valley erosion and hidden by later occupation. In spite of this, more than thirty deposits have been listed as preceramic and others will be found. Some may be strictly fishing sites but, on present data, all are classed as Early Farmer sites. The map (Fig. 9) indicates the more important or better-known ones.

Huaca Prieta, a village midden forty-five feet thick, at the mouth of the Chicama Valley (Plate 7), presents a good picture of life in these early times. The valley must have been quite different before settlement by intensive agriculturalists, with much more swampland, lagoons, wooded thickets and wider areas devoted to marginal desert vegetation than at present. Wild fruits and food plants, animals, and land birds must have been more abundant. Subsistence depended heavily on seafood but this is considered to have been insufficient to support the estimated population. However, there is surprisingly little evidence for the practice of hunting. Bones of land animals are not present in the midden and, though there are a few of sea lion and porpoise, hunting weapons are lacking. Evidence for weapons of any sort is limited to toy slings. A large part of the cooking was done with hot stones by roasting. Gourd vessels were common. Ceramics were completely unknown. The diet combined seafood, wild plants such as tubers of the *junco* sedge, cattail roots, various fruits, including the *lúcuma*, and several plants, *achira*, squash, gourds, lima and canavalia beans and chile peppers, most of which are believed to have been cultivated. Cotton, presumably domesticated, was common and was twisted into yarn with crude, whorlless spindles. Woven fabrics, present throughout the occupation, are rare, twined ones common. Other fabrics, made by looping and knotting, include fishnets and pouches. Structural designs occur in all techniques, some quite complex and sophisticated. Other products and implements include: twined reed baskets and mats, pounded barkcloth, bone bodkins, thorn needles and, made of stone, flake knives, perforated net weights, roughly shaped choppers, and, rarely, bowls and percussion flaked scrapers. The lack of hand-line fishing gear suggests lack of watercraft needed for its use at this site. The oldest burials were in shallow pits in the refuse, the bodies flexed. Later abandoned subterranean houses and storage pits were used for successive burials. Such structures were lined with cobbles or, at sites where stone was scarce, with rectangular adobes set on edge. Some evidence suggests that earlier houses were built above ground of cane and mud.

This simple culture pattern, with some local developments, overlaps the earliest coastal ceramic period. For example, at Huaca Prieta the use of hot stones in cooking continues into the ceramic period, twined fabrics compete with the new weaving techniques, and semi-subterranean constructions continue to be used along with constructions of cylindrical and conical adobes. The use of cylindrical and small biscuit-like adobes occurs with the first ceramic containers. These are simple olla cooking pots, irregularly colored from dull red to dark brown and black, showing lack of oxygen control in firing. The only decorative elements are appliqué ridges or ribs made irregular by pinching or notching. Pottery roller and plain stamps and figurines were also made. Jet mirrors, shell and bone beads, bone weaving tools and ornaments give further reason for believing that a population movement rather than a spread of ideas was responsible for the items new to the region. The only burials identified with this time contain a few simple artifacts as grave offerings. Bodies were either seated with legs extended in front or fully extended with arms at sides. At Aspero in Supe there is a structure which may represent an altar or religious site of this period. A large room, about four meters square, is connected by doors to two adjacent small rooms. The floor is of packed clay. The walls of uncut stone, crudely coursed and held together with mud plaster, are less than a meter high and about forty centimeters wide. A platform, 1.50 meters square and 50 centimeters high, in the center of the main room is built with uncut boulders set on end, with small stones filling the interstices. This base is covered with a clay plaster. Actually, pottery was not found with this structure, but discoveries of a lance point of chipped stone, llama bones, and maize serve to place it in the early ceramic period.

In many ways these coast sites apparently present a developmental sequence from the preceramic into the ceramic, but it is doubtful that this is a true picture of the origin of higher civilization in the Central Andes. It is more likely that these coastal sites merely reflect the important cultural developments that had occurred in the highlands. This becomes more apparent in the following discussion of the Cultist Period in which the Chavín style first appears. In art, architecture, and other aspects of culture, the contrast is great. It seems unlikely that so marked a change should suddenly emerge from such humble beginnings as presented by the Early Farmer sites. Nonetheless, all evidence points to a long period in time for these preceramic cultures.

CULTIST PERIOD

(*ca.* 1200 B.C.–400 B.C.)

Following the humble and modest beginnings represented by the coastal preceramic sites, the flowering of culture in the Cultist Period seems sudden and abrupt. Despite certain technological limitations, the ceramics are varied and well made. Judging by the few known samples, weaving is advanced. There is evidence of versatile craftsmanship and considerable sophistication in art and architecture. Subsistence is no longer dependent on fishing, gathering, hunting, and limited agriculture, but rather on agriculture with a wider range of plants. A marked increase in population occurred in some if not all regions, and from the eventual diffusion of a stylized feline motif and feline symbolism cultural unity is indicated. Part of this unity seems to have been of a religious nature hence the name "Cultist" for the period.

The Cultist Period includes many local cultures and sites which, in spite of their wide distribution, are linked by the Chavín style horizon. Some of the outstanding sites are: Chavín de Huántar in the North Highlands; great middens at Ancón, Supe, and San

FIG. 10. Principal Cultist Period sites.

Bartolo; various building units, such as Moxeke, Pallka, Sechín Alto, and perhaps Cerro Sechín itself, in Casma Valley; Pungurí and Cerro Blanco temples in Nepeña Valley; Guañape and related sites in Viru Valley; all of the Cupisnique culture sites in Chicama Valley; Chongoyape in Lambayeque Valley; and miscellaneous isolated finds in Piura, Cajamarca, and the Lima region. More extensive exploration will undoubtedly reveal a much wider distribution of the Chavín horizon and perhaps permit the inclusion of additional sites that are apparently ancient but lack the Chavín design, such as Pichalo on the North Coast of Chile.

There is abundant evidence for the relative antiquity of the Cultist Period. In Viru and Chicama valleys, the cultural remains follow immediately after the Early Farmer period and precede the Salinar and Mochica cultures. Likewise, the sites are stratigraphically older than the White-on-Red culture in the North Highlands and the Interlocking culture at Ancón. In general, Cultist materials are not mixed with other known styles, and have technological limitations which are not found later. The total period was one of long duration, perhaps eight hundred years. Of this range, the characteristic Chavín horizon cultures are estimated as between four and five hundred years by the guess-dates used here. These estimates are based on the exceptionally thick refuse deposits which range from 4.5 to 8.5 meters in Viru and Ancón. Within this long time range, many cultural advancements were achieved and with more study and material it is becoming evident that there are clearcut grounds for broad and regional subdivisions.

In this type of historical approach all cultures and sites that fall into the same relative time bracket, on the basis of stratigraphic evidence, are included in the period under consideration. In the Cultist Period the component cultures are somewhat uniform. All share the feline design of the Chavín horizon. Other similarities are due to technological limitations, to trade and diffusion, and perhaps to a common background and tradition. In spite of all this, each region presents local independence and variations which cannot be dismissed even when the period is considered as a unit. The significant regional differences will be emphasized in the subsequent cultural description of the period.

Cultist sites on the coast are generally located close to the shore or along the margins of the valleys, even in *quebradas* (ravines) which are now dry and stone covered. The highland sites likewise are in the small valleys rather than in the large basins. These marginal locations imply that the complete control of irrigation and agriculture had not yet been achieved. The flats of the coastal valleys were probably still brush-covered and swampy so that unskilled farmers could utilize only their boundaries. Furthermore, some of the regions which are now so arid were probably less so before the total flow of the rivers was channeled into irrigation systems. The sites are refuse deposits, cemeteries, and temples or other religious structures. Some of the latter are of considerable size, but there is still no convincing evidence for huge concentrations of people.

The large middens near the ocean shore prove that seafoods were still important in this period. They also provide us with the best data on the perishable items of this epoch which show a major development in agriculture. From middens near the Huaca Prieta comes evidence which indicates that maize was introduced into this part of Peru at the same time as the Cupisnique ceramics. With maize came several other new plants: peanuts, warty squash, pacai, and avocados. Other evidence suggests that manioc was also known. With these additions to the plants previously cultivated we have an impressive list.

Data on domesticated animals are less conclusive.

They may have had the dog though the evidence is not too positive. Certainly there is no trace of it earlier. The llama also may have been domesticated at this time, but, if so, its wool had not yet become important in textiles.

The Cultist used bone and stone extensively for tools. However, only stone mortars and pestles, plain and decorated stone bowls, and bone spatulas are found throughout the whole area. Adding the bone and stone implements from local sites, gives an inventory of grooved stones, hammerstones, long lance heads, both four-pointed and four-flanged club heads, stone boxes, and bone awls, needles, daggers, spear-throwers, and spoons. A long chonta palm bow was found at Ancón, but the spear-thrower was probably the more characteristic weapon.

Ceramics are now a constant association and these present certain similarities due largely to technological limitations. Vessels are basically monochrome, black, gray, brown, or red, often with thick walls and sometimes coarse tempering. The dark colors show that firing was in a reducing atmosphere in contrast to the general oxidized firing of subsequent ceramics. The commonest form, with greatest distribution, is a roughly egg-shaped cooking jar with inclined rims, thickened at the lip. More variation is evident in the other forms, open bowls, bottles, collar jars and stirrup-spout containers (Plates 8 and 9). Frequently, there is excellent, sometimes superb, symmetry. A fine appreciation of surface texture contrasts is shown by skillful use of roughened, scratched, punctate, and polished areas. Slip painted decoration is lacking except near the close of the period and then is combined with the older techniques. Designs consist of geometrical elements, circles, dots and features of the Chavín feline. Regional differences exist: emphasis on modeling and stirrup spouts occur on the North Coast, heavier wares and more rocker stamp-incised decoration are found on the Central Coast.

The few textiles collected show finer yarns. Spindle whorls were used and heddle controlled looms were probably employed for the first time. The fragments are virtually all made of cotton and demonstrate that the weaving techniques were competent although not as varied as in later times. Plain weaves, some with creped threads, are the most frequent and there are also monochrome tapestries, weft stripes, fringes, tassels, and embroideries. A more elaborate piece, found in a shell-heap at Supe, has a woven design depicting the Chavín feline.

From the textiles, the ceramic modeling, and the stone carving, it is clear that the typical Central Andean costume was not used. The figures are depicted without skirts, shirts, or footgear, and as wearing only belts, breechcloths, and some form of head covering, plus snoods. Feather headdresses have been found at Supe and some of the stone carving designs represent feather capes. On the North Coast the meagerness of clothing at Cupisnique was compensated for by an elaboration of body ornament. The graves contain stamps for body painting; cylindrical and pendent ear-plugs; bracelets; rings; many types of necklaces; wristlets; crowns; etc. The ornaments are made of many materials such as bird bone, turquoise, quartz, lapis lazuli, shell, bone, stone, and gold. All of these are well constructed and illustrate the artistic expression of the period. Pyrites or jet mirrors are found in all sites. Artificial skull deformation is also typical.

Metalwork is limited in materials and techniques. Gold was the only metal used and even this is not found everywhere. Thin hammered sheet gold occurs at Supe and pressed relief objects have been found in Viru and at Chongoyape (Plate 10) in Lambayeque Valley where the goldwork is more elaborate than at other sites and may be somewhat more recent. Gold cuffs, ear discs, and other objects are made by welding and soldering and decorated in relief with the Chavín feline motifs.

More perishable artifacts have been found in the middens and graves at Supe and Ancón. These include carrying nets, fish nets, netted bags, twined baskets, and totora mats, carved gourd containers, wooden boxes, and knobby sticks.

Most graves are simple pits containing flexed or extended burials. Variants, namely a simple stone lined and a shaft and chamber grave, are known only from Cupisnique where the skeletons are covered with red paint. Grave offerings are usually limited. Food is rarely included. Ceramics are either absent or limited to a few vessels. Other grave accompaniments are equally simple except at Cupisnique where personal ornaments are found in considerable quantity.

The domestic architecture is generally extremely simple, with circular or rectangular stone house foundations and stone-faced terraces for house platforms. One modeled Cupisnique vessel depicts a house with a gabled roof, straw thatch, and a thickened foundation wall. A structure near Huaca Prieta indicates that the walls were of adobe. Perhaps, when excavated, the site of Pallka in Casma, with its aggregate of many rough stone rooms, may prove to be an exception to this simple domestic architecture. The religious architecture is on the other hand quite elaborate. The buildings identified as temples are quite large, well planned, and extensively decorated. The coast temples are constructed of rough stones set in mortar, or of conical adobes, which vary greatly in size, but are always laid so that the flat bases form the surface of the wall. Several buildings in Viru and Chicama on the North Coast are constructed of conical adobes. These probably belong to this period, but so far they have not been excavated.

On the Central Coast no buildings of any magnitude can be assigned to this period. The best examples are found in Casma and Nepeña valleys where the sites of Cerro Blanco, Pungurí, and Moxeke are outstanding. All these buildings are constructed of rough stones and conical adobes. Each has such features as platforms, steps, rooms, clay columns, and decorated walls. The decorations are in polychrome fresco, in incised clay, and in high relief clay carving. The predominant design element is the ubiquitous Chavín feline.

The site of Chavín de Huántar, located in the North Highlands on a small tributary of the Marañón River, is the most elaborate construction of this period. The narrow valley in which Chavín is located certainly could not have supported a very large population, but the massive construction which covers a large area must have required many laborers. The several building units have a roughly symmetrical arrangement around a large sunken court, about forty-eight meters square, flanked on the north and south by raised platforms. The river has cut away the end of one of these platforms revealing a rubble construction with a few poorly constructed interior galleries. The exterior is faced with rough stones. Behind a raised terrace to the west of the courtyard is the "Castillo," the principal building, roughly seventy-five meters square and over thirteen meters high at the southeast corner. In order to maintain this height, the walls are inclined inward and are also set back in narrow terraces near the top. The exterior walls are finished with carefully dressed stones. The building was once encircled by a decorated cornice beneath which was a row of carved heads, each with its tenon for insertion in the wall. The interior of the Castillo has three floors, each with an elaborate series of stone-lined and covered galleries and rooms, as well as a special system of ventilating shafts which are found throughout the construction. The galleries are about one meter wide and 1.8 meters high. The rooms vary from two to four meters on a side. Ramps and stairways lead from one floor to another. One gallery still contains a carved prismatic stone known as the "Lanzón."

Many smaller buildings form part of this group, yet the site does not have the appearance of a village. Some habitation refuse is found near the structures, but actual house sites are few. Several house foundation walls on top of the Castillo are made of carefully dressed stone. The interior galleries and rooms contain no refuse nor other evidence that they functioned as dwellings. The symmetrical layout, the careful construction, and the carved wall decorations suggest a religious structure. Certainly, a unit like the Castillo must have been built according to plan. The first floor vents, galleries, and rooms were first constructed of stone, the spaces between the walls filled in with rubble, and the outside walls finished with dressed stones laid in horizontal rows of alternating thick and thin slabs. The second floor was added, following a similar pattern of galleries, rooms, and vents. Actually, massed man power would have been essential only to assemble the materials. The construction could have been completed over a period of time by a small group of skilled masons.

Although carving is reasonably abundant at Chavín de Huántar and at some other highland sites, it is not characteristic of the entire period (Plate 11). The carvings include human and feline heads in the round, with tenons for wall insertion, flat slabs for cornices and lintels, cylindrical columns, but no true statues. The carving, except for the heads, is in low, flat relief. The style is dominated by the feline motif represented in profile or in front view. The basic feline figure may be anthropomorphized or appendages may be added to identify it as a condor or a fish. Almost every detail of the design portrays another stylized representation of the feline head. Technically, this style is not very consistent for stonework, but suggests a repoussé metal technique applied to stone. In fact some authors see a stylistic technological sequence within the Cultist Period from the metal relief work of Chongoyape, through the clay relief of Nepeña and Casma, to the stone carving of highland Chavín.

Stone carving of any kind is rarely found on the coast of Peru; the outstanding exception is at Cerro Sechín in Casma Valley. This is a large construction composed of two principal terraces. The lower terrace has a central stairway flanked on either side by a series of carved monoliths between which are smaller stones, each with a face carved on one side. This carving style is unique in Peru. The designs are based on the human figure, and there is no suggestion of the Chavín feline. If, as present evidence suggests, this construction belongs in the Cultist Period, it must antedate the spread of the Chavín horizon.

In spite of certain features and similarities which characterize the Cultist Period as a whole, there is no evidence of over-all political unity. Instead, the social organization appears to have been based on family units grouped into small villages. It is not even demonstrable that the villages in a single valley were united politically. The general impression is that of a society which still devoted considerable effort to subsistence activities and directed its excess energy and limited leisure time towards art expression and religious practices. The art work, particularly the ornaments, seems individualistic in spite of the restrictions of techniques and the conventions of the Chavín horizon style. The religious practices find their major expression in the construction of temples, both local and regional. The religious importance of the feline concept is obvious. However, if the quantity of grave

35204

goods is significant, ancestor worship had not yet reached the prominence which it gained in later periods.

Large constructions like those at Chavín de Huántar do not in themselves imply enormous concentrations of population. As has been suggested, such buildings could have been erected by a small number of skilled masons and workers, once the necessary materials had been assembled. A religious pilgrimage pattern is implied, in which large numbers congregate during certain ceremonial periods in the year, contribute their labor service, and return to their respective settlements. The pilgrimage pattern still exists. For example, at Copacabana in Bolivia thousands assemble every August for religious celebration. At the time of the Conquest, Pachacamac, near Lima, was renowned as a pilgrimage center, and much of the archaeological evidence suggests the antiquity of this pattern.

A reconstructed picture follows. During one or more weeks in the year many people made the pilgrimage to a center like Chavín de Huántar for religious celebration. While great numbers were assembled, the building materials would be brought in, stones dressed, and some of the larger slabs put in place. When the ceremony ended and the pilgrims returned to their distant homes, specialized architects carried on the construction with a few local laborers. During the time of assembly, ideas and perhaps goods would be exchanged. At a minimum, the feline design, the primary symbol of the religion, would be widely distributed, without the implication of political unity.

As technology improved and as irrigation and agriculture became more firmly established, more attention was devoted to the local region. Populations increased and political organization advanced. Regionalism became marked and the pilgrimage pattern was abandoned. In each local area experiments in many types of controls were undertaken. The Experimenter Period lacked over-all unity. This tendency towards local development continued for a long time; in fact, until the Tiahuanaco horizon complex again represents, in appearance at least, a pan-Central Andean unity.

EXPERIMENTER PERIOD

(*ca.* 400 B.C.–0.)

The Chavín horizon, characterized by the stylized feline design, gives a definite unity to the Cultist Period. The exact origin of this style is unknown; in most regions it disappears as rapidly and mysteriously as it appeared. However, the Chavín feline reappears as a design element in the much later Mochica culture, so that presumably it continued to dominate the artistic expression in some marginal area of the Central Andes. The most likely section for such a survival is the Far North Coast, namely, in Lambayeque and Piura valleys where, unfortunately, full archaeological sequences have not been established. Elsewhere, the gap between the Cultist and Experimenter Periods is a sharp one, in spite of the fact that the undecorated utilitarian ceramics demonstrate a population continuum.

The Experimenter Period includes many local cultures, grouped together basically because they can be assigned to the same relative chronological position. However, they are also linked by some general characteristics as well as two horizon styles, namely, the White-on-Red and the Negative. The principal cultures and sites of this period are the following: the Salinar culture sites in Chicama Valley and the closely related Puerto Moorin culture sites in Viru Valley; Cerro de Trinidad and Baños de Boza, type sites of the

Chancay White-on-Red style; the North Highland White-on-Red style sites near Huaraz and at Chavín de Huántar; the Cavernas culture, represented at Paracas near Pisco Valley and at Ocucaje in Ica Valley; sites of the Chanapata culture near Cuzco; and the Chiripa culture site on the Bolivian side of Lake Titicaca. There is good evidence for placing these local

Fig. 11. Principal sites of the Experimenter Period.

cultures and styles in a time position between the Cultist and the Mastercraftsman Periods. A cultural sequence of Cupisnique, Salinar, Mochica has been established in Chicama Valley by grave stratigraphy. In Viru this is confirmed by refuse stratigraphy which places Puerto Moorin as post-Cupisnique and pre-Gallinazo. In the Chancay sites, the White-on-Red style gradually fades into the later Interlocking style—a sequence duplicated at Pachacamac. White-on-Red style graves are intrusive at the Chavín de Huántar ruins. At Paracas on the South Coast, the refuse of the Cavernas culture is older than the Necropolis culture graves. The Chanapata sites are known only to be stratigraphically pre-Inca, but the Chiripa culture can be shown to antedate both Early and Decadent Tiahuanaco.

Deep refuse deposits in Viru, Chancay, Paracas, and Chiripa point to a relatively long duration for the Experimenter Period, some four hundred years in the chronological plan employed here. This estimate is complicated by the uncertainty of the beginning and the termination of the period. The lower limit is unsatisfactory because of the apparent abruptness of the break with the Cultist Period. Only a few Salinar bone spatulas and some rare incised Cavernas ceramics indicate any carry-over of the Chavín feline design, and even in these it is an atypical variant. It is even more difficult to fix the upper limit because of the gradual transition into the technological controls and mastery of crafts that mark the next period. The specific changes differ in each region and undoubtedly occurred at different times. On the North Coast the Salinar culture soon divides into the Gallinazo and the Early Mochica. On the Central Coast a gradual transition is traceable from the Chancay White-on-Red to the Interlocking. The South Coast situation is not very clear, although the Cavernas culture contains the basic elements of both Necropolis and Nazca. The Chiripa culture in the South Highlands apparently develops into Pucara and Early Tiahuanaco. There is, then, no sharp cleavage between the Experimenter and the Mastercraftsman Periods. Rather, the first represents the beginning and the second the culmination of the same sequence.

The Experimenter Period sites are found in every major region of the Central Andes, which was not true of the Cultist Period. In all probability this may be due to differences in archaeological information and does not imply any sudden expansion of occupation. The sites include cemeteries, villages, habitation refuse deposits, and, more dubiously, hilltop fortresses and shrines.

On the whole, this period is characterized by experimentation in new techniques and new controls. This can be best observed in the technological achievements, in the crafts, in building, and in the agricultural methods. Similar experiments on the socio-political level are not so clear and probably were not of major importance until the technological controls were well crystallized. Superficially, some of the materials seem inferior to those of the Cultist Period, but a detailed examination proves these to be superior in technique, even though less artistic. Some artifacts have a reasonably wide distribution, but in general the period is marked by local developments, so that description of the period as a whole is difficult. The Cultist Period achieved unity through a religious pilgrimage pattern, but even this seems now to have disappeared. The two horizon styles that transcend the regional boundaries are both based solely on techniques. The White-on-Red horizon is little more than a technique of positive brush painting on ceramics that spread throughout the North and Central Coasts and the North Highlands. The slightly later Negative horizon is likewise a ceramic technique of resist painting that spread all along the Coast and into the North Highlands. In some areas these techniques were further improved and retained for a considerable length of time. Elsewhere they were tried and abandoned.

On the coast, the sites of this period are located on the valley margins and along the shore. The latter show a marked dependence on seafood, but there is now no doubt that irrigation was practiced, particularly in the upper narrows of the river valleys. The highland sites, like Chanapata and Chiripa, are associated with stone-faced terraces which are probably part of the cultivation system. Stone hoes are common. Several new plants and fruits can be added to those known previously: the frijol bean, quinoa, cañahua, and pepino, a sterile hybrid which can be propagated only by cuttings. Llamas are now common and one modeled clay animal at Chancay resembles a guinea pig. Coca, the important narcotic, has been found in a Cavernas tomb, as well as pots containing the dregs of some liquid like the corn beer, chicha. Dried meat found in coastal graves and a bin which contained quinoa at Chiripa suggest that methods of food preservation and storage were now known. In brief, the Experimenter Period is marked by greater dependence on agricultural subsistence, new techniques of cultivation employing terraces and irrigation, experiments with new plants, and the preservation of food.

Rough stone continues as a common building material, but, in addition, various types of hand-made adobes were used on the coast. These are conical or odontiform on the North Coast, dome-shaped on the Central Coast and blunt-conical on the South Coast. Modeled Salinar ceramics represent two house types; one, circular, with a flat roof supported by step-shaped side pillars; the other, rectangular, with an open front and a pent roof supported by cross beams and a central pillar. In Viru Valley there are small villages composed of clusters of three to five stone house foundations. It is also possible that honeycomb clusters of subterranean or semi-subterranean rooms were built of tapia and ball-like adobes. At least, these are the earliest types found in the succeeding Gallinazo culture. Underground dwellings are also found at Cavernas, Huaraz, and perhaps Chanapata. A unique type of village is found at Chiripa on the Bolivian shore of Lake Titicaca. It consists of fourteen rectangular houses arranged in a circle around a central court. The foundation walls, which are intact, are about one meter high and are built of small stones packed in clay. The upper walls were constructed of rectangular adobes and the roof of sticks and grass thatch. The side walls are double; their hollow interiors were used as storage bins, access to which was by means of inside rectangular windows. Deep vertical slots in the door jambs were for sliding wooden door panels (Plate 12).

Technological advancement in ceramic manufacture and decoration is evident. This by no means implies that the artistic accomplishment was any better, it simply means that a wider range of technical differences can be noted. There is a shift to open, oxidized firing and the decorative procedures which are possible with the resultant light-colored wares. Fired pigments come into use, at first in conjunction with the earlier incised decoration or as white or creamy painting on reddish slip or paste. Negative decoration, impractical on dark wares became popular. Because of its simplicity, knowledge of this process could spread without transmission of motifs or patterns—so it is not surprising that there are marked regional differences in its use.

Salinar presents a great range of vessel shapes, of which the most typical are stirrup-spout containers, jars with a spout and a bridge to a modeled figure, bottles with cylindrical necks and flat handles, and ollas (Plate

13). Modeling is an outstanding characteristic. The small figures which are almost caricatures are noted for their detail of facial expression. The modeled vessels portray birds, animals, and human figures in peculiar positions. All are disproportionate in detail, particularly in the treatment of the eyes. Incision, appliqué, punch, and white-on-red brush painting are also employed. The white paint is applied directly to the base clay. The designs are simple lines or triangles. Paint is also used to augment the modeled features of the vessels.

The Central Coast ceramics, best known from the Chancay sites, consist mainly of bowls with flaring lips, mammiform jars, flaring-sided cups, and plain jars. Incision is rare and modeling is limited to simple lugs. Some negative painting is found, but positive painting, either white zoned, or white-on-red, simple geometric designs, is the more characteristic decoration.

A long developmental sequence of Cavernas ceramics starts with Chavín designs and feline elements. Vessel forms include a drinking jar with a spout joined by a bridge handle to vented heads and figures, one and two-spouted bottles, with and without handles, varied bowl shapes and graters, egg-shaped storage and cooking jars, the last with thickened rims like those of the Cultist Period. Other items are figurines, drums, trumpets, panpipes and whistles. Modeling is sometimes suggestive of Salinar. Decoration emphasizes incision with lacquer-like, resin-based pigment colors added after firing (Plate 14). Negative decoration is common and use of white slip paint develops late.

The Chanapata ceramics are predominantly monochrome blackware: ollas with strap handles, open bowls with flaring sides, bottles, and plates. The major decorative techniques are incision, punctation, and appliqué. A simple cat, unlike the Chavín motif, is the characteristic design. Some positive painting presents both a red-on-white and a white-on-red combination, although it is not related to the Chancay style.

The typical Chiripa vessel is a flat-bottom open bowl, with perpendicular sides, and a thickened rim edge. Simple geometric designs are executed in a thick yellow paint on a red slip base (Plate 12). The color areas may be outlined by incision. A cat figure in appliqué relief, like Chanapata, is also common. This style, plus black paint and more emphasis on the modeled relief, forms the basis for the Pucara style.

Certain cultural traditions are either continued or established during this period. On the North Coast, the ceramic traditions of modeling, stirrup-spout, and hand manufacture continued and bichrome painting became established. Molds for increased production were developed later by Mochica potters while polychrome fired pigments start at the end of Paracas with the first Nazca wares.

Where textiles have survived and have been collected one finds them abundantly associated with all cultures of this period. The greatest quantity comes from Paracas Cavernas graves both at Paracas and in the Ica Valley. These reveal several well-developed techniques; double cloth, sometimes with supplementary yarns used to create the effect of triple cloth, patterned spräng or loom plaiting, gauze and abundant embroidery. Some are painted, others covered with tropical forest bird feathers imported from east of the Andes. The principal fibers are cotton and wool. Dyes on wool are often bright and varied. Designs are largely influenced by techniques and even on painted pieces are geometrically angular.

Among the various textile articles we find the basic Central Andean clothing pattern, turbans, headbands, hoods or snoods, shawls, sleeveless shirts, loincloths, and carrying bags. It is reasonable to assume that at this time the Highland inhabitants possessed adequate clothing although no actual specimens survive. As in later times, the principal fiber must have been wool.

In the north, modeled ceramics show turbans and other headgear, and knee-length skirts. Gallinazo fabrics from the Chicama Valley, made mainly of cotton, have fewer dyes and reveal less technical and design development than in the south. From all this it seems that Paracas culture placed great emphasis on the craft. The greater variety of fibers, techniques, and woven garments all bear this out. The South Coast also continues to be a versatile weaving center in later periods.

With greater attention given to clothing, there is less emphasis on personal ornaments than in the preceding period. Skull deformation is practiced in both Cavernas and Salinar. Some of the modeled clay figures depict tattooing, but face painting is not very common. Shell, bone, and stone beads are found everywhere. At Salinar circular and tubular earplugs, finger rings, and nose rings are added to the range of ornaments.

Metalwork, although still not very advanced, demonstrates some experimentation with new techniques and alloys. Simple hammered and cut-out gold objects are found in practically all of the sites. At both Chancay and Salinar a gold-copper alloy is used and pure copper makes its first appearance at Cavernas and Chiripa.

The sling and the spear-thrower are the most common weapons. Bone daggers are found in several sites, a wooden spear in one, and, at Chiripa, the bolas is still in use. The Experimenters made a great variety of bone and stone tools. The greatest range is to be found at Chiripa, but all sites have many of the standard implements. The bone inventory includes spatulas, needles, awls, daggers, spear-throwers, hooks, chisels, polishers, knives, and scrapers, some with serrated edges. Only Salinar has decorated spatulas. The stone artifacts consist of such utilitarian types as mortars, hammers, polishers, grinders, and scrapers. Shell seems to have been used only for beads. The Cavernas sites preserve certain of the more perishable artifacts: nets, calabashes decorated by pyrogravure, totora baskets and mats, painted leather containers, a circular strainer attached to a handle, and a five-stop flute. Clay panpipes are found both at Chancay and Cavernas.

There is still no evidence for stone carving in this period, although presumably the art carried over from the Cultist Period since it reappears in the Pucara and Tiahuanaco cultures in the South Highlands and in the Recuay culture in the North Highlands. Actually many carved stones in the highlands cannot yet be assigned to any specific period. Some of these may some day be identified as belonging to the Experimenter Period.

Direct pit burial was characteristic of the preceding period and is still a common type. However, there is now evidence of greater attention to the preparation of tombs. Some type of covering is usual. In Salinar, the elliptical graves are covered with inclined slabs. At Chancay the graves are covered with poles or rough stone vaults. Stone-lined box graves are commonly found underneath the house floor at Chiripa. Cavernas has more elaborate tombs cut into the soft rock. A typical tomb has a stone-walled upper chamber, 1.5 meters in diameter and about two meters deep. A passage cut through the soft rock extends some three meters below this before it broadens out into a lower chamber which serves as the burial vault. Some Cavernas tombs contain many bundle burials and artifacts. Elsewhere the grave accompaniments are relatively poor: one to three vessels and perhaps a few other artifacts.

It is extremely difficult to reconstruct the type of social organization in this period. Some of the Cavernas tombs appear to have been family vaults; these contain burials of both the rich and the poor, judging by the quantity and quality of the cloth wrappings. However, in general, there is little archaeological evidence of any sharp class distinctions. The arrangement of the house clusters, however, suggests an extended family pattern in which each unit was more or less equivalent.

Religion, too, seems to have been of no great importance. The feline cult of the Cultist Period disappeared and no new religious cult replaced it. The paucity of ruins which can be identified as temples or shrines, the relatively meager attention paid to grave construction and accompaniment, and the absence of symbolic design in the ceramics and other arts all confirm the impression of a poorly organized religion. Graves at Ocucaje in Ica Valley contain skulls cut in two halves, a practice which may imply either a religious custom or the preservation of war trophies. A medicine-man kneeling beside his patient is represented on one Salinar vessel.

Each local region can be distinguished on the basis of its ceramic styles, but there are no marked contrasts in development except at Cavernas which is perhaps more advanced in weaving techniques. Even with this exception, the regional culture patterns are not markedly different. Instead, the picture everywhere is one of relatively small populations, divided into family or extended family groups, which directed their major energies towards the development of agricultural methods, and towards the control of a variety of new techniques. The concentration of attention was therefore on the local region. Techniques developed outside its limits were rapidly accepted and applied locally, but there seems to have been no great pressure for widespread political or religious unity.

As experiments proved successful, the technological controls improved, and the population increased. When this happened, the geographical differences in size and fertility of regions became an important factor. Increased populations also created new problems in social and political controls. These new problems were solved in different ways in each local region, so that by the succeeding period, which marks the acme of technology and craftsmanship, each region has a distinctive pattern of orientation. As previously mentioned, it is not possible to determine precisely when this transition from experiment to mastery occurred. Doubtless it varied from region to region. However, there comes a point when it is clear that techniques have been mastered in all parts of the Central Andes and a new period has begun.

MASTERCRAFTSMAN PERIOD

(*ca.* 0–900 A.D.)

The long period of experimentation eventually culminated in the complete mastery of many techniques, particularly those relating to agricultural subsistence and the crafts. Since, as pointed out in the preceding chapter, similar experimentation was carried out in all parts of the Central Andes, it is impossible to determine exactly when the controls were finally achieved, but the quantity of artifacts of good quality suggest a substantial time duration for the Mastercraftsman Period. In the guess-dates used in this volume nine hundred years are allowed for this period, but the time span might easily be larger or smaller. The upper time limit is reasonably well established by the widely distributed Tiahuanaco horizon which is so uniform that it serves as a convenient time marker. Everywhere Tiahuanaco is either intermingled with or replaces the local culture of the Mastercraftsman Period, as has been demonstrated many times by stratigraphic excavation and by the analyses of the resultant collections.

In both the highlands and the coast the Mastercraftsman Period is characterized by the mastery of agricultural techniques, by ambitious monumental architecture, by skilled craftsmanship in ceramics, weaving, and metallurgy, and by a florescence of art styles. Despite this apparent unity on the technological level, regional differences are marked. Each sub-area may be

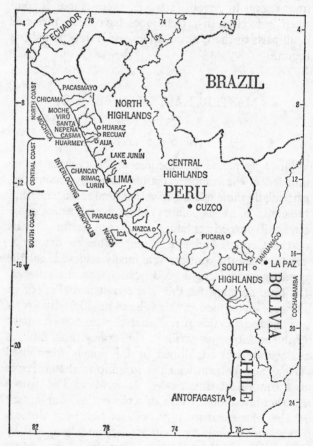

FIG. 12. Principal cultural divisions in the Mastercraftsman Period.

distinguished by its distinctive local patterns which were apparently strong enough to absorb alien influences and mold them into the dominant styles without interrupting the basic trends. Some design motifs, such as the feline, snake, sea-otter, and ray fish, are widely distributed, but their specific portrayal is in terms of the local style. In fact, regionalism is so strong that there are no horizon styles in this period. The diffusion, which certainly resulted from the ever-increasing contacts between peoples of the different regions, must have taken the form of a direct exchange of ideas rather than wholesale borrowing. In brief, the differentiation between regions is now of such magnitude that it is no longer merely marked by a contrast of local styles of manufacture and design, but, rather, by distinct patterns of orientation based on the same technological elements. Each local culture had a large inventory of techniques and controls at its command and these were selected and developed in terms of the particular regional pattern. For example, the absence of massive temple construction in the Nazca culture cannot be attributed to a lack of knowledge of building methods, but rather to a pattern which directed mass energy into other channels. At the close of this chapter two of the most distinctive patterns are described in some detail because they are important in the later history of the Central Andes.

The Mastercraftsman Period is represented by hundreds of sites and by extensive collections of artifacts. Since this period attained the peak of perfection in craftsmanship, the ceramics, textiles, and other art objects have been avidly collected by both amateurs and professionals, and are abundantly represented in museums throughout the world. It is not practical to list specific sites for this period since each major culture covers a rather extensive area. The Mochica culture is found in the North Coast valleys of Pacasmayo,

Chicama, Moche, Viru, Santa, Nepeña, and Casma
where it is evident that strong political as well as cultural unity existed. The Interlocking and Early Lima
cultures dominate the Central Coast, particularly in the
Chancay, Rimac, and Lurín valleys. On the South
Coast, the Necropolis culture at Paracas, near Pisco Valley, is closely related to the Nazca culture of the Ica
and Nazca valleys. The Recuay culture is found throughout the Callejón de Huaylas and in other parts of the
North Highlands. The South Highlands are the center
of the Pucara and Early Tiahuanaco cultures. The distinctive Tiahuanaco culture undoubtedly had its
origins in the period, but it will be described with the
next period which it so clearly dominates. Only the
Central Highlands, later so prominent as the center
of the Inca Empire, have no known cultural remains of
this period.

So vast is the quantity and variety of cultural material that detailed treatment of each culture is impractical. By and large the Nazca and Mochica cultures
are the best known; consequently, these are treated in
greater detail, particularly in respect to their contrasting cultural patterns. The other cultures are included
wherever possible. The technological achievements are
presented first as the basis for subsequent analysis of
the regional patterns of orientation.

In the Mastercraftsman Period subsistence is based
almost entirely on agriculture and there is every indication that the coastal valleys were completely conquered with respect to cultivation. In Viru, for example,
hundreds of sites of this period are found in all parts
of the valley, with the principal sites concentrated on
the valley flats. Some of these are small habitation
mounds; others are reasonably large villages. Irrigation
systems are intricate and suggest over-all planning. In
Chicama Valley one irrigation canal is over seventy-
five miles long; another, at Ascope, is conducted across

the wide mouth of a quebrada by means of an artificially constructed aqueduct, fourteen hundred meters long, fifteen meters high, and estimated to contain over 785,000 cubic meters of earth. Likewise many of the complicated arrangements of agricultural terraces in the South Highlands are assigned to this period.

In preceding periods the range of domesticated plants included maize, squash, beans, cotton, peppers, peanuts, manioc, coca, quinoa, cañahua, achira; and various fruits: pepino, pacai, lúcuma, and avocado. Additional plants and fruits were grown by the Mastercraftsmen: sweet potato, potato, oca, mashua, ulluco, jíquima, yacón, and lupines; tuna, granadilla, chirimoya, guanábana, tumbo, papaya, and pineapple. To be sure, some of these plants and fruits were undoubtedly known previously, but the evidence is now definite. In other words, the total range of Central Andean domesticated plants is now established, and no new plants are added until the Spaniards arrived. Likewise, the standard agricultural techniques include the digging-stick, the hoe, guano fertilizer, and probably every other method known in the Central Andes at any time. The psychological importance of agricultural subsistence is indicated by the common representations of domesticated plants in the art work, the frequent association of plants and religious symbols, and the pictures of ceremonies related to agricultural activities. Domesticated llamas, alpacas, and guinea pigs are numerous, and herding plays an important role in the subsistence. The gathering of wild foods no longer seems important, but fishing, with hooks, nets, and harpoons, is still a standard supplement to the food supply. Hunting, judging by the scenes on Mochica pottery, has now become a sport for the privileged upper class. The hunting scenes depict the use of deer nets and traps, spear-throwers and darts, clubs for sea lions, and blowguns for birds.

The advanced agricultural techniques and the size and number of habitation sites all suggest a large population. However, population pressure cannot have been very severe since many regions and valleys of considerable fertility were apparently only slightly utilized. It is of course possible that future archaeological work will prove that these were equally well populated by peoples with different cultures.

Permanent materials, such as stone or adobe, are used everywhere in house building. In the latter half of the Early Farmer Period underground structures were popular. Like those found in association with the Necropolis culture at Paracas, they had one and two rooms lined with stone and sun-baked adobes. In the earlier examples, entrance was through a short tunnel. Later, a stairway led to the rooms. Subterranean dwellings are also associated with the Recuay culture in the North Highlands. Some are long narrow galleries, lined and covered with stone slabs, and entered by a shaft at one end. Others have a central chamber surrounded by a number of small niche-like rooms. These are constructed of large and small stones, carefully chinked, plastered, and often painted. Still others have two floors underground, or a combination of a surface room and a basement-like chamber. Subterranean houses are also found in the South Highlands, but most villages consist of a number of rough stone surface dwellings. The North Coast Mochica ceramics portray houses built on terraces around open patios and with small rectangular rooms. The roofs are gabled and apparently thatched with straw or mats. The excavated ruins reveal clusters of rectangular rooms around some of the large temples. The walls are usually composed of mold-made rectangular adobes.

Villages of this period are not laid out according to a specific plan. An open scatter pattern is the most typical arrangement of house units. An exception is found in the North Coast honeycomb pattern of which the Gallinazo group in Viru Valley is a good illustration. This group consists of six artificial platform mounds, the largest of which is roughly two hundred by four hundred meters, and over five meters high. Its surface is covered with small rectangular rooms constructed of plain or cane-marked adobes. The rooms average about ten meters square, so that they number several thousand on this one platform. The layout is haphazard; new units were added in amorphous fashion from time to time. It does not follow that all the rooms were occupied simultaneously nor that each room represents the home of a single family unit. However, the group as a whole must have housed a sizable population.

The Mastercraftsman Period is generally characterized by the construction of large public works, usually identified as temples and forts. An exception is in the south where large fortified towns start in Paracas times but seldom have structures of large size. On the Central Coast, although time association for the many large pyramids and building units is not very satisfactory, some of the large pyramids and building units, like Pachacamac and Cajamarquilla, were certainly initiated during this period. For example, some thick walls built of hand-molded adobe and stone are decorated with frescoes with typical Interlocking designs of fish painted in white, yellow, red, and black. In the North Highlands some of the two and three-story temples with interior rooms, stone walls, and slab roofs, undoubtedly are assignable to the Recuay culture, although final confirmation of this identification is lacking. Consequently, our best knowledge of large scale public building is from the North Coast and the South Highlands.

The most outstanding Mochica constructions on the North Coast are found at Moche, not far from Trujillo.

At the base of a rocky hill, called Cerro Blanco, are two large buildings separated by a flat plain, once the site of a village. The first building, the "Huaca de la Luna," is a step-sided platform, eighty by sixty meters, terraced against the side of the hill. Graves with Mochica style pottery were uncovered at the base of this platform and some of the room walls on top are decorated with a fresco in black, white, red, yellow, light blue, pink, and brown. The design, in Mochica style, portrays shields, maces, darts, and the like, represented as if in revolt against human control. The second building, the "Huaca del Sol," is one of the largest single structures on the Coast of Peru. The base is a step-sided platform, two hundred twenty-eight by one hundred thirty-six meters and eighteen meters high; it is approached by a causeway six meters wide and ninety meters long. A step-sided pyramid, one hundred three meters square and twenty-three meters high, caps the south end of the platform. The Moche River has cut into this building, revealing a solid mass of rectangular mold-made adobes. In fact, the whole unit is composed of columns of adobes, piled up with little attention to binding, implying that it was constructed by organized groups of unskilled workers.

The Moche ruins are the most impressive, but there are many other examples of large isolated architectural units on the North Coast. Some are step-sided pyramids built on the village flats, others are platforms approached by a ramp; still others cap natural rocky outcrops and thus augment the impression of massiveness. Rough stones are used in the foundations and algarrobo logs may be inserted as binders, but the greater part of the construction is always of mold-made rectangular adobes. The outer walls are plastered and some are painted or decorated with cut-out arabesques. The decorated walls and the constant association of cemeteries imply that these structures were temples.

However, some of the constructions surmounting the high peaks may have served as forts.

In the South Highlands the architecture is more skilled and complex than the simple massive North Coast constructions. The temple at Pucara in southern Peru serves as an illustration. The basic materials are dressed sandstone and basalt blocks, although some adobe is also used. The over-all plan is somewhat complex. An inner court, about fifteen meters square, contains two subterranean burial vaults built of carefully dressed blocks and slabs. The vaults are entered through a doorway and a series of steps. This central

FIG. 13. Recuay-style stone statues of the Mastercraftsman Period. Statues in the Huaraz Museum.

court is at a lower level than the surrounding constructions which consist of a series of walls forming a horseshoe-shaped enclosure and contain small compartments with the doors facing the inner court. Each compartment contains one or two slab altars. The stone masonry is consistently of good quality, although the joining techniques so characteristic of the somewhat later Tiahuanaco are not employed. The identification of this Pucara building as a temple seems obvious. The North Coast building seems to represent mass labor, but Pucara gives the impression of being the work of skilled professional masons.

Stone carving is associated with all highland cultures of this period. In the North Highlands, carved statues and lintels are characteristic of the Recuay culture. The statues (Fig. 13) represent seated females and stylized warriors who carry clubs and shields. The figures are further decorated with finely incised designs in Recuay motifs. The Pucara sculptors carved human figures, animals, stelae, and slabs (Plate 15). The carving is competent and displays some attempts at realism, although it is not remarkable as sculpture. The stelae and slabs are usually decorated with frankly geometric designs. The few statues in Bolivia which are assigned to the Early Tiahuanaco culture have certain stylistic resemblances to those of Pucara. Again the statues are somewhat realistic and represented in kneeling or seated positions.

Throughout the Central Andes, the graves of this period, although differing in detail, are always carefully constructed and usually contain a large number of offerings. To be sure, all burials are not equally elaborate even in the same culture, since by this time there are marked distinctions in the importance of individuals. The materials placed in the graves are definitely ceremonial. For example, in both ceramics and weaving there is a sharp contrast between the utilitarian pieces and the ceremonial objects intended for interment. The deceased everywhere are buried in definite cemeteries; some are located in isolated spots, others in close proximity to the temples.

The typical Mochica grave is a rectangular box made of adobes. Niches may be built in its walls to hold grave offerings. The roofs are constructed of poles, a combination of poles and adobes, or rarely, of adobes arranged in the form of a true arch. The single or multiple burials are in an extended position and the grave accompaniments are usually numerous. The South Coast Nazca graves are pot-shaped, with a square or round shaft, which may be lined with poles or rough stones, leading to an enlarged chamber below. The burials are flexed and cloth wrapped. Burials of the Necropolis culture at Paracas were in stone-lined subterranean vaults similar to their houses. Some of these vaults contain forty or more elaborately wrapped mummy bundles. The Recuay graves in the North Highlands are either subterranean stone-lined boxes or underground galleries. The dressed stone burial vaults of Pucara in the South Highlands have already been mentioned.

Most museum collections of this period are from graves that have been systematically looted for years, and consequently, contain largely ceremonial objects. In general, knowledge of the utilitarian manufactures is decidedly limited. However, the Mastercraftsman Period is particularly noted for its skilled craftsmanship in ceramics, weaving, and metallurgy. There is no outstanding regional difference in technical abilities, so that the distinctions found represent local styles and preference. Each of the major crafts is described, then, in terms of its generalized technical achievement and its specific regional styles.

The ceramics are the best made and most competently decorated of those found at any time in the Central Andes. The pastes are fine and made from selected clays; the firing is done in open ovens with complete control of oxidation; and the thickness or thinness of the ware is entirely under the regulation of the manufacturer. Most vessels are covered with an over-all slip before the design is applied. Modeling,

incision, appliqué, and pressed relief are universally
known decorative techniques, but the principal distinguishing trait is brush work painted design. Polychrome painting is equally characteristic, although the
number of colors varies regionally. In general, the
ceramic design is depictive in that the modeling and
painting is intended to portray actual objects, animals,
birds, and figures. Occasionally the design approaches
true realism; sometimes, the basic naturalistic figure
is modified or stylized. Each major area has its distinctive series of shapes and designs which are readily
distinguishable.

The major diagnostics of the Mochica ceramics are
the stirrup-spout, the depictive linear brush design,
bichrome painting in white and red, and skillful naturalistic modeling (Plate 17). While the number of vessel shape categories is limited, the variations within
each are enormous. Roughly, sixty per cent of the
vessels in museum collections have stirrup-spouts, that
is, two arched tubes which meet in a single cylindrical
spout. The stirrup-spout is one of the North Coast
ceramic traditions, but it is distinguishable in Mochica
because of its consistent thinness and regularity of
dimension. It is found on globular containers, or, less
frequently, on angular-bodied, squat, cylindrical and
square vessels. It is also commonly found on modeled
containers which portray human heads, human figures,
animals, birds, houses, fruits, plants, etc. Other prominent ceramic shapes are head bowls without stirrup-
spouts, containers with a spout and an arched handle,
double bowls, dippers with conical handles, flaring-
sided (flower) vases, collar jars, and bowls. Although
virtually all vessels are made in molds, true duplication
is unusual. Painting, modeling, and relief are used singly or in any combination of the three techniques. The
bichrome painting is depictive, some designs showing
single figures; others, scenes. Three dimensional effects

are achieved in the modeling. Mochica design is basically realistic, portraying many details of the life of the times: fishing and hunting scenes, ceremonies, punishments, battles, modeled portraits of distinguished individuals, house types, animals, birds so carefully modeled that the species can often be identified, and representations of the gods and religious concepts. All these realistic representations permit considerable reconstruction of the Mochica culture. Further references to these designs will be made in discussing other aspects of culture.

On the Central Coast the ceramics have little variety. The predominant shape of the Interlocking culture is a beaker with out-flaring or out-slanting sides, painted in black, white and bright red on a reddish base slip. The characteristic design, after which the culture is named, is an interlocking fish, undoubtedly derived from a textile pattern. Other associated shapes are mammiform jars, double-spout vessels, constricted collar jars, and spout and handle jars. The Early Lima culture has few distinctive ceramic elements, but has, rather, a combination of features from both the North and South Coasts.

The Nazca ceramics (Plate 18) are characterized by globular containers with two short spouts and a flat connecting bridge, variants on tall, graceful goblets, complex stylized design, and polychrome painting in from one to eight colors on a background slip. There are twenty-five basic shapes; most of them are variants on shallow open bowls, tall goblets, double-spout jars, and a spout and bridge to modeled figure jars. Polychrome painting is outstanding, while modeling is decidedly secondary and not particularly distinctive. The commonest colors are various shades of red, yellow, gray, brown, violet, black, and white. The designs may be termed naturalistic in that they represent fish, fruit, birds, and other identifiable figures. Each design unit is usually outlined in black and filled in with other colors. The more elaborate designs include trophy heads, centipede-like figures, a human figure with a jagged staff and, most distinctive of all, an anthropomorphized feline with a mask. Nazca ceramics are excellently made, highly polished, and brilliant in color.

In the North Highlands, Recuay ceramics are characterized by post-fired, carbon-black, resist decoration applied to a red and white surface, and a stylized jaguar design with outlined angular body and a large head comb. The variety of shapes is so great that it is difficult to isolate the most typical ones. There are open bowls, conical-handled dippers, goblets, tripod bowls, jars with high flaring collars, jars with disc-like rims, containers with short collars and abbreviated bridges to modeled heads, double jars, and flat-topped jars with small modeled figures on them. Though inferior in quality to that of Mochica, the modeling is competent and has a wide range of subject matter. Besides the characteristic jaguar design and three-color negative painting, there are geometric, condor, and serpent designs painted in positive red, white, and black.

The Pucara ceramics in the South Highlands are distinguished by flat-bottom open bowls with diverging sides, a full cat figure design with profile body and front view face, and painting in thick black and yellow on a red slip wih the color areas outlined by incisions. Large goblets and jars and some smaller vessels are also associated; additional designs are composed of rows of profile human heads, running human figures with elaborate headdresses, men leading llamas, and anthropomorphized figures. The Pucara pottery is affiliated with the earlier Chiripa and the somewhat later Tiahuanaco cultures. Its relationship to the Early Tiahuanaco is not very close, although these two seem to be contemporaneous. Instead, the Early Tiahuanaco is characterized by long-necked decanters, flat-bottom spittoon-shaped bowls, and a fretted rim incense bowl with modeled puma heads. The designs, peculiar animals, birds and geometric patterns, are painted in a polychrome on buff, employing glossy, burnished white, black, red, brown, orange, and yellow.

Although cloth is preserved only in certain favorable sections, there is considerable indirect evidence of competent weaving everywhere in the Mastercraftsman Period. For example, though no fabrics are preserved in the highlands, weave daggers and spindle whorls are numerous, and the incised designs on many stone statues represent complex textile patterns. Cloth is best preserved on the South Coast which, consequently, furnishes the fullest evidence for the textile arts. Fine weaving seems to have been a widespread tradition. Regional emphasis on techniques made twill more popular on the North Coast in Mochica times than elsewhere. Most Mochica cloth is of single-ply cotton, commonly paired, a feature used in various constructions. These include, in addition to twill, double cloth, tapestry, brocade, gauze, plaid, and embroidery. Clothing depicted on pottery shows large, bold designs so the elaboration of detail seen on some of their tapestries may be a late feature.

The textile art reaches its highest development on the South Coast. Both cotton and wool fibers are extensively employed. Since the Central and South Highlands are more favorable environments for the breeding and herding of llamas and alpacas than the North Highlands, the South Coast peoples always had an abundant source of wool for weaving, a circumstance which may account for some of the emphasis on this craft. In their totality, the textiles of Nazca and the Necropolis cultures present almost every weaving technique known in the Central Andes at any time. Over-all embroidery is the most characteristic decorative technique, but brocade, warp and weft stripe, gauze, lace, double cloth, and tapestry are all common. There are also many types of braiding and three dimensional needle knitting. Polychrome design is the rule and as many as one hundred ninety hues in seven color ranges have been identified. Most designs are complex, but the embroidered figures are particularly elaborate, resembling the polychrome painted designs on Nazca pottery in many details. In fact, the textiles of the South Coast represent one of the greatest artistic achievements of the Central Andes. The demonstrated skills in spinning, dyeing, and weaving techniques rank these textiles among the great arts of the world. The known quantity of woven fabrics is almost unbelievable. Furthermore, many of the garments were woven exclusively for the mummy bundles, rather than for the use of the living.

The woven parts of clothing include breechclouts, belts, slit neck shirts, wrap-around skirts, large shawls, rectangular pieces folded and wrapped as turbans, woven headbands, and other forms of headdress. The Mochica ceramic designs depict a similar clothing pattern for the North Coast, with, if possible, even greater emphasis on the elaboration of headdress. Indirect evidence from other areas confirms the conclusion that by the Mastercraftsman Period, the basic Andean pattern of male and female costume was established throughout the Central Andes. Closely related to costume are personal ornaments which show elaboration and variety. Ornaments and details of dress seem to mark individuals of different rank and importance and also to identify local groups and specialists. The variety of headdresses has already been mentioned as characteristic. These include plain bands, turbans, skull caps, animal and bird skin caps, and some attachments like feather fans and metal crests. The Mochica ceramics suggest that the headdress symbolized messengers, wise men, fishermen, agriculturists, priests, warriors, and rulers. Face and body painting is a common practice; again it seems that the design detail served to distinguish rank and association. Some of the South Coast mummies are tattooed. Elsewhere the ceramic designs represent facial incisions and punctations which probably signify tattooing. Artificial skull deformation is a widespread custom. It has been suggested that this was a mark of rank, but actually, undeformed skulls are so rare that the practice seems to have been fairly universal. Earplugs, noseplugs, and lip plugs are found in every region. Other types of ornaments such as beads, necklaces, anklets, rings, feather plumes, collars, and tweezers for depilation are also widely distributed. Ceremonial or burial masks of clay, cloth, or metal are also associated with every culture of this period.

The metallurgists worked with silver, copper, and gold, and made alloys of copper and gold, copper and silver, and silver and gold (Plate 16). It is noteworthy that bronze, the alloy of copper and tin, is still unknown. The range of techniques includes soldering, hammering, embossing, casting, gilding, and annealing. Some regions, particularly the South Coast, were not as advanced as others in metalwork. In general, metal objects were used only for ornaments. The Mochica are exceptions, since they used copper for spear points, digging-stick points, battle axes, and some other tools.

Many minor crafts were undoubtedly advanced, although archaeologists have not devoted much attention to them so that our knowledge is somewhat restricted. The Mochica tombs contain incised clay whorls, figurines, whistles, trumpets, and panpipes; ceremonial stone axes and club heads; intricate examples of inlaid shell mosaic; incised and carved bone tubes; and some carved wooden staff heads and other objects. Other sites preserve decorated calabashes and a variety of baskets which, although competently made, are not very elaborate in technique.

There is also evidence of advancement of knowledge in other fields. An ideographic means of communication has been suggested for the Mochica. This is based on the frequent depiction on ceramics of variously marked beans and activities in which beans obviously play an important role. An alternative suggestion is that variations in the markings of beans were used in divination. Whatever the reason similar beans appear as design elements in the Necropolis culture of the South Coast and in the Tiahuanaco culture of the South Highlands. Many skulls from the South Coast and the North Highlands have pieces of bone cut out, and since the edges of the cuts show subsequent growth of the bone, this trephining operation was obviously successfully controlled. The Mochica ceramics record other surgical practices, namely, bone setting, limb amputation, and circumcision. The artists also depicted many types of diseases and their cures, some, apparently, with medicinal plants. The ceramics also display medicinemen curing patients by means of massage and by sucking out disease objects.

The designs on stone carving and ceramics and, in some places, the actual specimens, show that feather capes, masks, and other special costumes were worn in ceremonial dances. Many of the ceremonies are directed by priest-like figures and are accompanied by musicians. These designs and the preserved artifacts present a fair inventory of musical instruments, including drums of various types, tambourines, and flutes, panpipes of both clay and reeds, gongs, clappers, rattles, shell trumpets, and both straight and coiled clay trumpets (Fig. 18).

Religion is highly developed and organized in the Mastercraftsman Period, as witnessed by the ceremonial paraphernalia, the elaborate grave equipment, the temple constructions, and the depiction of priests and anthropomorphic divinities. The feline is the most universal religious figure represented, but many others depicted in the modeling, painting, and carving seem to suggest a hierarchy of gods. Nature worship is certainly prominent in the religion and the elaborateness of burial indicates an equal importance for ancestor worship. The Mochica ceramics represent many sacrifices of prisoners and the widespread distribution of the trophy head design suggests that the taking of trophy heads was part of the religious practice.

A marked increase in population occurred in the Mastercraftsman Period, but the organization and control of agricultural subsistence was adequate to produce an excess supply which permitted leisure-time activities. In other words, when technology had advanced to a satisfactory level in terms of the local economy, attention was shifted to socio-political organization and the utilization of leisure time. Many different patterns for such organization are theoretically possible and each major area may well have had its own distinctive type. On the basis of existing evidence three emerge clearly, namely, the Mochica pattern on the North Coast, the Nazca-Necropolis pattern on the South Coast, and the Tiahuanaco pattern in the South Highlands. The characteristics of the first two patterns are presented here; the third, the Tiahuanaco, is reserved for the next section, since it forms the basis for the subsequent pan-Central Andean horizon.

The Mochica socio-political organization and leisure-time superstructure emerged as a sharply divided class system in which a small upper group directed the labor of the masses. The ceramic designs suggest many specialized groups, such as rulers, wise men, messengers, warriors, priests, weavers, potters, fishermen, musicians, doctors, and prisoners or slaves. Certain symbols are regularly associated with some of these groups. A combination symbol composed of shield, mace, and darts identifies the warriors. The messengers are represented by centipedes, birds, and dragonflies. A fox or a cat-like mask usually distinguishes the learned men, and a jaguar is commonly the symbol of authority. Specialized groups in themselves do not necessarily imply a strong class system, but in this case there is additional evidence for rather marked differences in the ranking of the groups. The costumes of important individuals are definitely more elaborate than those of the commoners. Furthermore, the "rulers" often combine the attributes of political, religious, and military authority. The leaders are pictured as seated on raised daises under special sun shelters, as carried in litters, or as seated on rafts which are towed through the water by menial swimmers. Guests of inferior rank dine at a lower level than the important chiefs. Servants are often depicted as lizards. Both the rulers and the gods are approached with an attitude of reverence —the hands clasped as if in prayer, the head inclined towards the ground. The chiefs occupy prominent positions as leaders of ceremonies and as supervisors of hunting and fishing parties. The graves of such important individuals are markedly richer and more elaborate than others in the same cemetery.

The Mochica erected immense public buildings and temples which display only limited architectural skill, but certainly suggest well organized mass labor. The adobes were made in molds and piled up in columns. One vessel shows a group of weavers working under the direction of a supervisor, so simple mass production methods were applied to the textile craft. Ceramic production is not so well documented and we can only deduce that potters were similarly organized. The ceramic painting and modeling reflect a great interest in mundane affairs. Even the anthropomorphized deity engages in agriculture, fishing, and hunting, and fights with demons as a symbol of the "good." Since the chief is portrayed as both a political and religious leader, many of the ceremonies and religious beliefs served to bolster the upper class authority. Many scenes represent systematic and severe punishments, including mutilation, stoning, exposure, and execution or sacrifice. Nude prisoners are pictured with ropes around their necks, but even here the more important individuals are carried in litters. The Mochica women occupy a definitely subordinate position. They are never represented in social or ceremonial scenes, but are portrayed as engaged in the menial tasks of weaving, domestic work, and burden bearing. The warrior group, on the other hand, is particularly prominent. The warriors have distinctive headdress and garments and carry copper battle axes, maces, darts, shields, and spear-throwers. Battle scenes are common and illustrate the Mochica aggressive tendencies.

The Nazca-Necropolis pattern on the South Coast presents a sharp contrast to the Mochica. The social organization and the leisure-time activities appear to have been directed essentially towards the preparation of special grave materials in an elaboration of ancestor worship. There are no large scale buildings and the simple structures use hand-made rather than mold-made adobes. The greatest emphasis is placed on textile weaving, a craft which requires an enormous expenditure of time, particularly for the more elaborate pieces. Increased production in hand weaving can be achieved only by increasing the number of weavers, so that the vast quantity of Nazca-Necropolis fabrics suggests that a large part of the population was involved. Although artistic and technical standards of weaving are exceptionally high, almost every fabric achieves them, which again implies numerous highly skilled weavers. Various fabrics must have been woven especially for interment, rather than for other purposes. Some garments show no signs of wear, others do. Some are unfinished and certain turbans are so large that they appear to have been made to fit the mummy bundle rather than the living.

Many motifs in both textile and ceramic design are essentially mythological in nature and often have long records of use and modification. None was used in a way implying rigid class distinctions. Some individuals were honored more than others and were buried with a greater number of costumes and ornaments. Such persons were not set apart and are found among groups of people of lesser rank, men and women together. The grouping seems to have been by families perhaps over a number of generations. In preparation for burial successive wrappings were used which prompted an erroneous suggestion that this was done at different times.

The reality of these two regional culture patterns is confirmed by their later history. The Nazca-Necropolis pattern did not expand, but rather was confined to the three South Coast valleys of Pisco, Ica, and Nazca. The expanding Tiahuanaco horizon complex, whatever its nature, mingled readily with the Nazca style to produce new types of textiles and new combinations of ceramic shapes and designs. In fact, Tiahuanaco completely absorbed the Nazca-Necropolis culture so that it never re-emerged. The Mochica, on the other hand, became aggressive at the end. They spread their culture by military conquest from the original center of the Chicama and Moche valleys until they controlled the North Coast from Pacasmayo to Casma. The Mochica culture mixed very little with the Tiahuanaco. In fact, the meeting of the two cultures appears to have resulted in a struggle for survival in which the Mochica were temporarily eclipsed or, more likely, withdrew to such northern valleys as Lambayeque and Piura. At least the Mochica style and the Mochica pattern soon re-emerged in the modified form of the Chimu culture which persisted up to the time of the Inca conquest.

The Mastercraftsman Period in general marks the culmination of technological advancement. A successful formula for subsistence and crafts had been achieved, and attention was shifted to the control of man units rather than development of additional techniques. The remaining cultural history of the Central Andes is, then, that of different types of political and social organizations. The next period is marked by confusion and political expansion out of which the Tiahuanaco formula becomes pan-Central Andean in scope. This is not based on any radical change in technology, but is rather a new form of social, political, or religious organization.

EXPANSIONIST PERIOD

(*ca.* 900–1200 A.D.)

The shift from technological advancement to manipulation of man-hour units and political organization had begun even before the close of the Mastercraftsman Period. With this change in emphasis, expansion in the form of conquests of new regions became profitable. This general tendency for expansion and aggression is not limited to one region, but, except for the Nazca culture, seems to be general throughout the Central Andes. As previously mentioned, the Mochica had occupied five of the major North Coast valleys. Still farther north, the local cultures of Lambayeque were spreading their influence to neighboring regions. In the North Highlands, both the Recuay and Cajamarca cultures were increasing their territory to the extent of strong influence and, in some cases, actual penetration on the coast of Peru. The several Central Coast valleys were united stylistically, if not politically, by the Interlocking culture. This widespread expansion resulted in considerable conflict and confusion. In some regions the irrigation systems seem to have broken down and the populations diminished and scattered. In fact, the peoples of the Central Andes apparently became engaged in serious internecine warfare.

The Tiahuanaco culture, presumably developed in the Central and Southern Andes, starts the spread of its influence which characterizes the whole Expansionist Period. The exact nature of this expansion cannot be finally determined, but the archaeological materials include the diagnostics of the Tiahuanaco horizon complex in all six of the major areas of the Central Andes. The problem of interpreting the nature of this expansion is complicated by the fact that by the close of the Mastercraftsman Period, each region had a well-established local culture represented by a sizable population. Irrespective then of the type of Tiahuanaco expansion, a merger with each of the local cultures would be anticipated and this is precisely what occurred. However, the Tiahuanaco horizon presents a complex, not merely a single style, and the fact that the various components are so readily recognized in such widely separated areas certainly suggests some form of political expansion, even though the integration was religious and priest controlled. Considering the type of cultural development everywhere in the Central Andes, this wide distribution in all probability was effected over a relatively short span of time, nor is there any indication that the unity, political or otherwise, endured for any great length of time. Instead, the local cultures were so strong that they soon re-emerged as independent organizations. The assignment here of three hundred years for the duration of the

Expansionist Period is largely guesswork; it might have flourished for a longer or even shorter time.

In order to present an adequate picture of the long recognized pan-Central Andean Tiahuanaco horizon, the highland Bolivian site of the same name must first be described. The ruins of Tiahuanaco have long been considered as the type site for the culture, partly be-

FIG. 14. Principal centers of the Expansionist Period.

cause they have been extensively covered in the literature, partly because the culture here is well isolated. It seems highly improbable now that Bolivia was the center of distribution for this horizon. The bleak altiplano near Lake Titicaca has an altitude of almost fourteen thousand feet, which is too high for the cultivation of many plants, although quinoa, potatoes, and oca can be grown, and there is pasturage for llamas and alpacas. Today, the region supports a scattered, although reasonably large Indian population; presumably the situation was not very different in the past. However, the Tiahuanaco site appears to have been a major ceremonial center, rather than a city or large village. This would enhance its importance even though it was not the political or distributional center. In most regions, the Tiahuanaco elements are intermingled with local styles, but the Bolivian site is an exception, and thus offers the best illustrations of the basic culture. Chiripa, Early Tiahuanaco, and Pucara cultures all antedate Tiahuanaco in the South Highlands and contribute, in part, to its final formulation. This must have been initiated at least in the Mastercraftsman Period since some designs are shared in common with the Mochica and Nazca cultures. However, Tiahuanaco as a whole belongs in the Expansionist Period which it so thoroughly dominates.

The ruins of Tiahuanaco, located about twelve miles south of Lake Titicaca in Bolivia, are composed of four major structural units and numerous minor ones scattered over a large area. The largest unit, called Acapana, is a natural mound, about fifteen meters high, which was re-shaped into a step-sided pyramid and faced with stone. The over-all groundplan measures two hundred ten by two hunded ten meters and has the appearance of a step-sided triangle. House foundations rest on top of the mound and there is also a large artificial reservoir, with an overflow canal built of dressed and fitted blocks. The unit appears to have been a fortress which served as a place of refuge in time of siege.

Immediately to the north of the fortress is a large rectangular unit, one hundred thirty-five by one hundred thirty meters, called Calasasaya (Plate 19). This was at one time a raised earth platform or terreplein faced with a dressed stone wall of slab uprights and smaller filling blocks. Today most of the smaller stones have been removed and the earth fill has eroded so that the ruin has the appearance of an inclosure of upright pillars. An inner court, sixty by forty meters, is still discernible and is approached from the east by a megalithic stairway consisting of six slabs. The best preserved wall on the west side of the unit may possibly have been added at a slightly later time. Several stone statues and a decorated monolithic gateway, the "Gateway of the Sun," are associated with this unit.

A smaller inclosure, sixty by fifty-five meters, west of Calasasaya, is called the Palacio. It contains many dressed and fitted stone blocks, as well as a painted stairway. The fourth major unit, Puma Puncu, another platform structure, lies some distance southwest of the others. It is built of great slabs and stone blocks, some weighing over one hundred tons. Although badly destroyed, remains of cut-out seats, decorated blocks, and broken monolithic gateways are still identifiable. The nearest source of the sandstone used in this construction is over five kilometers distant. Organization and skill were needed to transport and place these immense stones in precise positions.

The major construction units are in themselves symmetrical, but their relationship to each other is not. The units appear planned, the over-all arrangement haphazard. The architecture is massive as illustrated by the solid raised platforms and the stone-faced pyramids. Both basalt and sandstone slabs and blocks are ground down to a smooth dressed finish. Stones are fitted by means of notches, joints, and copper cramps placed in cut-out T and I-shaped grooves (Plate 20). Not only is stone sculpture associated, but it is also one of the architectural features. Other Tiahuanaco specialties are decorated monolithic gateways, megalithic steps, cut-out step-sided wall niches, and decorative blocks arranged in mosaic patterns. Both surface conduits and underground drainage canals are found in the vicinity of the buildings, and some subterranean rooms are lined with dressed stone and entered by stairways. On the whole, this Tiahuanaco masonry is the most skilled and complex found in the Central Andes.

The stone carving at Tiahuanaco includes pillarlike statues, relief slabs and blocks, decorative friezes on gateways, and both animal and human heads with tenons or blocks for wall insertion. The statues are stiff and conventionalized and little attention has been given to sculpture in the round (Plate 21). The figure is usually in a standing position with the hands placed on the chest. The squared head has a raised headband, T-shaped eyebrows and nose, and eyes with wings or tear bands. Fine incised designs on the body and waist bands represent woven garments. These incised designs and the low relief friezes on the gateways illustrate the style which is commonly considered as typical of Tiahuanaco because of its wide spread. The designs include front view human figures with a staff in each hand, profile running figures with masks and flowing capes, profile puma and condor figures, and a series of characteristic appendages composed of puma, condor, or fish heads. That these designs are basically derived from textile patterns is confirmed by the tapestries of this period. It is of interest that at the Tiahuanaco site, the ceramic designs are usually distinguishable from the stone series incised with textile patterns, and more local in distribution. Other styles of stone carving, such as realistic human figures and geometric relief slabs, are also found at Tiahuanaco, but are not definitely associated with this time period.

There have been only a few systematic excavations at Tiahuanaco. The graves described are simple pits containing a few pieces of pottery, but more elaborate graves undoubtedly existed and perhaps some of the subterranean rooms served as burial vaults. However, fairly large private collections of grave pottery have been assembled. The ceramics are characterized by flaring-sided goblets, squat, open bowls, annular base libation bowls, modeled puma and llama vessels, tall vases, and open bowls with wide flaring rims (Plate 22). The ceramics are well fired and highly polished. All vessels are covered with a red slip and painted in polychrome designs of two to eight colors, although black, white-on-red are the basic combinations. The designs are usually outlined in black, or black and white, and other colors are added to fill in the figure. In contrast to the stone incised patterns, the ceramic designs are simple: profile pumas, human heads, and condors, or combinations of these elements.

Textiles are not preserved in the rainy altiplano, but, as mentioned, the stone carving designs are evidence that this craft was advanced. The metallurgists employed gold, silver, and copper with competence and skill. It is possible that bronze first appeared at Tiahuanaco, since Bolivia is about the only source of tin in South America, but thus far the analyses show only pure copper artifacts, even for the cramps used in fitting the stone. Decorated stone bowls, incised snuff tablets, clubs, pounders, polishers, and axes are all common. Bone and shell objects are numerous, but all the more perishable types of artifacts are not preserved.

The cultural pattern implied by the archaeological remains at Bolivian Tiahuanaco is that of a well integrated and powerfully controlled religious organization. The large construction units required organized mass labor, careful advanced planning, and skilled masons. The site has every appearance of a ceremonial center, so that it is logical to assume a religious direction. There are many indications that Tiahuanaco was built at intervals and that much of it was never completed. This suggests once more the religious pilgrimage pattern, in which great masses of people assembled at certain times of the year and contributed the labor of hauling, dressing, and placing the large stones. In the interim periods, skilled masons worked on the fitting, joining, and carving. The Tiahuanaco art style, represented by stone carving and ceramic painting, is highly conventionalized, little varied, and rigidly limited. Chavín style was limited in motifs, Tiahuanaco is limited by conventions. The designs are doubtless symbolic but they are also impersonal. They confirm the impression of a formalized and well organized religious control.

The type site of Tiahuanaco presents a unique combination of masonry, stone carving, and ceramics, but there is good evidence for the spread of some Tiahuanaco diagnostics, both in the highlands and on the coast. Other sites have been found on the islands and shores of Lake Titicaca. Lucurmata, on the Bolivian shore, presents a terraced platform and a small temple built of dressed and fitted blocks. Cemeteries near Cochabamba prove that Tiahuanaco expanded into the eastern cordillera of Bolivia. In the Calama oasis of North Chile, Tiahuanaco is represented by textiles, polychrome ceramics, and incised wooden snuff tablets. Likewise, Tiahuanaco style ceramics have been found near Arequipa and Chuquibamba in southern Peru.

The recently discovered site of Wari, near Ayacucho in the Central Highlands, may well prove to be one of the most important Tiahuanaco centers. Preliminary reports describe Wari as an enormous area covered with rough stone walls, some of which are still twenty feet high. Dressed stone tombs, simple upright statues, and thick polychrome pottery with elaborate Tiahuanaco designs are also associated. The central location of Wari, plus its apparent size and complexity, makes it a favored candidate for the true center of expansion, particularly for the coast region. Materials pertaining to the Tiahuanaco horizon complex are found in quantity in all the coastal valleys from southern Nazca to northern Chicama. Pacheco in Nazca and Pachacamac and Ancón on the Central Coast are outstanding sites, but it is impractical to list all the others. In the North Highlands, many sites, like Wilkawaín, near Huaraz, contain Tiahuanaco horizon materials. It is interesting that their stylistic affiliations are with the coast rather than with other parts of the highlands.

The highland sites of this period are represented by building units, stone sculptures, and cemeteries, but the coast sites thus far known are largely limited to cemeteries. This situation is due in part to the lack of adequate archaeological work, but it may also reflect the nature of the Tiahuanaco expansion. This whole period seems to have been one of great confusion, and it is unlikely that the unification represented by the Tiahuanaco horizon was a well organized political one. Somewhat later, the Inca perfected the techniques of conquest and incorporation, but at this point political organization was still experimental. Consequently, ambitious building projects would not be expected, but instead, the existing constructions would be re-utilized. If the expansion were truly religious, the priest leaders would probably try to maintain the authority of the recognized highland ceremonial centers rather than establish new ones. This is, of course, speculation; but, as yet, major buildings on the coast have not been assigned to this period and there is ample evidence that earlier constructions were re-used. The recent work in Viru Valley adds to the general picture of conditions at this time. Though sites are numerous, they are located on the margins of the valley. This may indicate that the valley flats were under total cultivation, but it is more likely the result of a temporary breakdown in the main irrigation system. Other evidence suggests a marked decline in population. Reorganization at the end of the period is demonstrated by finds of some villages composed of clusters of forty by sixty meter rectangular enclosures which contain interior subdivisions.

Numerous coast and highland sites of the Expansionist Period are united by the Tiahuanaco horizon complex, as well as by stratigraphic evidence which places them in the same relative time span. For example, at Moche on the North Coast an Expansionist Period cemetery is found on a platform of the Huaca del Sol constructed by the earlier Mochica. A Wilkawaín-Tiahuanaco building in the North Highlands is superimposed on a Recuay culture subterranean gallery. On the South Coast, Tiahuanaco mixes with the Nazca-B style which marks the end of the Nazca sequence. Much more data on the chronological placement of the various sites are also available.

The diagnostics of the Tiahuanaco horizon complex have previously been briefly mentioned, but deserve more detailed treatment. Ceramic traits are obviously the best criteria since pottery looms large in the collections and is universally preserved. All sites of the Tiahuanaco horizon have some ceramics with the characteristic shapes of the flaring-sided goblet and the squat flaring-sided cup; a red slip over-all base, common black and white painted design, and some use of four or more colors; the black outlining technique for design figures with other colors used as fill; and a high polished finish. Equally widespread are distinctive design elements derived largely from the stone incision style at Tiahuanaco, such as the front view figure with a staff in each hand; the running profile figure, with cape and bird mask; the puma and condor figures; the step design, scroll, and trident; and appendages of animal and bird heads. Furthermore, wherever textiles are preserved, there are some samples of tapestry with distinctive Tiahuanaco designs. On the coast, other non-Highland ceramic shapes, decorated with Tiahuanaco designs, have a wide distribution: a spout and round-handled jar, thick U-shaped urns, face bowls; modeled animal bowls, although not like the Highland types, collar jars with and without relief faces, double jars, and containers with double spouts and connecting flat bridge. In spite of the numerous horizon components, local styles are equally prominent at most sites. For example, an incised redware is abundant at Ancón on the central coast; two-color negative ware at Wilkawaín in the North Highlands; and pressed relief blackware on the North Coast.

The architectural features of the Central and South Highlands have already been described. It has been pointed out that large scale building on the coast is not yet associated with this period, even though some of the constructions at Pachacamac on the Central Coast and at Chanchan on the North Coast were probably initiated in this period. In the North Highlands, however, this period presents many one-room aboveground house sites with walls of rough stone and roofs of large slabs. At Wilkawaín a three-story temple was once ornamented with a projecting cornice and a row of carved stone puma heads. Each floor of the temple has half a dozen rooms and a ventilation shaft. The walls are made of split stone laid horizontally in alternating thick and thin rows. The slab roof is gabled. The construction in general follows the North Highland stone building tradition which was initiated with the Chavín culture.

The graves and burial types vary locally. On the Central Coast direct pit graves contain mummy bundles with false heads adorned with masks of metal, wood, and clay. Urn burials are found on the South Coast, but there are also log-covered subterranean chambers hung with tapestries. At Wari in the Central Highlands, subterranean boxes lined and covered with dressed stone slabs served as graves. Similar boxes lined with rough stone are found in the North Highlands.

On the coast the admirably preserved textiles illustrate skill in most of the known techniques, but the tapestries are most characteristic and among the finest made in the Central Andes. Other commonly employed techniques are brocade, warp pattern, double cloth, painted cloth, square and flat braiding, velvet-like pile knotting for caps and headbands, interlocking warp, double cloth, and tie-dye patchwork. Both wool and cotton fibers are used. Some colors are quite brilliant, but tans, browns, light oranges, and pale blues are more typical. Many of the tapestry designs are so similar to the incised stone motifs at Tiahuanaco, that they might easily have been used as the models for these.

Many other artifacts found present a great variety of wood, shell, bone, and stonework (Fig. 15). Metalworkers developed silver plating, continued to use earlier techniques, and may have increased copper production for such new applications as cast copper tie bolts in masonry (Plate 20).

The over-all unity represented by the Tiahuanaco horizon is soon interrupted and derived local styles appear. However, the coast is somewhat reunited towards the close of the period by the spread of the Black-White-Red horizon, represented by a geometric painting style for ceramics and a few characteristic shapes, such as the flask, and the container with spout and bridge to modeled figure. This horizon style forms a minor element in the ceramic collections throughout the coast and in the North Highlands, but its com-

Fig. 15. Miscellaneous prehistoric Peruvian artifacts; carved and painted box, comb, spoons, wooden and ceramic ear spools.

ponents no longer even suggest any form of political unity.

The Expansionist Period is then distinguished by the widespread Tiahuanaco horizon complex, which certainly reflects a dominant, formalized religious impact, and suggests a loose political unity as well. Some have used the phrase Tiahuanaco Empire, but it is doubtful that the unity and duration were of sufficient magnitude to justify such a designation, in spite of the fact that the unification is greater than at any earlier time. The Tiahuanaco horizon, while widespread, is not all inclusive. The far North Coast valleys of Lambayeque and Piura were not affected, but continued to develop locally, perhaps inspired by the residue of Mochica culture. Cajamarca and Huamachuco in the far North Highlands were also out of the range, and in this same time period their inhabitants constructed sizable buildings and developed a distinctive ceramic style. It is of even greater interest that in spite of the proximity of Wari, the Cuzco region of the Central Highlands remained totally independent of Tiahuanaco influence. This suggests that the local Early Inca culture was already sufficiently advanced to resist even such strong outside influences.

Whether political, religious, or merely stylistic in basis, the unity of the Tiahuanaco horizon was relatively short-lived. The local culture of each region had not been entirely eradicated and reformulation soon begins again. This was not achieved immediately, but only after a period of some struggle. The new culture is not a pure re-emergence of the old, but rather a mixture. None of the technological techniques is lost and the reorganization continues on social and political lines. In some parts this takes the form of large concentrated populations which in many ways reflect a city pattern.

CITY BUILDER PERIOD

(*ca.* 1200–1450 A.D.)

Following the Tiahuanaco dominated Expansionist Period, local cultures re-emerge in the six main geographic divisions of the Central Andes (Fig. 16). The disintegration of whatever type of unity the Expansionists had imposed was succeeded by new struggles for power so that the formulation of local cultures did not follow immediately. This is illustrated by the fact that the styles which finally appear are more than simple derivatives of the Tiahuanaco horizon. For example, the Chimu ceramics on the North Coast present a fusion of a number of styles: some from the earlier Mochica, some from the Expansionist Period, some from more local styles of the far North Highlands and the far North Coast. Despite its diversity of origins, the Chimu style which ultimately crystallizes is unified and distinctive.

Throughout Peru this new regional formulation is based on political organization rather than technology. There is now evidence for large, well organized populations living in planned building units in a pattern which can be designated as urban, even though large cities are not found everywhere. The established subsistence techniques were extended so that a more expanded terrain was irrigated and cultivated than ever before. The population may have reached a new peak, but the shift from rural to urban habitation makes this difficult to verify. Since all cultures now possess adequate technology and all are concentrating on political controls, the balance of power depends largely on the extent of territory. Consequently, it is not surprising that the North Coast cultures become stronger than those of the Central and South Coasts, since the northern valleys are larger and have a more permanent water supply.

For the City Builder Period, it is no longer practical to list individual sites, since a single culture dominates and is extensively represented in every major area. The archaeological evidence for the cultures and their distribution is partially verifiable from the records of the

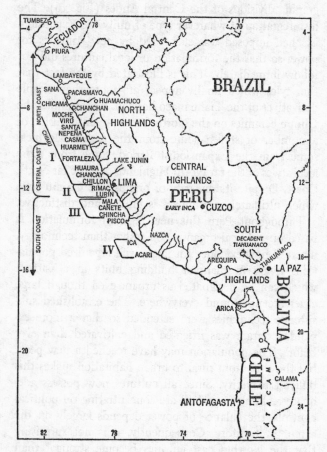

Fig. 16. Principal centers of the City Builder Period.

Spanish chroniclers who list the names and locations of the tribes conquered by the Inca in their expansion. The Chimu who dominated the North Coast had their political center at the large city of Chanchan in the Moche Valley. The Chimu or Chimor territory, just before it was conquered by the Inca, extended six hundred miles from Tumbez south to the Chillón. As the relevant archaeological material within the area has marked differences there is reason to doubt that it had been unified for any appreciable length of time. To the south, a small but powerful state occupied the Rimac and Lurin valleys. Farther south, the people in the valleys of Mala, Cañete and Chincha were united, and had their main center of government in the Chincha. In turn, still another state centered in Ica is reported as composed of the Ica, Nazca and Acari valleys, a region with an established record of cultural and perhaps political unity. Regional cultures in the highlands are less well known although there are many large stone constructed villages, like Marca Huamachuco in the North Highlands, which are pre-Inca but which lack distinctive styles. An Early Inca culture has recently been isolated in the Central Highlands, although it is still not well known. Presumably evidence for the antecedents of the Inca Empire will eventually be clarified in this region. In the South Highlands, particularly around Lake Titicaca, the Tiahuanaco culture was not seriously interrupted, but continued as a local development, although there are no longer indications of strong organization. Around Arequipa and in North Chile are the remains of the Atacameño culture. These regions were not capable of supporting very large populations, but the general cultural development is similar to that in other parts of the Central Andes. The extensive flats of the coastal valleys were the most suitable for large concentrated populations. The highlands, on the other hand, might support equally large populations, but not in the same concentration. Consequently, the city pattern reaches its highest development on the coast.

The City Builder Period cultures and sites fall into the same relative time bracket, as verified by stratigraphy and other dating evidence. For example, their late position is well demonstrated by the fact that the local styles ultimately mix with the Incaic. On the North Coast typical Inca aryballoid jars are made in the Chimu blackware as are many Chancay and Ica vessels. Whether such mixture occurred prior to the Inca expansion or as a result of the Inca conquest does not affect the relative sequence. The duration of this period is another matter. In this account, a guess-date duration of two hundred fifty years is assigned to the City Builders. The numerous massive structures which pertain to this period might suggest a longer duration, but, on the grounds that man-unit labor was now well organized and that the architecture is not particularly complex, the buildings might well have been completed in a relatively short time.

The period is designated City Builder because of the enormous ruins of planned villages. Perhaps the largest and certainly the best known of these cities is Chanchan near Trujillo on the north coast. These ruins cover about six square miles and contain ten distinct units, some as large as four hundred eighty by three hundred seventy-five meters. Between these units, which are not symmetrically arranged, are irrigated areas, cemeteries, numerous small structures and totora reed marshes. The ten major units differ in detail, but each contains approximately the same features. From one to three high walls, some still nine meters high, surround each unit. Within the inclosures are symmetrically arranged streets, houses with gabled roofs, large pyramids, small cells, cemeteries, gardens, and stone-lined reservoirs. Some insist that Chanchan was a ceremonial center rather than a city, but irrespective of its function, there must have been a large number of fairly permanent residents.

Chanchan is the largest of the Chimu cities. There are many others of great size, such as Pacatnamú or La Barranca in Pacasmayo Valley and El Purgatorio in Lambayeque Valley. All of these share such features as symmetrical planning, rows of houses, streets, pyramids, terraces, decorated walls (Plate 25), steps, ramps, and reservoirs. On the Central Coast other cities, like Pachacamac and Cajamarquilla in the Lurín and Rimac valleys, are comparable in size and plan to those of the north. The smaller valleys of the South Coast did not support such large cities, but centers like La Centinela in Chincha Valley and Tambo Colorado in Pisco Valley resemble the North Coast towns in general plan and combination of features.

From north to south, all of the coast cities, although differing in size, are similar in the planning, the general rectangularity, and the combination of pyramids, stairways, terraces, and courts. Building materials are everywhere identical. The rectangular mold-made adobes are small and square on the South Coast, large and flat on the North Coast, but identical in technique of manufacture. Tapia walls, in which the clay is tamped into large blocks between plank forms, are commonly used for inclosures and terraces, and algarroba logs are used as lintels and wall binders. The techniques of wall decoration are widespread. Ornamental niches are cut out of the walls and mosaic arrangements of rectangular adobes form decorative frets. Walls may be painted in solid color or with designs. Most characteristic are clay arabesques in which intricate small unit designs are cut out of a thick clay plaster. The small geometric designs, typically birds and fish, are arranged in textile-like patterns. The most famous arabesques are found at Chanchan, but there are equally good examples from the Central and South Coasts.

In this period the elaborateness of the graves reflects the importance of the deceased. Many graves are simply excavated pits, usually marked by an upright stick or paddle. Others are subterranean chambers roofed with poles. These contain more elaborate burials and greater quantities of grave goods. The burials are in seated flexed positions, wrapped with cloth to form a bundle, on top of which is a stuffed false head adorned with a painted face or with a mask of clay, wood, or metal.

Craftsmanship is still at a high level of competence, but lacks individual artistry. Instead, attention seems to have turned more and more to quantity production at the expense of quality. In ceramics, for example, the colors are reduced in number to monochrome on the North Coast and to black, white, and red on the South Coast. Shapes also have a more limited range. The design style is generally geometric; a widespread characteristic is the application of textile derived patterns. This decrease of attention to expressive individual art may have been due to the stultifying effects of the Tiahuanaco conventionalizations. In other ways it represents a shift of emphasis from the artist as a craftsman to the artist as a technical worker. In spite of these generalizations about craftsmanship throughout the Central Andes, each region has distinctive local styles.

The Chimu ceramics, although varied in detail, can be classified under a few basic shape categories: the stirrup-spout, now squared in cross-section, with a small modeled animal at the spout base; a double-whistling jar; a globular container with taper spout and flat handle; a vessel with spout and a bridge to a modeled figure; ollas; and plates (Plate 27). Some of these shapes, like the stirrup-spout, are carryovers from the Mochica culture; others, like the spout and bridge, are introductions from the Expansionist Period. The Chimu ceramics are commonly mold made and typically polished red-ware or smoked blackware. Painting is rare, but decoration is achieved by modeling, pressed relief, stipple, appliqué, incision, excising, and paddle marking. The modeling is still somewhat depictive, but the skills of the Mochica culture are no longer present.

The Chancay ceramics on the Central Coast are made of a thin porous red or orange clay which is coated with a scaley white slip over which textile derived patterns are painted in black or dark brown. The typical shapes are straight-sided goblets and face collar jars with flat side handles. The commonest design elements are bands, stripes, dots, wavy lines, cross hatch, serrated, diagonals, and small birds and animals. On the South Coast, Ica ceramics are generally painted in black, white, and red. Open bowls with angular bodies, round bottoms, and beveled rims are the most typical shape, but also common are constricted flaring collar jars and globular vessels with long tubular collars ending in slightly flaring rims. The designs are either geometric units or small birds and fish arranged in diagonals or panels in imitation of textile patterns (Plate 28).

The ceramics attributed to the Atacameño in Peru and North Chile are characterized by constricted collar jars with two body handles, and one-handled pitchers. Again, the designs are geometric combinations of triangles, diamonds, scrolls, and steps, painted in black and white on a red base. The Atacameño ceramic style has sometimes been considered as a forerunner of that of the Inca. However, many of the pieces considered Atacameño are most common outside the Atacama area and are found unassociated with plainware types used in that area. This indicates incomplete data so until Atacameño sites are systematically excavated, we must avoid theories about their culture. Elsewhere in the highlands, the ceramic styles are not particularly distinctive, as previously mentioned.

Woven fabrics are now produced in quantity, but the ambitious, elaborate weaves are less frequent than in some of the previous periods. The coast regions are united by their great use of all cotton weaves and by the quantity of painted, tie-die, and double cloth. Embroidery is still common, but is now applied to limited areas or to figure outline. Border fringes are typical although needle knitting is no longer practiced. Tapestry is used to finish borders and for small inserts in the centers or in the corners of the cotton pieces. Gauzes, brocades, and pattern weaves are abundant. The textile designs are everywhere similar in the conventionalization of small bird, fish, and geometric figures, and in the arrangement of units in horizontal bands, diagonal rows, and within squares, diamonds, lozenges, and frets. Over-all coast similarities are striking, although detailed studies permit the differentiation of textiles from the North, Central, and South Coasts. Featherwork is also typical of this period on the coast. The feathers are sewn on a base cloth and designs are produced by arrangement of different colored feathers, sometimes resulting in mosaic-like patterns.

Metalwork is more abundant than in previous periods and some new techniques are added to the earlier inventory. Bronze, or the alloy of tin and copper, is now known, and the casting of copper became widespread for the first time. Gold, silver, copper, and bronze are all used in making such ornaments as masks, earrings, beads, crowns, and breastplates. The Chimu earplugs are long cylindrical tubes of gold, decorated with fine incised designs. At one end is a circular disc with hammered relief figures augmented by attached bangles. Goblets, bowls, and plates are made of silver and gold. There are also a great many utilitarian artifacts of copper and bronze, illustrated by points for digging-sticks, club heads, knives, and needles. Many other artifacts are made of shell, bone, stone, and wood. Basketry is common. Decorated calabashes are particularly typical, some ornamented by pyrogravure, others by mosaic insets of beads and seeds.

The existence of an urban pattern in itself suggests a strong social and political organization. The maintenance of a city must have been difficult under conditions in which it was necessary to transport all food by llama or by individuals on foot and in which markets, monetary units, or formal exchange patterns were apparently unknown. The erection of pyramids composed of billions of adobes and of cities covering many square miles required organized labor. Certain sections of the cities seem to have been religious centers, others the headquarters of administrative units. Definite class distinctions are indicated by striking differences between dwellings in the same site, by marked contrasts in the quantity and quality of grave goods, by variations in clothing, and by the few records left by the Spanish chroniclers. The separated walled-in units of Chanchan and other sites suggest that social groups, of *ayllu* or clan type, persisted within the political superstructure. The wide distributions of these regional cultures and the high degree of similarity of materials within a region imply over-all political unity. Although the nature of this unity is unknown, its roots lay in the traditional experience with centralized authority, the authority needed to plan and control the irrigation systems. There is also evidence for formalized religious organization, although in general this seems secondary to the political organization.

Rivalry and conflict would be the inevitable result of a series of expanding local political organizations. Although the City Builders of the coast seem far stronger than their Highland neighbors, subsequent history proves otherwise. In the next period the Highland Inca not only conquered and incorporated all parts of the Central Andes, but extended their political empire well beyond its borders. There is remarkably little archaeological evidence for the development of the Inca organization in the Central Highlands. The Early Inca culture, recently isolated, is estimated to cover the time period of 1200 to 1438 A.D. The few known sites of this culture contain carelessly executed ceramics with simple designs, rough stone walls, beehive-shaped tombs with crude corbeled vaults, and a limited inventory of metal, bone, and stone tools. Future archaeological work will certainly enlarge this picture. There is still no knowledge of cultural development around Cuzco in the Mastercraftsman Period, although it was presumably of sufficient strength to resist the Tiahuanaco influence in the Expansionist Period and to continue through the City Builder Period until it became the center of the Inca Empire.

IMPERIALIST PERIOD

(*ca.* 1450–1532 A.D.)

The Inca Empire marks the final formulation of Central Andean culture which persisted up to the time of the Spanish conquest (Fig. 17). The political system in previous periods may have been a confederacy, a feudal state, or a military band organization. However, the Inca had a true political empire which united the enormous territory from northern Ecuador to the Río Maule in Chile under a single ruler, thus encompassing not only the Central Andes, but much of the Northern and Southern Andes as well. As mentioned before, little is known about the specific origins of the Inca culture. The Early Inca culture in the Cuzco region is not very impressive and is not the only stem for the development which followed. Inca mythology contains several accounts of their origin, but while these are interesting, they have little historical reliability. Actually, the question of precise origin is only of academic interest since the basic roots of Inca civilization are found in the archaeological past of the

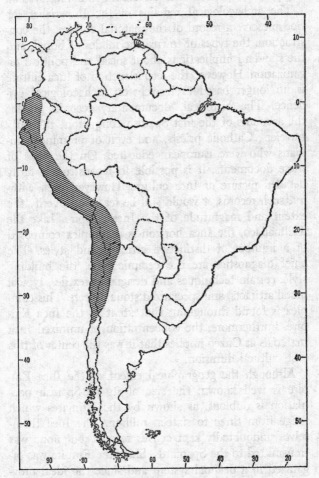

FIG. 17. Maximum expansion in the Imperialist Period.

Central Andes, as demonstrated in the previous chapters. The complete gamut of Inca technology had been developed and the shift of emphasis to political organization had occurred in earlier periods. The Inca contribution was little more than a reformulation of the political pattern into an empire building system.

The archaeological remains of the Imperialist Period preserve a record of the material culture, the construction, the types of towns, the modes of burial, and the standard implications about social and political organization. However, the reconstruction of Inca culture is no longer based exclusively on archaeological evidence. The historical, documentary records present the accounts of the first Spanish conquerors, the early travelers, Catholic priests, and even of prominent Indians who were European educated. On the basis of these documents, it is possible to reconstruct a fairly detailed picture of Inca culture. However, even without such records, it would still be feasible to verify the extent and magnitude of the Inca Empire. Like the Tiahuanaco, the Inca horizon is a complex composed of a number of distinctive artifacts and styles. The chief diagnostics are the ceramic type, the building style, certain techniques and designs in textiles, typical metal artifacts, and specialized stone objects. This complex is found throughout the extent of the Inca Empire. Furthermore, the concentration of unmixed Inca materials at Cuzco implies that it was the center of this vast cultural diffusion.

Although the geographical extent of the Inca Empire is well known, the size of its pre-Spanish population is dubious, as shown by the estimates which range from three to sixteen million. The Inca themselves undoubtedly kept census records, but none was transmitted to the Spaniards. Since the Empire was organized in a decimal system and since the ideal province had forty thousand workers representing about two hundred thousand inhabitants, the population could be easily computed if the number of provinces contained in the Empire were known. The first Spanish census, taken in about 1571, gives a total of about 1,500,000 Indians for the Central Andes. Since this census was taken some time after the Spanish conquest, it raises the question of the rate of reduction of Indian population during the years of struggle. Two estimates have been made in the 1946 "Handbook of South American Indians." George Kubler favors a two to one reduction ratio, based on comparisons with Mexico and the absence of serious epidemics, and thus arrives at a total pre-Spanish native population of three million. John H. Rowe prefers a four to one reduction ratio, based on records of specific provinces, and arrives at a figure of six million. Adding in other parts of the Empire, it would not seem unreasonable, then, that the population was not less than three and a half million nor more than seven million. Some authors have claimed that the populations were larger in the pre-Inca periods but there is no archaeological confirmation of this, nor is it likely since the Inca had the same technical and agricultural knowledge as their predecessors.

The early Spaniards recorded the traditional lists of Inca rulers, together with miscellaneous information on the reign and conquests of each. John H. Rowe has made a study of these documents and arrived at the following list of Inca rulers with their dates of reign:

1. Manco Capac
2. Sinchi Roca
3. Lloqui Yupanqui
4. Mayta Capac
5. Capac Yupanqui
6. Inca Roca
7. Yahuar Huaca
8. Viracocha
9. Pachacuti Inca Yupanqui (1438–1471)

10. Topa Inca Yupanqui (1471–1493)
11. Huayna Capac (1493–1525)
12. Huascar and Atahualpa (1525–1532)

The information about the first eight rulers is hazy and inconsistent. Rowe considers the year 1250 a reasonable date for the first ruler and believes that the first eight represent a local Cuzco development corresponding archaeologically to the Early Inca culture. The true Inca Empire was thus created between the time of the ninth ruler, Pachacuti Inca Yupanqui, and the Spanish conquest, that is, in less than one hundred years. Undoubtedly there had been raids outside of the Cuzco region in earlier times, but the first territorial conquest was the Lake Titicaca region campaign in 1445. The incorporation of most of the other areas occurred after 1470.

When the Inca began this expansion, many of the coast cultures were well united politically, and the Highland groups, while less concentrated, were organized into protective confederacies. The Inca military conquest encountered varying degrees of resistance. Many years of fighting were required to conquer the Highland tribes and even then garrisons had to be constantly maintained to prevent rebellion. Other groups were less resistant and some of the largest, like the Chimu on the North Coast, were incorporated by passive persuasion. Many of the marginal groups, like the Chiriguano in the east and the Araucanians in Central Chile, were never actually conquered.

The Inca conquests were not inspired by population pressure, but rather by a desire for economic gain in the form of new administrative posts, new produce, new labor supply, and more soldiers, and by the necessity of strengthening the position of the ruling class. The conquests were carefully planned. A propaganda campaign usually preceded the military aggression. Official emissaries endeavored to point out the benefits of Inca control and missionaries attempted to make converts for the official sun worship. If these were unsuccessful, the army entered in mass formations of eight to ten thousand soldiers and effected the conquest by siege, by cutting off the food supplies, by building forts, and by pitched battles. The army was well organized and discipline was severe. All officers were from the upper class, but the soldiers were commoners. All able-bodied men were subject to the draft, and it is estimated that one-tenth of the adult male population was in the services. The families of the draftees were supported by the state. Military instruction was given in the use of all weapons: bronze battle axes, slings, bows and arrows, spear throwers, lances, hard wooden clubs, and clubs with stone or bronze heads. Metal helmets, thick jackets, and shields were used for protection. All of the weapons had been used for many years throughout the Central Andes, so that success of the Inca is not ascribable to superiority in weapons, but rather to superior military organization.

The captured province was systematically incorporated into the Empire system. A census was taken and a rough relief map of the terrain was modeled in clay. Villages were frequently shifted and new towns were built. The administrative officers were usually members of the Inca caste, but every effort was made to continue the previous local rulers in office. To assure their loyalty, their sons were taken as hostages to Cuzco where they received the formal, upper class education. The Inca imposed their sun-worship religion on the new subjects, made the Quechua language the official one, and required Inca style dress, although local distinctions were permitted. If the conquered peoples continued to be rebellious, the Inca resorted to the system of *mitimaes* whereby whole villages were transplanted to another district and replaced by pacified

populations. As each new district was conquered, the
network of roadways was extended to include it, so that
ultimately the whole Empire was linked by connecting roads. Some of the roads were paved, some hewn
out of the bed rock, and some merely indicated by
markers. Rivers and gorges were crossed by means of
suspension, pontoon, and cable bridges. Inns for the
travelers were maintained at intervals along the road.
Widespread communication was effected by means of
professional runners, the *chasquis*, who covered as
much as one hundred fifty miles a day by running in
relays. However, the Inca Empire did not endure long
enough to provide a true test of the effectiveness of
this system of pacification and incorporation.

In the Imperialist Period, subsistence was based
on intensive agriculture, which by this time had passed
through the stages of exploitation and conservation and
reached that of restoration. No new plants were domesticated, but all those known previously were still
grown. Likewise, irrigation, terraces and other techniques were little changed, although the digging-stick
was slightly improved by the addition of a foot bar and
a handle. The importance of agriculture was recognized
and intimately linked with other aspects of culture; a
great proportion of the laborers were so engaged and
the work was done in groups rather than individually.
For example, the planting season was determined by
solar observations; the priests fasted to insure good
crops; public religious ceremony accompanied the
first planting and the harvest. The ruling Inca and
members of the upper caste made agriculture a symbol of honorable labor by breaking the first ground
themselves. The Inca used personal service as a form of
taxation and agricultural work became the economic basis of the system. Each family cultivated not only its
own plot of land, but also worked on the fields assigned

to the church and the state, the produce from which supported the political superstructure.

The common foods prepared in Inca times are still used by the contemporary Indians and had undoubtedly long been known. Llama meat was cut into strips and dried as *charqui*. Potatoes in the high altitudes were frozen into *chuño*, which could be preserved for long periods of time. The basic dish, called *chupe*, was a corn or potato soup with other foods added to form a stew. Corn was toasted, popped, roasted, and used in many other ways. For example, *t'anta* was a cornbread, *minta* a sweet cornbread, *yahuar çancu* a cornbread mixed with blood for ceremonial occasions. A corn beer, *chicha*, was also prepared for religious and secular celebrations. Tobacco was utilized only in the form of snuff for medicinal purposes, but the narcotic *coca* was of great importance. Coca chewing among the Inca was a restricted upper class privilege; the commoners were permitted to use it only on special occasions.

In the Imperialist Period, each district produced more than was needed to support the local population and this surplus was stored in state granaries throughout the Empire. Careful records were kept of production and storage since the surplus was used to support the aristocracy, the priests, and the special artisans, and the army and all laborers who were working on public projects or in the mines. The surplus also provided social security on the occasions when a district was stricken with famine because of crop failure.

All cultivable land was divided into three parts. The first, and usually the smallest area, was assigned to the support of the priests and the temples. The second was the property of the state, acquired by confiscation or as the result of new irrigation projects. The third, and usually the largest portion, pertained to the local villages for their own support. The village land was divided into strips of equal size, each considered large enough to support only one couple, so that additional assignments were made for each child. Since the village lands were controlled collectively, only a house and perhaps a garden plot belonged exclusively to the family.

There was no monetary system. Local markets allowed simple exchange of goods on a barter basis, but even this practice was not very extensive. To be sure, great quantities of produce were transferred from one region to another, but this was state property and state controlled business. Foreign trade likewise was a state monopoly.

The herding of llamas and alpacas continued to be an important subsistence activity. Here again, a distinction was made between individually owned animals and state flocks, the tending of which was another form of tax payment. Along the coast and around Lake Titicaca fishing was a common addition to the subsistence, but hunting everywhere had become a sport restricted to the upper caste.

Extensive building activities are characteristic of the Imperialist Period. These range from irrigation systems, agricultural terraces, roads, and bridges through various types of habitations to large public centers, temples, and forts. The dwellings of single families were generally one-story rectangular buildings, with walls of rough stone or adobe, floors of trodden earth, and gabled roofs with grass thatch. Such houses had narrow doorways, and niches and pegs in the walls, but no windows. The house furnishings were very meager, consisting of a single platform bed and such utilitarian objects as grindstones, clay braziers, animal skins, and rush mats. A compound of several such houses was occupied by the extended family, and a village consisted of a scattered group of such compounds. In general, the Imperialists were not urban dwellers, although some of the religious and administrative centers reached respectable sizes, and were planned and constructed by special architects. One of the best known town centers is Machu Picchu (Plate 29), built on a high ridge near Cuzco. The ruins present a conglomeration of terraces, house compounds, courts, stairs, terraces, and temples. Most of the construction is done with rough stone, but some of the important units are built of carefully dressed and fitted stone. The best houses have windows, carefully built niches, stone wall pegs, and narrow doorways capped with stone lintels.

The large public buildings for religious or administrative purposes are quite ambitious affairs, but even so all of those better known can be assigned to the one hundred year period of Empire expansion. In the Coast buildings, large rectangular adobes were used, but in the Highlands stonework of many types was utilized. In Cuzco alone there is a megalithic style with large slabs and blocks of irregular sizes and shapes carefully fitted together; a similiar style but with smaller stones; walls built of unit blocks, either dressed smoothly on all sides or left slightly rounded on the outer face (Plate 30). These different building styles do not imply a sequence since their employment seems to have been functionally determined by the purpose of the construction, whether it was intended to support a heavy superweight, to be a free standing wall, or to have some other function. The architects planned the buildings by making clay models. In viewing the finished structures it is worth bearing in mind that they were produced without benefit of any iron or steel tools; that the available bronze was of little or no use in stone cutting. Quarrying was a laborious process of pecking and hammering stone against stone until the desired block was so nearly free that the final cleavage was simple. Most of the dressing and fitting was obviously done at the last moment at the construction site. Many of these walls have stood for over four hundred years, testifying to the skill exercised in their construction. The quality of the masonry is a remarkable achievement, although it does not surpass that of some of the earlier periods.

Craftsmanship was still at a high level of competence, but the artistic quality does not match the earlier achievements. Each family among the commoners made the pottery, textiles, and other artifacts necessary for its own use. Selected specialists produced the finer work for upper class and ceremonial uses. These specialists were supported by the state, but were not organized into craft guilds, nor, so far as can be judged, was their position particularly favored in the social system. The art style of this period is distinctive and is identifiable in every craft.

The ceramics are well made, highly polished, and polychrome painted with black, white, red, yellow, and orange. Except for small, stylized butterflies, bees, and animals, the design is frankly geometric, consisting of serrations, bands, diamonds, checkers, triangles, cross hatch, circles, and dots. The vessel shapes are standardized. Most characteristic is the aryballoid jar with its conical pointed base, vertical, flat side handles, tall flaring collar, and animal head body nubbin (Plate 31). Shallow bird-handle plates, straight-sided goblets, pedestal base beakers, one and two-handled pitchers, and bottles are also common. This typical Inca ceramic style is found throughout the widespread Empire.

The weaving is competent; control of all earlier techniques is demonstrated, but the number of truly fine pieces is limited. Among the best examples of the weavers' craftsmanship are ambitious tapestry ponchos decorated with small design units. Warp patterns and repps (see p. 208) are very common. The clothing pattern previously established is continued and details of dress, particularly in headgear, distinguish class, special occupation, and regional residence. The woven articles include breechclouts, mantles, waistbands, headbands, poncho shirts, rough blankets, belts, bags, and slings.

Metalwork now included quantities of both utilitarian artifacts and ornaments. The collections of gold ornaments demonstrate great skill in workmanship and this is verified by the early Spanish descriptions. The utilitarian objects are now commonly made of bronze and include club heads, digging-stick points, tweezers, chisels, flat-headed pins, discs, and needles. New methods of gilding and casting are added to the techniques previously known. Stone carving is not associated with this period, but stone artifacts are numerous. The most distinctive are bowls, club heads, stellate-shaped mace heads, and small carved llamas with holes in their backs for offerings. Wood is also used extensively. The wooden kero, or goblet, decorated by lacquer inlay, is a most characteristic container.

The Imperialist Period placed great emphasis on social and political organization. Actually, the system developed was little more than a formalization of tendencies already initiated in the Central Andes. The family and extended family were still basic units. Several extended families were united by a local village group, or *ayllu*, which theoretically controlled the real property. The *ayllu* is sometimes called a clan, but actually it lacks the kinship unity and other characteristics of this unit of social organization. Instead, the extended patrilineal family within the *ayllu* was the most important kinship group, and also cooperated in labor, controlled the education and marriage of the children, and supported local religious cults. The entire village, however, also had certain social and religious functions which increased in importance when the Inca formalized them. For example, the Inca made marriage within the village compulsory. Furthermore, the village was made an economically independent unit of sufficient strength so that it has survived up to the present day.

The economic system was based on the organization of man-power labor units. The population was classified into twelve age grades to facilitate the maintenance of a labor census. Those classed in the able-bodied age grade were taxed by being assigned a specific quantity of labor service such as agricultural work on the state and church fields, army service, herding, or work on a public building project. Records were kept of each individual's contribution. The assignments were made in terms of quantity rather than time, so the man who could use the assistance of his children finished sooner than the others. The system also encouraged exchange of labor on a cooperative basis, particularly in the form of individual arrangements for substitute laborers. In most cases this made little difference since the work was performed in groups, and the tasks demanded little skill. In fact, much of the planning consisted in reducing the work units to the unskilled level.

The political system, usually described as pyramidal, was based on the labor unit. Ten laborers formed a work group under the supervision of a foreman. In the ideal pattern work groups corresponded to the village or *ayllu*, under the direction of a head man. In turn, ten village units formed a tribe, under the supervision of a high-ranking official. Such pyramiding continued until large units corresponding to the four quarters of the Empire were attained. The ruling Inca formed the apex. In the functioning of this system each administrator reported to his immediately superior official, and so on up to the Inca. In reverse, the Inca's orders filtered down to the laborers. Administrative officers of the same magnitude were not organized in any way. Instead this vertical political organization was cut across by the sharp class distinctions which had by this period assumed the rigidity of a true caste system.

The upper caste contained two classes: the Inca aristocracy, the original conquerors and their families and the nobles, composed largely of the previous rulers in the local districts seized. The lower caste included all the commoners, the basic mass of the labor population. The outstanding distinction between these castes was in the privileges accorded them. The upper caste had finer garments, more permanent houses, gold and silver service; but food was abundant for all, and coarse clothing, adobe houses, and ceramic vessels do not imply poverty. The differences in privilege, however, were numerous. Not only were travel, dress, marriage, and celebrations regulated for the commoners but they were forced to perform all the manual labor. The upper caste controlled all of the higher administrative and religious posts, were permitted several wives, performed no labor, and were treated with extreme reverence and homage. Formal education was limited to the upper group. Little mobility was allowed in the system so that it was virtually impossible for a commoner ever to enter the upper caste. Even those selected as specialists in weaving or metallurgy remained in the lower caste. The ruling Inca himself had absolute authority and was considered divine. His symbols of authority were a special mace, a feather headdress, and other distinctive insignia. Most of the Inca rulers, judged by achievement, were outstanding men. The caste system had become so dominant that in reference to any aspect of the Imperialist Period, distinction must be made between upper versus lower class.

Archaeological information about customs and ceremonies of the life cycle is at best meager and conjectural, and even with the addition of the Spanish records the data are still limited. It is known that children were considered an economic asset and, therefore, desired. The mothers observed certain prenatal taboos, but there was no special ceremony at the birth of a

child. The infants were kept in cradles until old enough
to walk, and weaned at about two years of age. At this
time a special naming ceremony was performed by the
family and close relatives. The infant's hair was tied
into bunches which were cut off singly by the participants who contributed gifts and selected a name. Most
of the names were those of animals, natural objects,
places, or particular qualities. In the upper caste,
special titles of rank were added. Children played with
tops and balls, and competed in footraces. Education
for the commoners consisted of practical home training in those crafts and techniques necessary for self
support. In the upper caste, education was formalized
under the supervision of special wise men who taught
regular courses in history, mathematics, religion, and
language. The twelve age grades, previously mentioned,
were not recognized in local custom. However, the transition from youth to adulthood was an occasion for
rigorous tests in the upper caste. Among the commoners marriage was a family affair arranged by the
parents within the village unit. The families concerned
held simple home ceremonies; once or twice a year the
marriages were officially recognized by the Inca over-
lord at a public ceremony. Death and burial were
family affairs among the commoners but the occasion
for elaborate public ceremonies among the upper caste.
Pits, caves, and bottle-shaped graves were used for
burial; important individuals were buried in a seated
position, wrapped with fine cloth, and accompanied
by many offerings.

The Inca calendar was based on the solar year and
the lunar phases, but was not recorded. In contrast to
the Maya, however, their observations and calculations
were not elaborate. Although lacking any form of writing, numerical records were kept of the quantity of
crops raised, the size of the herds, the population totals
in terms of age-grades, and many others. The exact

system of calculation is not known although it had a decimal basis. Boards with various box-like divisions have been found which were probably used as a form of abacus for calculation with beans or pebbles. Whatever the system of counting, the totals were recorded on the *quipu*. This consisted of a base cord with a series of attached strings on which half-hitch knots represent decimal units. The numbers from one to nine were recorded at the extreme tip of the string, and the tens, the hundreds, and sometimes the thousands were proportionately closer to the base cord. Strings of different colors represented specific categories of objects. On some *quipus* the total for a group of four or more strings was recorded on another on the opposite side of the base cord.

In examining the religious beliefs and practices of the Imperialist Period, a distinction must be made between the local village cults, maintained by the commoners, and the formal state religion directed by the priests of the upper caste. The distinction is in elaboration and formalization rather than in the basic beliefs which are, in both cases, concerned with the agricultural cycle, nature worship, and especially ancestor worship. The gods in the official state religion were arranged in a hierarchy. Viracocha, the leader, was considered to be the creator of the world and to reside in heaven. The Sun, second in importance, was the protector of the crops. He was represented by a golden disc with a hammered relief face. Thunder followed as the god of weather and warfare, appropriately represented by a club and a shield. The Moon, as the wife of the Sun, held an important position. Many stars were identified as lesser gods and some constellations, like the Pleiades and Lira, had special functions. The Earth and the Sea had apparently been important gods in earlier periods and continued to be prominent. There were many ghosts and spirits, both good and evil, but these were outside of the formalized hierarchy.

The state religion was in the hands of a priest group, arranged in a pyramidal system in which the upper caste occupied the top positions. The priests as well as the religious temples and shrines were supported by the commoners. The principal ceremonies were calendrical, at least one for each month, and more important ones for the new year and the solstices. Other ceremonies were held on irregular occasions such as the death of the ruler, the inauguration of his successor, and the initiation of warfare. The public ceremonies were elaborate, several day affairs organized by the priests for the benefit of the commoners. East and west were the most important ceremonial directions. The gods were approached with special attitudes of worship in which the priest faced the image, bowed, and stretched out his arms. Fasting and confession were regular duties of the priests. Offerings and sacrifice were important in the ceremonial. Prisoners captured in warfare were sacrificed or children were offered by their parents for this purpose, but this practice was not carried to extremes. More common was the sacrifice of llamas and alpacas selected for their particular color or markings. Food, coca, clothing, gold and silver objects, and other things were burned on the altars as sacrificial offerings. The ceremonies also included the consumption of special ceremonial foods, chicha drinking, and coca chewing.

The most elaborate ceremonies were held in Cuzco and involved many participants. The priests and privileged members of the upper caste conducted parts of the ritual within the temples. The commoners were restricted to special sections of the city where they observed only the public phases of each ceremony. Groups of warriors in full regalia engaged in violent activities in order to drive off evil spirits. There were parades, games, and dances at every performance, and sometimes the mummies of the important deceased were removed from their burial vaults and carried in the parades. The ceremonies started at sunrise and

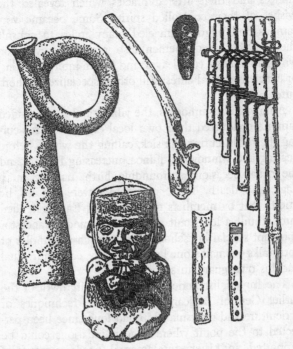

FIG. 18. Musical instruments: panpipes, flutes, whistles, and a horn.

closed at sundown with a ritual bath for all the performers. Special chants and songs were composed for the dancers who were specially trained groups with elaborate masks and costumes of skins or feathers. The music, all in the pentatonic scale, was provided by skin drums, bronze gongs, copper bells, bone flutes, panpipes, trumpets, and whistles (Fig. 18).

Apart from the hierarchy of priests in the state religion many lesser priests presided at local shrines. These were actually medicinemen or soothsayers who, under the influence of liquor and narcotics, went into trances and then uttered oracles which revealed the wishes of their controlled spirits. Some became very famous and pilgrims traveled many miles to consult them. Other medicinemen also practiced divination with llama lungs, coca leaves, and dream interpretations, or effected magical cures; still others specialized in herb cures.

Among the commoners, the village and the extended families conducted their own local ceremonies for curing the fields, curing the sick, calling the winds, before beating and winnowing quinoa, increasing fertility and the ritual occasions surrounding birth, naming, marriage, and death. These ceremonies were not led by priests, but by members of the village. Each extended family built a local cult around the founding ancestor and kept special household fetishes, such as bundles of cornstalks or small stone llamas. Finally, each individual had his own guardian spirit.

The Imperialist Period is a natural outgrowth of the earlier Central Andean patterns. The techniques of agriculture and craftsmanship had long since been perfected to the point where large populations could be supported and their fundamental needs successfully met. Likewise, the shift of emphasis from technology to manipulation of labor units had passed through a reasonable period of experimentation. The Imperialist pattern was only one of the possible formulations, but certainly a logical one. An objective evaluation of the Imperialist system is difficult. It consisted basically of a sharp dual division between a large lower caste of workers and a small privileged upper caste. The commoners were organized around the *ayllu* or village which became a self-sufficient unit for the support of its members, the production of the necessary housing, clothing and other artifacts, the maintenance of local government and of local cults. National government, economic security, and protection were under the control of the upper caste. The gap between these castes was ever increasing, until no equality was admitted. Knowledge and education as well as the skilled productions in the arts and crafts were controlled by the upper caste. When the Spaniards replaced the upper caste, following the conquest, there was naturally a rapid breakdown in craftsmanship and education.

The Inca Empire had existed less than one hundred years before the conquest, which probably furnished insufficient experience to perfect final controls. Had it been uninterrupted by the Europeans, modification might well have occurred and the size of the Empire unit might easily have been reduced. However, it is doubtful that the fundamental pattern would have changed greatly since it had been maintained for several centuries. There were, to be sure, signs of weakness in the Inca political system itself. The pyramidal structure, while efficient, failed to provide *esprit de corps* or communication between officers of the same rank. The regimentation in the Empire was excessive in spite of the guarantee of security. It certainly appears that the commoners' loyalty to the upper caste was not very great. A final weakness was the failure to establish a fixed rule for succession in the rulership so that immediately prior to the conquest there were two contenders who had already divided the Empire. The Spanish conquest has always seemed amazingly rapid, reflecting, in part, some of the fundamental weaknesses of the Imperialist system.

AFTERMATH

The year 1532, when Francisco Pizarro and his followers initiated the conquest of Peru, marks the end of the archaeological and the beginning of the historical epoch. The more dramatic incidents of the conquest are well known: the bold seizure of the Inca ruler, Atahualpa; the golden ransom paid for his release; the assassination of the Inca; and the collapse of the Inca Empire. Although amazingly rapid, the conquest was not as simple as this historical condensation implies. The initial shock was followed by forty years of active resistance during which the balance of power was often delicate. However, the Europeans eventually won and the four hundred years since the conquest have made many profound changes in the Indian culture.

One of the immediate effects of the conquest was a marked reduction of the actual numbers of Indians, whether one selects the estimate of three and a half million or seven million for the maximum population of the Inca Empire. In fact, the census records, such as they are, show unrelieved loss up to 1796 when an all-time low of under seven hundred thousand was reached. Following the wars of independence, however, the situation was reversed and the Indian population increased at a rapid rate so that today there are some six million in the area once included in the Inca Empire. The vast majority of these, roughly five and a half million, are the Quechua-speaking peoples in the highlands of Ecuador, Peru, and eastern Bolivia. In the Lake Titicaca basin, there are five hundred thousand Aymara speakers, and along the Desaguadero River, which drains the lake, are still a few remnants of Uro speakers. Today these Indian populations form an integral part of the several countries. After four hundred years of European influence, the contemporary Indian cultures obviously do not represent a direct survival from the past. Rather, these cultures are distinctive blends of elements from the ancient times, from the Colonial Spanish and from the recent Republican period. Although it is not the intent to present any detailed picture of this long historical period and the modern scene, some of the major changes and survivals may be briefly described.

The Spanish superimposed a new culture, a different language, and a contrasting physical type on the indigenous inhabitants of the Central Andes. The European conquerors became a new ruling caste, with economic, political and religious controls. The sharp caste differences which had divided the Indian populations were eradicated and a long leveling process was inaugurated ultimately reducing all Indians to a single lower class. In the Imperialist Period, travel for the commoners had been limited by law to strictly Empire business. Such restrictions were not maintained after the conquest, resulting in great mobility of the Indian population. This was motivated both by the desires of the Indians to escape tax payments and too great Spanish influence, and by the Spaniards' need for miners in the mountains. In time, there was considerable displacement of the Indian population, particularly since the coastal valleys were the most suitable for European commercial crops and for urban settlements. Today, the coastal region has a Spanish and Mestizo population, while the Indians are concentrated in the highland sections. The Europeans also introduced many new techniques and new methods of power control which effected the Indian culture, such as the principle and use of the wheel, ocean travel, firearms, the true arch, writing, iron and steel, frame looms, and new domesticated animals. Of equal importance was the systematic imposition of a new religion on the Indians. The success of the church was amazing, since by 1650 the

Indians were pronounced to be Christianized and no longer a field for intensive missionary activity.

A comparison of the Imperialist Period culture pattern with that of the contemporary Indians reveals other specific changes and survivals. Relatively few changes have occurred in the subsistence pattern. The Central Andean domesticated plants were well adapted to the different environments and knowledge of their cultivation was deeply ingrained in the Indian population. The Spaniards brought few practical substitutes for such high altitude plants as potatoes, oca, and quinoa. Barley, alfalfa, and a few other cereals have been introduced, but on the whole, the modern Indians still raise most of the old plants. Since food habits are generally conservative, there has likewise been little change in the preparation of the standard foods. The old agricultural tools were simple, inexpensive to make, and effective, and consequently they are still in use. For example, nothing has replaced the digging-stick for cultivating the fields on the steep mountain slopes. Old methods of terracing and irrigation are still practiced. For Indian agriculture, the chief innovation has been the introduction of the wooden plough and oxen as draft animals. On the other hand, European domesticated animals, including the pig, chicken, burro, horse, cattle, sheep, and goats, were vastly superior to any known in the New World. The Indians have accepted most of the new animals, but have not abandoned the llamas and alpacas.

The construction of temples, public buildings, and similar major projects was taken over by Spanish architects, although the Indians still furnished unskilled labor. The Indians continue to build their own houses, however, much as in the past. The simple rectangular room with frame and thatch roof is now made of adobes, and several such units are arranged in compounds for

[19] Tiahuanaco ruins and decorated gateway. Panorama, taken in 1896. Courtesy of University Museum, Philadelphia; others, Courtesy of Harry Tschopik, Jr.

[20] Typical wall construction and detail of sockets for cast copper cramps or tie bolts in stone paving at Tiahuanaco.

[21] Monolithic statue from Tiahuanaco. Discovered by Wendell C. Bennett.

[22] Coast and Highland Tiahuanaco vessels. A, Pacheco; B, C, F, Pachacamac; D, E, G–L, Bolivian highland.

[23] A fortress of the City Builder Period at Paramonga, constructed of clay bricks. Courtesy of W. R. Grace and Company.

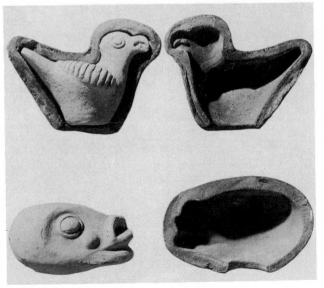

[24] Molds for ceramic manufacture.

[25] Clay arabesque wall decorations at the ruins of Chanchan. Many walls were so decorated, but most of this decoration has been destroyed by rains.

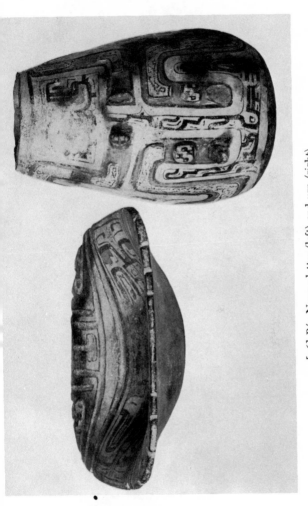

[26] Río Napo platter (left) and urn (right).

[27] Chimu blackware water jars. At left, two men boxing; center, an example of mold-pressed decoration; at right, two men on a balsa raft.

[28] City Builder ceramic styles from the Central and South Coast. A, F, Ica style; C, D, Chancay Black-on-White style; B, Negative painted Recuay vessel of the Mastercraftsman Period; E, late vessel from Pachacamac.

[29] The famous Inca citadel of Machu Picchu.

[30] Types of Inca masonry. Top, Machu Picchu; lower left, Fortress of Sacsahuamán; lower right, a street in Cuzco.

[31] Inca artifacts: lacquered wooden kero, ceremonial stone llama form container and bowl, two very typical pottery containers, a pitcher and aryballoid water or beer jar.

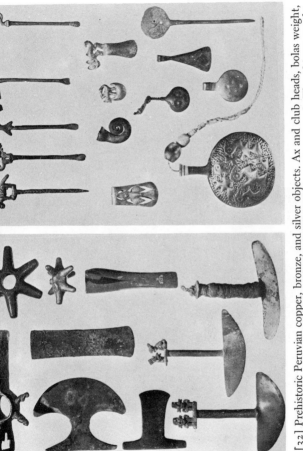

[32] Prehistoric Peruvian copper, bronze, and silver objects. Ax and club heads, bolas weight, knives, chisels, and ear spools are cast; tweezers and pin are hammered. The objects on the left are one quarter their original size and those on the right one half.

[33] Paracas Necropolis embroidery. Top, poncho shirt with heavy shoulder fringe; center, mantle borders, with foundation fabric completely hidden by the embroidery; bottom, half of a large mantle. Center, *Courtesy of Museo Nacional de Antropología y Arqueología de Peru.*

[34] Poncho shirt, shaped by inserting additional warp at center of fabric (North Chile); cape, shaped by expanding the warp; upper half, cotton, warp faced; lower half, eccentric tapestry; boy's shirt, tapestry; woman's work basket; detail of interlocked warp loom.

[35] Peruvian fabrics. Top, gauze weaves, the center one from a Paracas Necropolis grave, the others later; center, double cloth; bottom, late period painted cotton compared with Paracas Necropolis painting (Courtesy of John Wise); lower right, tie-dyeing.

the extended family. The scatter village pattern is still common.

One of the major changes in craftsmanship has been due to the fact that ceremonial objects are no longer manufactured. Most utilitarian artifacts are, however, still made by each family. The ceramics are coarse and poorly decorated, but made in the old techniques. There are also some professional goups who now use the potter's wheel. Everywhere some weaving is still done on the old types of girdle-back and belt looms, although the European foot treadle loom is also common. Sheep wool is now used as extensively as llama wool. For the most part, the weaving is limited to coarse homespuns. Practically all native metalwork has now disappeared, but wooden bowls and other artifacts, decorated calabash containers, baskets, and mats are still commonly made. There have been many changes in the clothing pattern, but the breechclout, shirt, head-dress, and carrying bag are still standard parts of the Indian costume.

The Indians of today, as in the past, are largely engaged in farming. Some are independent farmers, living in small isolated communities; others are peon farm laborers on the haciendas. The residence pattern and the social organization is reminiscent of the old *ayllu* village group. The village consists of a number of scattered house compounds and the residents recognize definite territorial claims. Individual ownership of land is now the common practice, but the group as a whole assumes the responsibility for the defense of its territory. Marriage within the village is still the rule, so that the members are united by many kinship ties, as well as local cult practices. The village is a self-sufficient unit and any form of inter-village unity is decidedly weak.

Indian languages have persisted with amazing tenacity. Many groups speak only their native language, although the number of bilingual individuals increases every year. Mythology too has survived along with this linguistic persistence. Catholicism was accepted as the official religion long ago, but local superstitions and rituals have survived with only slight modifications. The Indians still decorate llamas and march them around the fields in a curing ceremony. Children receive names at a simple ceremony in which the infant's hair is tied in bunches which are cut off by relatives who leave small gifts. The threshing of quinoa is initiated by a medicineman who calls the proper winds. There are many medicinemen who specialize in medicinal herbs, predict future events with coca leaves, and perform magical cures. Such practices do not constitute a formalized religion.

The Indian population of Ecuador, Peru, and Bolivia maintains a distinctive culture, even though modified by many years of European influence. One of the major problems faced by the contemporary Andean countries is the incorporation of the Indian population into the national scene. The cultural past of these Indians is characterized by its high achievements. There is every reason to believe that their future achievements can be even higher.

PART 3: TECHNIQUES

One measure of the cultural development of a people is their technical skill. This does not imply that culture and technology are synonymous or that we can take something like the metallurgical knowledge of a group and use it to calibrate a scale for measuring their culture. It will, however, if we have sufficient information, indicate whether the group has adapted itself to its environment and available natural resources, whether it has been receptive to cultural suggestion, or whether the members of the group were themselves inventive and ingenious. For better comprehension we must sometimes compare the technological development not only according to contemporary standards but in terms of the total record of human achievement. A technical comparison will often furnish the key to understanding and appreciation; hence, this short resume of three of the crafts. As our knowledge is still far from complete, the section on each craft should have been prepared by a specialist who could evaluate the published data and point out where further work is needed. In a limited way this has been attempted and if the following comments stimulate interest, they will be justified.

CERAMICS

Clay suitable for ceramics is available in most coastal valleys and highland basins of Peru. Most of it is derived from igneous rocks of the Andes, while some, in the Cuzco Basin and Nazca Area, is from marine tertiary formations. Due to the great variation in topography, water flow, and rainfall, materials from these sources must have been locally modified and differentiated. A comparative study of available clays might serve to explain some of the marked regional differences in ceramics. Is the seeming inferiority of some Central Coast wares due to absence of good clay obtainable in quantity, rather than to lack of skill or interest? Is the great emphasis on color in Nazca wares the result of a more varied supply of materials, or, is it due to fondness of color evident in the textiles and traceable to the post-fired treatment of earlier wares of the same region? Were these colors unavailable to the Mochica artisans? Answers to these questions would furnish a better understanding of the ceramic record.

Ceramic processes have been reconstructed from an examination of archaeological specimens and from our knowledge of modern methods. The clays are soaked, kneaded, pounded, and, when necessary, stored until they become more evenly plastic. In some areas the clay is first dried, then crushed and ground as an initial step. Some clays can then be used without further modification. Usually a grit temper is added rendering them more workable, less liable to crack as they dry, and better able to withstand the sudden temperature changes of simple or primitive firing methods. Tempering materials in the Andean Area depended on what was available and the type of product planned. Crushed stone and potsherds, sand, mica, and sometimes shell were employed. Where these were lacking, as in parts of eastern Peru and Ecuador, siliceous material from the burned bark of certain trees was used.

The methods of shaping vessels varied, and depended on the desired size and form and on regional or period practice. The coil method, widely employed throughout the Americas, was common in Peru, but the coil marks were usually smoothed out. In coiling, the vessel base is first formed by hand, and the sides raised by adding cylindrical strips of clay, either row by row or spirally. As the strips are added they are flattened, shaped, and united by pinching and scraping, or by tapping with a wooden paddle, while the inner surface is supported with an "anvil" of stone or other material. In another process, direct shaping, a prepared lump of clay is modeled into the desired form either by hand pressure or with paddle and anvil. In both methods the base of the vessel usually rests on a slightly concave pottery plate or a large potsherd. This enables the potter to rotate the clay as it is worked. In the construction of some vessels the rotating motion must have been fairly rapid, for the scratches and tool marks on the surface of unpolished pieces closely resemble those on coarse wheel-turned products. The symmetry of many of the finer pieces supports the same conclusion.

Mold-made pottery is particularly characteristic of the Mochica and later period products of the North Coast of Peru. Very few molds have been collected, so we must rely on finished products for our knowledge of molds. Modeled jars and figurines, fruits and vegetables, were reproduced in piece-molds, generally of two parts. More complex piece-molds were used where details or under-cut parts of the original object made them necessary. The molds were of fired clay, so they could be used repeatedly. Broken vessels show that the sections were joined after removal from the molds, none shows slip casting. Spouts, handles and some ornamental details were made separately and were often cast (Plate 24).

Once shaped and smoothed, some vessels were then coated with a clay wash, a thin slip to impart a desired color, a finer surface, or to form a base for painted decoration. The material used is normally a fine clay or pigment chosen for color qualities. These are prepared by grinding and washing. The latter is a simple process;

the finer material being held in suspension, is poured off and allowed to settle. The same methods were presumably followed in the preparation of pigments and clays used for painted decoration.

There is no evidence that the Peruvian potters, like some of their central American fellows, intentionally used such dispersants as lye or gums to deflocculate or further separate the coarser and finer clay particles. After application both slip and painted details were burnished, the exact procedure probably varying with the type of product and effect desired.

Slips can also be used to create a better bond between such features as handles and spouts and the body of a vessel. Although so used in Old World ceramics, none of the American potters, as far as we know, was aware of this fact.

Ceramic paints first appeared in the Andean Area in the late Cultist stage and were combined with the older decorative procedures, incising, grooving, roughing, appliqué, and modeling. The red and blackish colors first used were restricted to incised or grooved design areas. This practice spread gradually, and was used in the ceramics at Pucara. Before it reached the Nazca-Ica Area we find incised details colored, after firing, with powdered mineral pigments mixed with resins to form a lacquer-like coating. The colors so obtained are often outside the color range of the local fired pigments.

Firing is a relatively simple procedure. All of the Andean wares can be reproduced in an open fire, and do not necessarily require kilns. Where production was on the scale which this craft attained, some form of kiln was probably used at times though as yet none has been reported. The terms "oxidized" and "reduced or controlled" firing have been too loosely used by archaeologists in writing about Andean ceramics. If fuel and unfired clayware are so arranged that all or most of the carbon present is burned away in an open fire, an oxidized ware results. As most clays used contain iron compounds these will, in oxidized wares, usually be in the form of ferric oxide and the ware colors will range from cream to red, depending on the amount of oxide present. The same clays, fired to the same temperatures without oxygen, may be colored light to dark gray or even bluish because the iron compounds will be reduced to ferrous oxide. Actually most Andean wares, loosely classed as "reduced" owe their dark tones more to retained or adsorbed carbon than to reduction. They can be duplicated, with or without some degree of reduction, simply by smothering the fire with such organic material as leaves or grass or just earth if all the carbon in the fuel has not been burned. Without such covering the same pieces would come out oxidized. Both procedures were employed by Andean potters with varying frequency in different periods and areas.

After firing, various techniques were employed to enhance the products. The application of powdered pigments and lacquer-like finishes has been mentioned. Some Mochica potters added decorative details with a water-soluble black substance, readily destroyed by careless washing. More common was negative "painting". This relatively simple procedure has been reconstructed by Robert Sonin. A design is painted on a fired, "oxidized", vessel using a fine, fluid mixture of clay. When firm, this forms a resist, protecting parts of the surface. The exposed areas can then be blackened simply by smoking or they can be coated with various water soluble substances. When held over a fire these substances will char or deposit carbon on the surfaces. The clay resist scales off and a carbon negative image of the design remains. Because this black readily burns away, it is never found on cooking pots. If this treatment is applied to a surface that already has two colors fired on as slips, or as slip versus paste color, it results in an effect that has frequently and inaccurately been called "three-color negative".

Students of ceramic technology will find much of interest in the Andean Area. Without the potters' wheel great skills and artistry were developed with the alternative procedures. Similarly the lack of glazes meant that surface treatment was restricted to a certain line of development which reached a refinement unexcelled anywhere else in the world.

METALWORK

Out of the vast treasure offered in futile ransom by Atahualpa, a treasure with a present-day bullion value of over eight million dollars, even the Spaniards were constrained by admiration to keep a few objects intact. Subsequent centuries of tomb robbing undoubtedly yielded thousands of equally fine pieces, yet virtually all have been reduced to ingots. The fraction surviving shows that by the sixteenth century Andean smiths possessed a wide range of technical skills developed by trial and error over a long period. These skills are perhaps more amazing to modern metalworkers than they were to the Spaniards.

Gold, silver, and copper were the principal metals, with tin, lead, and platinum used in lesser degrees. Placer mining yielded most of the gold and all the platinum. Native copper and ores were extracted from open pit and shallow shaft mines with the simplest tools. Examples of these were found with the remarkably preserved body of a north Chilean copper miner killed by a cave-in. Long known in the museum as "the copper man", he and his crude implements are mute testimony to the patience, labor and danger involved in such mining.

The extent to which smelting of ores was carried out is still to be established. Remains of small smelting furnaces, *huairas*, have been found in Highland Peru, Bolivia, Northwest Argentina, and Chile, situated on hill slopes so that prevailing winds would increase the draft. In these the charge of ore and charcoal was placed. Burning charcoal on platforms before the air intake vents raised the temperature of the air as it entered. These furnaces were adequate for reducing high-grade ores, carefully selected carbonates and oxides, and, in some instances, sulfides which had been desulfurized by roasting. The molten metal was tapped from the bottom of the furnace and cast into small ingots for trade and subsequent working.

Among the alloys disclosed by analysis the most common are gold-copper and gold-silver-copper, usually called *guanín* or *tumbaga*, silver-copper, gold-silver, copper-tin (bronze), and in Ecuador, gold-platinum. Except for the latter, more study is needed to determine which alloys were intentional. They vary considerably in the proportions of each metal yet enough of the combinations have lower melting points and other desirable qualities, such as mold-filling, hardness, malleability, and color, to indicate an awareness of the results.

The Indians treated metals mechanically, thermally, and, to a limited extent, chemically. Mechanical treatment included the crude shaping of nuggets by hammering or grinding (perhaps the earliest techniques); cold hammering for making sheets, stretching ax and knife blades, and strain hardening (tempering); pressing or hammering of thin sheets over or into carved matrices; repoussé decoration and chasing; incising; foil sheathing of wood, bone, and shell objects; metal inlays and incrustation with turquoise and other stones; clinching or joining thin sheets of metal by folding the edges over each other and hammering; stapling and lacing with thin metal strips; and raising vessels in one piece out of a sheet of metal. The principal types of thermal treatment were melting in clay crucibles and casting in open and closed molds; soldering; wash-gilding by flowing a molten gold-copper alloy over pre-heated copper; and annealing, an essential step in all cold-working processes involving any considerable amount of plastic deformation.

When alloys containing base metals are annealed, oxides form on the surface. These are best removed chemically by dipping the piece in an acid "pickle." This procedure, obviously used in pre-Hispanic times, must have led to the discovery that objects made of gold-copper alloys could be given the color and appearance of those of nearly pure or high gold content. Such change can be effected with acid baths as the acid not only removes the oxides but also the surface copper leaving the gold in place. When finished, sometimes with burnishing and polishing, such *tumbaga* pieces have been mistaken for examples of gold plating, and, by the unwary, as solid gold. Whether or not any were made with the intent to deceive, the process did broaden the utilization of gold. Examples are more frequently found in the areas where the casting of gold was practiced to a greater extent than in the Central Andes, specifically, Colombia and northwards into southern Central America. Where silver was available and was worked, silver-copper alloys were similarly treated to modify the color. Not infrequently all three types of treatment, the chemical, thermal, and mechanical, were employed to finish a single object.

The greatest refinement of the casting process was practiced by Colombian goldsmiths in making certain hollow objects. The first step was to form a porous core of powdered charcoal and clay, corresponding closely to the shape of the object to be cast. When thoroughly dry, this was covered with a wax coating of uniform thickness, with details added to complete an exact model. To provide openings for the pour and air vents, wax rods were attached to the model; and at the same time, small wooden pegs or thorns were inserted through the wax into the core to hold it in position within the mold during the rest of the process. The wax was then "faced" or coated with fine charcoal paste, and completely covered with clay and coarser charcoal, forming the mold. When dry, and all was ready, the mold was heated to melt out the wax and facilitate the flow of the molten metal, which was then poured in, filling exactly the space formerly occupied by the wax model. Such molds can be used but once and must be broken away to free the "lost wax" (*cire perdue*) casting. This was finished by cutting off the excess metal remaining in pour and air vent channels, burnishing and polishing, and, if necessary, removing the core and plugging the holes left by the core supports.

Two-stage casting with metals of different melting points was known in the southern highlands. Examples are boleadora weights with decorative or functional frames of copper set in lead. Elaborate mace heads from the Lambayeque area on the coast show great skill in the creation of separate interlinked elements, probably cast simultaneously with separate pours.

Platinum, with a melting point well over 1700 C., was not used in Europe until the nineteenth century. Long before, the Indians of Ecuador had learned that by alternately and repeatedly heating and hammering fine platinum and gold grains together, they could produce a homogeneous mass. The principle of this process, called sintering, was later rediscovered and forms the basis of our modern powder metallurgy.

Relatively few of the tools used by Andean metalworkers have been collected. Among them are care-

fully made stone hammers of varied size and form, clay
crucibles, stone and porous clay molds, carved wood
and stone patterns for shaping sheet metal, chisels,
punches, and burins. These last were made of stone in
earlier times, and later of bronze and copper, as were
the blowpipes that served in place of bellows, as described by Spanish chroniclers.

The types of metal objects made by these gifted
artisans are extremely diverse as shown in Plates 4, 10,
16, and 32. The oldest illustrated, the gold Chavínoid
pieces from Chongoyape, may have been made before
500 B.C.; the most recent, a cast copper decorative
detail showing a man on horseback (Plate 32) dates
from the late 16th century. Throughout this long period gold was used for ornaments, containers and vessels, and in Inca times to adorn important structures.
The metal, without being diverted into a monetary
system, was a medium of artistic expression for things
more of the spirit than for material needs.

TEXTILES

Among the varied prehistoric products of Peru perhaps the most challenging and interesting are the textiles. The record of these textiles probably spans a full
5000 years and much research is needed before it can
be fully understood and appreciated. In addition to the
large collections already available for study, a vast
amount of material remains to be recovered from the
many arid sites of the coastal area. These however are
not inexhaustible and it is distressing to note that the
Peruvian government permits the destruction of this
heritage through the extension of irrigation without
thought of the consequences.

The development of a textile tradition in Peru resulted from a fortunate combination of at least three

factors. Excellent fibers were available from both plant and animal sources. Climatically, even in coastal areas, the temperature fluctuation is sufficient to make clothing desirable and, in some areas, essential. Finally the improvement of agriculture and the prehistoric development of irrigation provided enough leisure to permit the creation of fine and complex fabrics.

In the second and third millennia B.C., if not earlier, textiles were the primary media for artistic expression. In subsequent centuries textile production became almost a competition in ingenuity, yet continued as an honored and remarkable combination of art and craftsmanship. Even today a few Peruvian weavers maintain this tradition and still have pride in their work.

In terms of modern technology the old Peruvian fabrics are outstanding for several reasons. Almost every known technique of modern weaving was used as well as a number which are either impossible or impractical for mechanical looms. The spinning ranks among the finest known in the world and the large range of colors is evidence of exceptional skill in dyeing. Obviously, technical developments of this order were based on a great pride in weaving and a widespread appreciation of quality, as shown by the frequency with which examples of excellent workmanship occur in the collections. The following notes are intended only as a brief outline of our present knowledge and do not cover the subject fully. A real appreciation of their technical and artistic merits can only stem from first-hand experience with the textiles themselves.

FIBERS

Studies of the contents of the strata of refuse dumps in widely separated localities have yielded basic data on the occurrence and utilization of the different fibers. In the Viru and Chicama valleys, in the great deposits of debris left by an early farming group who knew neither maize nor pottery, cotton is the principal fiber. Bast, perhaps *Asclepias,* was sometimes blended or plied with it. Twisted sedge, used in open mesh coiled pouches and mats, served for cordage. From this evidence it is clear that the Peruvian textile craft is based on the use of cotton and not on wool or any other fiber.

This explains the cotton-wool ratios in the analyses of other series of Andean textiles for which chronological data are available. One set of these from northern Chile, covering the entire period from the introduction of weaving to the sixteenth century, shows proportionately much more cotton than wool in the oldest fabrics than in the more recent. This is also true of the Paracas textiles checked by O'Neale; the older series from the Cavernas graves contained more cotton than wool as compared with the later Necropolis material. Still older mummy wrappings from Ancón and Supe are all of cotton, except for a single piece in which a little wool is used. The latter may be contemporary with the Cupisnique textiles from the Chicama Valley, among which no wool has as yet been found. Considered in terms of the still older preceramic fabrics, all this evidence clearly establishes cotton as the oldest textile fiber.

Modern Peruvian spinners are said to distinguish by name six naturally colored varieties of cotton, ranging from light tan to reddish brown and gray. At least several of these are known from the Preceramic and Cultist periods as examples occur among the Chicama and Supe finds. Used with white cotton in patterns and designs they have been and still are important to the weavers for they eliminate the necessity of dyeing in those shades.

To a people possessing the tradition of cotton spinning and weaving the value of wool would be obvious once they moved into the habitat of the animals producing it, namely, the Peruvian highlands southward from the Ecuadorean border. We know nothing of the wild forms of the llama and alpaca, but the wool from their wild cousins, the vicuña and guanaco, is very soft and fine. Parts of their coats are pure white and as white wool is much more easily dyed than cotton, the utilization of wool may have stimulated the use of dyes.

Wool from the vicuña was secured by great round-ups of these animals. It was so highly prized for its fineness that its use in Inca times was reputedly limited to the nobility. Because of this tradition many of the finer fabrics have automatically been classed as vicuña without proper verification. Recent research by Mr. Truman Bailey leads him to believe that many of the prehistoric fabrics formerly classed as vicuña are of selected alpaca wool. He also reports that it is more difficult to hand spin vicuña wool than alpaca; in explanation, the spinners say that this is so because "the vicuña is a very active, playful animal," and that its wool retains these characteristics.

Guanaco wool is found in textiles from north Chile, but we do not know how it was secured. Young guanaco are easy to tame, but they never seem to have been domesticated. Was this because their habitat is largely marginal to the area of intensive farming and weaving? If the young of the wild llama and alpaca, living within that area, were as easily tamed, it is quite possible that a growing interest in wool was the major incentive for the domestication of these animals.

Domestication ultimately increased the yield of white wool and extended the range of the animals beyond their natural habitat. It may be impossible ever to date the beginnings of domestication, but such finds as the sacrificed llama burials beside a Cupisnique period structure in the Viru Valley show that some animals were being brought down to the coast during that period. It would be interesting to know if there was a simultaneous spread of weaving into the highlands, where no other fibers were available and warm clothes were needed.

Human hair was at times employed in twisted and braided cordage but is so completely lacking in some periods as to suggest that some groups may have had taboos against its use. Sedges and reeds, and bast fibers from *fourcroya* leaves were employed to some extent in all periods, mainly for cord and rope. Their use, in part, antedates the textiles, for fishlines of unidentified bast have been found with the remains of a non-agricultural preceramic fishing culture in north Chile.

DYES

The variety of colors which were ultimately used in the fabrics testifies to the skill achieved in dyeing, a skill so advanced that it is tragic that so few data on the subject were recorded after the conquest. O'Neale, comparing Paracas Necropolis dyed yarns with the Maerz and Paul color charts, distinguished one hundred ninety hues. Uneven fading undoubtedly accounts for some shades, but the record is nonetheless impressive. Truman Bailey, gathering surviving information and experimenting with native plants, has prepared two hundred fifty color formulae which may well duplicate most of the ancient ones. To these must be added another important source, the cochineal insect, which before the invention of synthetic dyes was an important item of export from Peru and Mexico. There is also reason to believe that a shellfish dye secured from the *concholepa* was used.

Virtually nothing is known of dyeing procedures. Mordants were used to an undetermined extent and permanent brilliant and lovely colors were produced.

The only attempt yet made to identify the mordants used seems to confirm an early historic mention of the use of alum for this purpose.

As these ancient peoples possessed no carding equipment, the dyeing of raw wool stocks was not common, for the process is apt to tangle the fibers. Raw stock dyeing of cotton, unknown in modern industry until recent years, was practiced, a technique which may explain the remark of a sixteenth century writer that a blue cotton was grown. He must have observed the several natural shades of cotton on the plants and seeing the natives spinning blue cotton, assumed that it was also grown. It was not mentioned by later writers, who were more familiar with the cotton plants and were not concerned with dyeing processes. In 1946 a possible explanation of this old error was found in the Museum collection in a Peruvian work basket that contained cones of dyed blue cotton prepared for spinning. In 1947 survival of the practice was noted in Bolivia and the Chicama Valley. In order to prevent tangling of the fibers, the cotton is dyed with the seeds still attached. When dry, the subsequent handling of the fibers is no more difficult than the undyed cotton.

Some data on the chronology of dyes are available. Blue is the only dye found on the preceramic textiles of Chicama. A red pigment was applied to yarn before weaving and to finished pieces, but this is not a true dye. No further advance has as yet been noted on the succeeding Cupisnique textiles, but in the old Supe and Ancón series a little true red dye is found in addition to the blue. In the Paracas Cavernas group, ten or twelve colors are noted; while in the Paracas Necropolis series, the range of colors reaches its maximum. In the oldest textile series from northern Chile, except for a single example of red and a questionable yellow, only natural shades of wool and cotton are found. Subsequently, there was a gradual increase in the use of dyes, with this maximum use so late that a marked time lag in their diffusion from the north is obvious.

The yarns of the oldest textiles are all rather coarse and uneven. The debris in which they occur in the Chicama Valley contains thousands of twigs and wood fragments; yet not a single recognizable spindle and no spindle whorls have been found. In the same valley, women are occasionally seen today twisting coarse yarn, using an unworked straight shoot of a local shrub for a spindle. In making coarse yarn they are used without a whorl. The lower ends are continually held and twisted by the fingers of the right hand while the left hand draws and lays the fibers from a bunch of cotton tied to the end of a stick or distaff. The identification of these simple spindles would be impossible unless found with yarn in place, so it may well be that the earliest spindles were similar.

In the interval between preceramic time and this decadent modern survival spinning was developed to an art yielding yarns several times finer than are produced by modern machines using the same staples. The delicate spindles of wood and thorn used in spinning these fine yarns were equipped with whorls so small that their identity as such has been questioned. In operation, the lower end of the spindle rested in a special cup of pottery, gourd, or wood which, as Crawford has emphasized, minimized vibration and strain, a requisite for fine spinning of cotton. This method is still used, though the spindles are crude by contrast and the yarn produced is heavier.

In spinning wool the modern spinners all use free-swinging spindles, and though such spindles are found archaeologically, we do not know whether the finest of the old wool yarns were created in this way.

Whether the spindle is revolved clockwise (S twist) or counterclockwise (Z twist) is, of course, optional, but preference is usually shown for one or the other. In doubling single ply yarns, the direction of twist was consistently reversed, so that the spinner's fingers were trained to work in both directions. As the fibers can be spun in either direction, there seems to be nothing to dictate direction of twist other than local custom. A small random sampling indicates that the S twist predominated in preceramic and Cupisnique fabrics and was fairly common in later yarns on the North Coast, while in old Supe, Paracas, the North Chilean, and modern yarns the Z twist predominated. Sometimes S and Z twist yarns are combined in a single fabric, perhaps intentionally. A further recording of twist seems warranted and should yield useful comparative data.

Data on the use of distaffs are meager. In the sixteenth century, the Inca used a forked stick. More carefully made slotted wooden distaffs, one with wool still in place, have been found occasionally. Today one sees some spinners with a crude roving or roll of prepared cotton or wool looped about the left wrist and hand, drawing out and laying the fibers with the left fingers, while the right hand operates the spindle and stretches the fibers while spinning progresses. Others fasten a bunch of prepared cotton to the end of a reed, about thirty inches long, which is held between the left arm and body, leaving the hands free to manipulate the fibers. Some such simple distaff was perhaps used to hold the conical bunches of prepared cotton so frequently found with the late period work baskets. They may also have been wedged in the carved forked sticks, as portrayed in the sets of miniature spinning and weaving equipment made of silver.

When we marvel at the quality of the yarns produced with such simple tools, it is interesting to note that the use of hand-spun yarn is still economically justified in Peru. Hand spinners, according to Truman Bailey, can produce one hundred grams of yarn per day at a cost about thirty per cent less than similar but inferior machine-made yarn.

LOOMS AND WEAVING

As yet, no one has made a comprehensive study of the loom types still in use and of their distribution in Peru. Such a survey would be invaluable in interpreting the archaeological material.

It is generally agreed that most of the excavated fabrics were constructed on backstrap looms like the modern ones used in the Central and Coastal valleys. However, in the Southern Highlands and in Bolivia, the loom bars are tied to four stakes driven into the ground so that the warp lies horizontally. Less common is a frame-loom set vertically.

Of these three types, only the first permits the weaver to control the warp tension automatically, an important feature. In its essentials, this loom (Fig. 19) is an exceedingly simple device, consisting of two sticks, called loom bars, with the warp stretched between them. The lower bar, tied to a belt passing behind the weaver's back, rests above the lap, while the upper is suspended from a post or other support. As the work progresses on a long fabric, the warp is unrolled from the upper bar and the finished portion is rolled on to the lower.

In warping these looms, the yarn was, and still is, first wound with a figure-eight motion between two stakes. The figure-eight crossing, called the lease, automatically separates the alternate turns and creates two sheds, greatly simplifying the remainder of the preparatory work.

After the yarn has been warped off, it is laced fast to the loom bars in such a way that when completed,

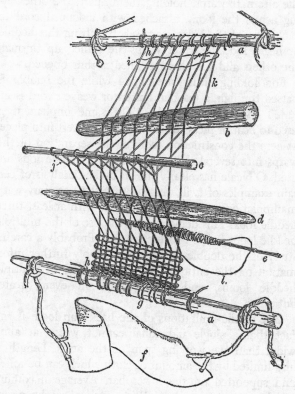

Fig. 19. Diagram of a backstrap loom: *a*, loom bars; *b*, shed rod; *c*, heddle rod; *d*, batten or sword; *e*, bobbin; *f*, back strap; *g*, warp lashing; *h*, heading string; *i*, lease cord; *j*, leash cord; *k*, warp; *l*, weft.

all four edges of the fabric are finished off, sometimes so uniformly that side and end selvages are indistinguishable. Usually, however, the end selvages incorporated the cord or yarn, which, with the lashing, held them against the loom bars.

For plain weaves, the control of the warp sheds is accomplished with two sticks, one inserted between the alternate warps, holding them apart; the other, lying across the loom, attached with a looped cord to each yarn of the lower warp set. By lifting this heddle or heald rod, the lower warps are pulled up through the others and the alternate shed is thus opened.

For holding either shed open while the bobbin is passed through, a wooden batten or weave sword is inserted and turned on edge. The same implement is used to beat or press the newly inserted weft into place. Where the construction requires the separation of the warps into several sheds, two or more heddle rods are used. O'Neale has clearly shown by her analysis of certain examples of twill weaving that the necessary warp manipulations must have been made with at least three heddle rods. This demonstrates the use of the multiple heddle loom in the Mochica period. Probably a careful study of the double-cloths would supply further information on the antiquity and distribution of multiple heddle looms, and might show an even greater antiquity.

One of the limitations of the backstrap loom is the fact that a single individual cannot weave a fabric wider than the working span of the arms. Length is also limited by the amount of cloth which can be rolled and supported on the lower bar. Average maximum widths seem to be about thirty inches, so the occurrence of large fabrics like the Paracas specimens which have widths up to seventeen feet eight inches and lengths of eighty-seven feet, indicate that some other type of loom was used. Truman Bailey has recorded the use of a super backstrap loom which is roughly three times the normal width and was operated by three women working as a team. The limitations of such a loom would be in the length rather than in the width.

WEAVING TECHNIQUES AND CHRONOLOGY

Very recent excavation has yielded an adequate sample series of farbrics from the preceramic horizon already referred to. Unfortunately, our data still depend on field notes and an analysis of uncleaned specimens as they were excavated. Cleaning and further study will add detailed information, but should not appreciably change the rate of occurrence for the techniques listed below:

	Per Cent
Twining	78.3
Looping and loop coiling	10.1
Fish nets, knotted	7.5
Plain cloth, warp face weave	3.7
Plain cloth, warp face with warp floats	0.2
Netted pouches	0.2
	100.0

(This list does not include matting and basketry.)

Twining as a technique has been used with many materials other than spun yarns, and survives today mainly in mat and basket construction. From its world-wide distribution and some archaeological evidence, it is believed to be one of the oldest methods of creating a fabric.

The principle is simple. The weft is always worked in pairs intertwined between the warp elements, and, if tightly twisted, they will remain in place even when the weft rows are widely spaced. In the old Peruvian material, the wefts are nearly all short, crossing the fabric only once; with their ends tied together at the selvage, forming a row of knots at the edge. There is no simple mechanical method of placing the weft; it must be done with the fingers, and, as the warp does not have to be manipulated, a heddle is useless.

Twining, as shown by these old fabrics, was highly developed. By crossing and arranging the warps, and by varying their size and grouping, differences in texture and pleasing effects were created. There are designs of considerable complexity but none is constructed in the manner of the Chilkat blankets of North America, in which the wefts carry the pattern.

The contemporary woven pieces are surprisingly small. Eight inches is about the maximum width, and, except for belting, lengths do not seem to exceed twice the width. All are warp faced, i.e., the warp yarns, more closely spaced than the weft, predominate at the surface. Patterning, as with the twining, is limited to warp manipulation. Most common are stripes of warp floats done with alternate yarns, a movement resembling that employed in modern huck weaves. Occasionally some intricate figure was made in this technique.

It is highly significant that in virtually all the woven pieces at least some detail is accomplished by twining. This may be limited to several compact twined rows to hold the warp ends together or, in addition, may appear as twined weft rows separating woven areas. In some textiles twining and weaving occur side by side, with the same weft yarns used in both areas. Other warp faced examples reveal the use of short wefts, with the ends tied in knots along one selvage, exactly as in the plain twining.

The impression from this material is that twining is definitely the predecessor of weaving; that the heddle was unknown, and that weaving did not evolve from twining, but developed with it as an outgrowth of the experimental manipulation of yarns. The invention of the heddle was, in all probability, the critical factor in further development, for without it weaving could not compete with twining.

A sudden increase in the frequency of woven pieces occurs in the Cupisnique, or Cultist Period debris lying above the primitive material mentioned. Their size and the less compact spacing of the warp imply the use of the heddle, while finished end or loom bar selvages and a number of techniques not used earlier mark a break in tradition. One would scarcely expect these techniques to appear simultaneously had the development occurred in the neighborhood of the Chicama Valley. As they first appear in the Chicama Valley associated with Cupisnique sherds, the first maize, warty squash, and a number of other culture elements, it is clearly interpretable as influence from another area in which weaving had evolved well beyond the preceramic technical accomplishments.

A careful analysis of material from this horizon is needed, but has not yet been made. The fairly common continued occurrence of twining may be a local feature resulting from cultural fusion or, perhaps, Cupisnique weavers were actually not far removed from the pre-pottery stage. Completely new at that time in Peru was gauze lace made by twisting adjacent warps before inserting the weft. Design areas within the gauze are woven in to match the plain weave adjoining the gauze.

Another less practical device for creating design was to wrap cotton lint around certain portions of the weft just before it was laid in place, resulting in a compact figure set in a relatively loosely woven field. Only two later pieces show this patterning method. One is the fabulous Paracas "altar" cloth at the Brooklyn Museum with its central figures wrapped on the warp before weaving; the other is a Nazca item incorrectly described by O'Neale. This is quite distinct from the wrapping or "facing" of yarn with yarn in late period slings and hair nets.

Another regionally new construction was tapestry,

which can be briefly defined as the use of independent wefts for each color or pattern area of the design. Also present are the simplest devices for varying the appearance of plain weaves: the use of warp or weft stripes and a combination of the two to form plaid. The weft yarns are usually paired singles.

The series of textiles from Supe, perhaps close in age to Cupisnique, add to the known technical data. As with Cupisnique, warp-faced fabrics are in the minority, about thirty per cent of the total. Apparently a higher percentage of Supe fabrics has paired single ply wefts and some also have paired warps. Brocading, the insertion of secondary wefts in addition to the ordinary weft at the places where the pattern falls, was known, but embroidery seems to be lacking. Tapestry is more common than yet noted among Cupisnique fabrics and is found in several forms. One example, a Chavín stylized condor head set in a plain weave field, is cleverly executed with eccentric and slit techniques. At least three shades of naturally colored cotton were used in it, the over-all effect enhanced by the contrast between the compact weft of the figure and the loose weave of the adjacent fabric. Others have interlocked geometric areas of loose tapestry in which, contrary to accepted tapestry procedure, the wefts are not beaten tightly together.

The Paracas Cavernas textiles here assigned to the Experimenter Period are probably not quite as old and among them, in addition to those mentioned for Cupisnique and Supe, are several more techniques. One, which became very popular much later, is double cloth. In this, two separate webs of contrasting colors, each with its own warp and weft, are woven together. Pattern is created by interlocking the two webs, a tedious procedure on any hand loom. The complexity of the oldest known examples shows complete mastery of the process and indicates an earlier developmental stage.

This concept of double cloth was carried still farther by the Peruvians who produced a triple cloth and a narrow quadruple cloth belting.

This Cavernas lot also adds embroidery and warp float patterning to the list, comprising in all a remarkably broad range of techniques for such an early culture level. The contrast with the preceramic fabrics is obvious. Plain twining survived in Chicama, while in the south twining was limited in the Paracas Cavernas material to basketry, matting, and elaborate twined lace. With weaving, the break is so marked that at present it can only be explained by postulating technical evolution outside the area, which would mean that the late preceramic textiles were, in their time at least, outdated survivals. There is such slight chance of recovering old fabrics outside of Peru that if we are to locate the area of development, careful attention must be paid to the associated non-perishable items. Perhaps the answer lies along the potsherd trail which may ultimately reveal the origin of the Cupisnique-Chavín ceramic techniques and designs.

The textile development subsequent to the Cupisnique-Supe-Cavernas stage shows marked differences by period and area, not so much the result of technical development as in the emphasis on and increasing perfection of some device already in use. An excellent example is the superb embroidery of the Paracas Necropolis period when this art became fashionable almost to the point of exclusion of other techniques (Plate 33). Great numbers of intricate and complex embroideries were prepared and laid away with the dead; pieces which were never again equaled in quality or in the use of color.

The omission here of published data is not intended to slight or question the work of others. The identification of weaves and trends in the Mastercraftsmen and later periods is so comprehensive a topic with so many incomplete details that it is inadvisable to attempt to encompass it at present. As an alternative, some comments can be made on certain techniques which have not already been discussed.

Plain Cloth: Regional trends are well exemplified by comparing the products from the northern coasts of Peru and Chile made during the period of Inca control. At the time of the Spanish conquest and afterwards, an undetermined but high percentage of plain cloth from Chicama was made with paired elements, using single-ply cotton yarn, a custom well established at least as early as the Cultist Period.

On the North Chilean coast, where the influence of Inca culture was scarcely felt, sixteenth century and earlier plain weaves are entirely warp faced. Most of them are of two-ply wool yarn, and only one in a series of nearly eight hundred has paired wefts. This again is founded on long established local tradition, with a slight variation seen only among the oldest textiles, four per cent of which are square count, the rest warp faced.

At Pachacamac, plain cloth associated with Inca pottery is predominantly warp faced and made with two-ply yarns. Paired warps and wefts of single ply S spun yarns are elements apparently introduced from the north during this period. Cotton is six to eight times more frequent than wool, with the latter most abundant in the textiles associated with the highest concentration of Inca sherds.

Repp: Plain cloth in which the warps outnumber the wefts and predominate on the surface is referred to as warp faced. This generally has a ribbed appearance which can be accentuated by the use of heavier weft yarn. This effect, called repp, is sometimes mentioned as a feature of Peruvian fabrics and is indeed quite common. The term should perhaps be limited to those fabrics in which the weft is heavier than the warp and until some such distinction is made little can be said about it other than that it naturally follows the distribution of warp faced textiles.

Twill: The rarity of the occurrence of twill in existing collections has occasioned some speculation. O'Neale, in the only report on Peruvian twill, discusses the seventeen examples known to her. As its production required at least three heddle rods, the work of setting them up may have limited its popularity. Perhaps far more twill was woven than has been assumed for most of it was collected in Mochica tombs, notoriously poor in yielding textiles. In the light of our present knowledge, however, it is clear that though the Peruvians did master the application of this technique, its distribution is restricted.

Pattern Weaves: The creation of well executed, intricate patterns with the warp is a challenge to the weaver's ability; yet in spite of the difficulties involved, it became very popular and still remains so in the southern highlands. Though known to some degree throughout Peru in all periods, the finest warp patterns are generally from the South Coast and are relatively late. The similarity of designs in modern and fourteenth to sixteenth century specimens is often striking and should give a good check on the conservatism of such textile design. In North Chile this technique appears with the first painted pottery.

Weft or bobbin patterns are not so difficult to create and, though widely used, never were as popular as warp patterns. Much more common are the brocades, possibly because the use of supplementary wefts permits a more varied application of color than in plain bobbin patterns.

Tapestry: When the Spaniards entered Peru, tapestry was definitely in fashion as, in a sense, it then was in Europe. The Peruvian products, however, were technically far superior in every detail. Usually made with cotton warp and wool weft, they frequently have over two hundred weft per inch and some exceed two hundred and fifty. One with an average of 327 per inch has weft crowded together at the rate of 500 per inch in some details of the pattern. It would be impossible to create such a fabric without having perfect yarn for the warp. In this case a three-ply cotton yarn, with seventy twists per inch, was used. The warp count is sixty-seven to the inch. Roughly, contemporary European tapestry, by contrast, seldom exceeds eighty-five weft per inch, and modern examples much fewer.

In a sense, this is an unfair comparison, for the European products were primarily pictorial wall hangings in which fineness of weave and the condition of the under surface were not very important; whereas in Peru, tapestry was employed for clothing, belts, and bags. In these, careful finish of both sides and compact yet light construction were naturally appreciated. The extreme fineness of weave, however, is only one aspect of the Peruvian product. Every conceivable device applicable to tapestry construction was employed with care and skill. As an example, one finds in the Nazca area that the structural weakness of slit or kelim tapestry has been overcome by using hidden wefts. By using paired warps a fine hard-spun single-ply cotton can be woven in so it does not show through the wool weft of the pattern unless the fabric is torn or badly worn. These have sometimes been inaccurately classified as "embroidery to resemble tapestry." Actually, there is no recognized name for this technique and, as often happens with Peruvian material, one has to be suggested. In this case "reinforced slit tapestry" is adequate, if we can agree at which limit the construction is technically something else. Some pieces show the reinforcing yarns inserted only where the slits are largest. In others a continuous fine cotton weft is inserted regularly, with two or more pairs of tapestry weft between the picks of cotton weft. When only one pair of the pattern weft separates the fine cotton yarns, the latter are usually carried beyond the pattern and form a plain weave area. Such pieces are certainly not tapestry, although they reproduce its appearance exactly.

In addition to the more conventional types of tapestry, some very delicate pieces have been found showing interlocked tapestry construction in which warps and wefts are single-ply crepe twist, cotton. They are sometimes so loosely woven that, as far as texture goes, the fabric can be considered a voile, yet the construction is essentially that of tapestry. Since this technique has no parallel in modern weaving, again a term has to be proposed and in this case perhaps "sheer tapestry" is preferable to calling it interlocked plain weave. One of the two examples in the American Museum of Natural History is very rare among known Peruvian fabrics in showing what is called "Swedish" or two-way interlock. In it, the locking of the weft produces a ridge or wale on the reverse side of the fabric. In the other, the wefts interlock around a warp.

The antiquity of tapestry has already been mentioned in comments on the Cupisnique-Chavín fabrics. As yet, we know little about it during the interval preceding the Tiahuanaco or Expansionist Period. In both known Paracas periods, it was virtually ignored, furnishing a good example of the influence of fashion on the occurrence of a technique. Certainly a people possessing such skill in spinning, dyeing, and weaving ignored it only by intention.

Somewhat later and far to the north there is some evidence for its use in the Mochica period. To what extent, remains to be discovered, but from then on, all down the coast, it appears with increasing frequency. The major development seems to have come with the spread of the Tiahuanaco influence from the southern highlands. Beautifully executed pieces with characteristic figures of this period are among the most easily identified of all Peruvian fabrics. Though the stylistic influence of Tiahuanaco faded in time, the manufacture of tapestry continued, receiving new support with the second wave of highland conquerors, the Inca. It is interesting to note that while the Inca ultimately dominated a larger area than their predecessors, they seem to have had less influence on the general textile development. The only marked Spanish influence on the Peruvian textile record immediately after the conquest was in tapestry design. The Spaniards recognized and appreciated the native product, if not the patterns, and soon had weavers making tapestry hangings and carpets for their homes. These products, in which ideas from two unrelated cultures have been blended, merit special study.

Interlocked Warp Pattern: This construction which, like tapestry, can yield a pattern identical on both sides of the fabric is peculiar to Peru. It has sometimes been called "patchwork" or "weft scaffolding," but as the pattern is set up in the warp before inserting the weft, the term used here seems more appropriate.

A unique unfinished example in the American Museum collection has a rather intricate two-color pattern laid out with the aid of taut scaffolding yarns, set like the rungs of a ladder, parallel to the loom bars and presumably held in place by supplementary bars set at right angles to the regular ones (Plate 34, lower right). Warping was done very much as one inserts the weft in one-way interlocked tapestry, with the warp spanning one or more "rungs" as the pattern required. The interlocking turns of the contrasting yarns also encircle the scaffold yarns. In other words, if all the warps were pulled out of a finished piece of interlocked tapestry, the weft would then resemble this type of interlocked warp fabric before the insertion of the weft. It is obvious that if the final product is to be smooth, warp tension must be perfectly distributed and, except for unusually large areas, the weft must be inserted without benefit of a heddle and in most cases was done with a needle.

Several types of interlocked warp are distinguishable on the basis of the weft manipulation. In the most elementary, the warp is close together and a single weft runs the full width of the fabric. In these the scaffold yarns are either left in place or the weft substituted for them. Others show the use of different weft colors, matching the colors used in the warp. In these the sides of the color areas may be woven as slits, then stitched up; or the different wefts may be interlocked between the warps.

The complexity of some of the patterns in this weave are astounding, considering the labor involved and the limitations of the plan by which they were laid out. In fact, they are excellent examples of the extremes to which Peruvians carried their loom work. The interlocked warp technique is found among Paracas Necropolis fabrics and continued to be made until historic times, demonstrating how fixed in their tradition was a willingness to attempt the difficult.

One justification for the term "patchwork" is to be seen in the garments made of small tie-dyed units. All the units in any one garment were warped together on scaffold yarns without interlocking the warp turns. After weaving in the wefts of each unit, the removal of the scaffold freed the "patches" for dyeing and left the warp end loops open for reuniting. So far, there is little to indicate that this "patchwork" was used before the Tiahuanaco period, and nothing to show that it was not consistently used with tie-dyeing.

Interlocked Darning: Another product which at first glance seems to belong to the interlocked warp group and has been called "interlocked plain weave" and "multicolored patchwork," was created entirely by darning without any preparatory warping. O'Neale has described one piece from the Paracas Necropolis period, which must have been made by darning on a temporary grid of both vertical and horizontal scaffold yarns. Others seem to have been done with only horizontal yarns as a guide but until an unfinished example is found, there will be doubt about certain steps in the process.

As a group, they can be distinguished by the impossibility of identifying warp from weft. In any given area of the pattern, the yarn laid in one direction as "warp" turns and serves as "weft," as in darning. Parts of this "weft" may be used to extend the pattern and, in doing so, they become the "warp." Hence, warp and weft yarn is continuous in each area and the warp-weft counts are equal. The patterns are squared geometrically and the colors are clear and contrasting. One might expect such fabrics all to be small, yet a fragmentary example in the American Museum apparently measured thirty-two by eighty-eight inches when new.

Shaped Fabrics (weaving to shape): We are all so conditioned to cutting cloth to a desired size or shape that few of us realize what a relatively new concept this cutting is in terms of our total textile history. The Peruvians, like all ancient weavers, wove their fabrics to the length and width needed for a particular garment or purpose and never cut or tailored them. As the normal product was rectangular, this had a rather depressing effect on clothing styles. Their response to this limitation was to weave cloth to the shape desired. Examples of this practice constitute a larger and more important group than is generally realized.

Of several methods, the most rudimentary is based on a very simple principle; fanning or spreading of the warp between the loom bars, which, if evenly done, yields a trapezoidal product. The side selvages were curved as desired by varying the tension of the weft during weaving. Loin cloths, quite similar to very modern French bathing suits, were woven by keeping the center of the warp close together and spreading the ends so that the finished corners could be tied over the hips. Poncho shirts, some over twice as wide across the shoulders as at the bottom, were made by spreading the center of the warp before weaving. To avoid loose construction where the spreading became extreme, additional warps were laid in as needed. The Museum collection contains one large shirt of this type from North Chile (Plate 34); woven in one piece, it is eighty-four inches across the shoulders by thirty-eight across the bottom. For every hundred warps running the full length of the loom, fifty more were added at the center.

Other irregularly shaped pieces were made by setting the loom bars so that one side selvage was longer than the other. Uniform construction was maintained by carrying some of the weft rows only part way across the loom. The same weft manipulation was used in pieces which appear to have been warped between two curved loom bars for the production of capes which are wider in the middle than at the ends.

Although no record has been made of the number of techniques employed in conjunction with shaping, the list includes tapestry, double cloth, two-faced warp pattern, and interlocked warp. The oldest occurrence yet noted is in pre-Tiahuanaco material from North Chile. By the time the Spaniards arrived with the concept of tailored garments, the shaped fabrics were more widely used than has hitherto been realized. One cannot help wondering where this phase of costume design would have led had it not been interrupted.

Resist Dyeing: Tie-dyeing or "plangi" has already been mentioned in connection with patchwork. This basically simple process consists of binding portions of a fabric with yarn or fiber before dyeing as protection from the dye, and thus creating a pattern. If a small portion of fabric is bunched and bound, then dye-free circles result. When the binding is applied to folded and rolled cloth, straight lines can be created. Several colors can be used successively by properly planning a sequence of dyes and bindings, but only two colors, in addition to the natural color, have so far been reported. The resist process with wax to stop the dye penetration, known as "batik," has not been positively identified in Peru.

Ikat: Another and more complicated resist dyeing process is made by dyeing the pattern on the warp before weaving commences. For precise results, the whole fabric must be carefully planned in advance. The exact number of warp yarns required is calculated and these subdivided into lots which are grouped, tied, and dyed together for each division of the pattern row repeats.

From the present South American distribution of ikats, south central Chile, Bolivia, north Peru, and Ecuador, one might expect to find more examples from pre-Spanish times than actually appear. Only a very few have been collected, most within the Chimu area, and none is older than the late Coastal Tiahuanaco pottery, if that old. This and other reasons suggest that it was introduced into Peru later than and independent of "plangi" tie-dye. Most pieces show retouching after weaving, when dyes were painted on parts of the design as if in an attempt to create the appearance of a polychrome ikat.

Both warp and weft ikat are known in Central America, but the latter has not been found in Peru.

Painting: This is an older method of decorating fabrics than resist dyeing. Though plain red pigment was used in lieu of a dye in preceramic days, the creative application of pigments has not yet been reported earlier than Paracas Cavernas. Afterwards, it is found rather widely distributed in the different areas and periods. Perhaps its greatest use was in copying the effects achieved by some structural method such as the reproduction of tapestry designs. Rectangular wall hangings of cotton cloth with large bold and weird painted figures have been found in late Central Coast sites (Plate 35).

Feather Work and other Surface Decoration: Quantities of feather-covered fabrics have been found, mostly in post-Tiahuanaco graves. In some cases, the feathers have been cemented fast but the more usual method was to attach the feathers to a cord and stitch this to a woven fabric row by row. Some of the feather work is strikingly colorful. Quite common are feathers from domesticated macaws and parrots, some of the latter a yellow variety which is now extinct. Other feathers are from tropical rain forest birds which must have been brought a considerable distance. A study of such material ought to yield information on trade contacts.

Correspondingly late fabrics are also occasionally decorated with sheet metal discs and plates. Most of these are of interest only in that they reveal a trend which has little real appeal from an esthetic viewpoint. Beaded fabrics are virtually unknown and are limited to a net construction.

After the Paracas period, embroidery declined in quality. Examples of a later use are the pieces which look like brocade, but are actually created by embroidery. The stitches do not overlay the surface but are inserted under the warp parallel to the weft. Selective choice of the warp creates a secondary pattern over the embroidery yarn unrelated to the figures formed by the latter. One example shows two such independent patterns on opposite faces of an area with the original weft completely hidden between them.

Miscellaneous Techniques: A number of special techniques or devices are employed only occasionally or for some particular purpose. As is true of most weaving processes, a description without detailed illustrations is almost wasted effort, so only a few of these special techniques will be mentioned, without attempting to explain fully the methods used.

Tubular weaving is a term applied to a group of belts and straps in which the weft, in passing the warps, forms a spiral so that the finished product is in the form of a flattened tube. Almost invariably, these have warp patterns with the pattern yarns carried along inside the tube and brought to the outer surface when needed. If the pattern units are spaced with plain weave areas and the pattern warps do not shunt too frequently from one side to the other, the product is quite round in section. Where the pattern warps are used continuously and are frequently shifted from one side to the other, the result is a flat strong strap with rounded hollow edges. This latter, popular in late Inca times, was commonly used for coca bag straps and is still made in parts of Peru, Bolivia, and Chile. However, where a bold pattern was created with solid color areas, the fabric is virtually a double cloth woven with a single continuous weft.

Another tubular construction, but basically distinctive, appears as a finish on warp end loops. In these cases, the insertion of the weft does not stop at the heading cord or rod, if one was used, but is continued around it. Actually, the original heading cord must have been removed to provide working room. The final result is a tubular warp end finish, seldom over a quarter of an inch in diameter; yet, in spite of the small size, one finds carefully executed weft patterns in them.

Other special edgings, such as narrow woven ribbons with fringe, were created by carrying the weft out around one or more temporary warps just as fringes are made on power looms today. Late fabrics from the North Coast have loose spun weft so the finished fringe consists of open loops. The earlier Paracas Necropolis examples are of two-ply weft which has been uniformly over-spun in the doubling so that after the temporary warps are removed each loop closes or twists shut. This, too, is still standard procedure for modern fringes of the same type and calls for carefully prepared yarn.

A rather common practice which sometimes leads to misunderstanding was the combination of several techniques in one fabric. A number of Late period shirts from the South Coast were set up in the looms with interlocked warp border units at each end, with the warp between them spaced in groups. When the weft was inserted, it remained exposed where it crossed the spaces between warp groups and this exposed yarn was, in turn, used as warp for the construction of tapestry rows so that a tapestry-on-weft was created. The same procedure is found in small bags from Nazca in which rows of fine warp pattern parallel the weft of such tapestry rows. Nearly identical specimens have rows of fine interlocked warp patterns instead of the tapestry rows; at least, that is what they appear to be.

A few examples of looped pile weave shirts of cotton have been found. The outer surface of the one in the Museum collection has rows of inch-long loops formed by drawing out a supplementary weft yarn from between each warp of one shed. The regularity of the loops implies the use of a gauge rod or stick and as the loop rows are well spaced with plain weave, it is clear that the objective was a shaggy-surfaced fabric which would not be too warm for comfort.

Looped pile of wool is extremely rare. An unrelated type of wool "pile" occurs in extremely coarse, heavy, Late period, shirts and shawls (?) from northern Chile. They are warp-faced fabrics in which tufts of alpaca wool were wrapped twice about every other warp in each alternate shed as the weft was laid in. The free ends of each tuft were loosely twisted and are sometimes about ten inches long. A finished garment is about as handsome as a mangy bearskin, but is probably much warmer, if the American Museum specimen, weighing twelve pounds, is typical. One has only to experience the great diurnal temperature changes in the interior of the Atacama Desert to understand the reason for such heavy fabrics.

The only compact and patterned pile is a non-loom product. Brightly colored spun wool yarns are caught in a tightly knotted web at each knot, and are trimmed off evenly a quarter of an inch or less above the surface. The ends, when untwisted, form a soft pile of good quality, completely hiding the base fabric. Actually, the technique had only a limited application in hats, headbands, and bags, most of which date from the period of Tiahuanaco expansion.

If, as it appears, the foundation for this pile was usually made by knotting various cords together, it differs from the bulk of the knotted and looped Peruvian products which were made with a single element. In these, a number of techniques were used; the commonest in most periods was netting, because of its use in fishing nets. It also had other, more refined application as in very delicate lace-like hair nets. Knitting and crocheting, the single element techniques most common today, were not used, which is rather surprising when one observes how both have been accepted since the conquest. The somewhat misleading term "needle knitting," used in reports on Peruvian textiles, refers to an embroidery stitch. Although it duplicates the turns and loops of knitting, it is not made by interlocking one loop with another. The direction of build-up is opposite to that in knitting and is accomplished by drawing the end of the yarn, threaded in a needle, through the necessary turns. Maximum perfection of this process is found in the "three dimensional needle knitting" of the Paracas Necropolis period: small, delicate, multicolored, elaborate figures in the round which must be seen to be believed.

Utilization of multiple elements, in braiding or plaiting, is found most commonly in slings, and ropes, and to a lesser degree in flat bands. As in weaving, nearly every conceivable elaboration was developed beyond the dictates of necessity. Anyone interested in plaiting should find in the Peruvian examples much more that is worthy of study than has yet been described.

In the preceding comments, the finished fabrics have been mentioned only incidentally. In view of the wide range of techniques, it is surprising to find such a limited range of loom products in terms of their use.

At the time of the conquest, a well-dressed Inca man might wear sandals, a loin cloth, a knee-length poncho shirt, a belt, a rectangular shawl or cape, and a headdress or headband. Lacking any form of pockets, he carried his chewing coca in a small cloth bag—a minimum of six separately woven fabrics, each created for its specific purpose and none cut from a larger piece.

His wife, if equally well dressed, might have five fabrics in her costume: a rectangular mantle worn wrapped around the body reaching from the shoulders to the ankles, a belt, a shawl similar to the man's, a headband, and a kerchief used for various purposes but mainly to carry things.

The number of items per person does not seem ever to have been appreciably larger. Marked regional and period variations of style, because of the absence of tailoring and the limitations of shaped weaving, are observable mainly in the application of structural or decorative techniques. Thus we find that almost every technique was at one time or another employed to some degree in every article of clothing.

No one has so far secured figures showing the ratio of garments to other textiles. A guess of ninety-five per cent may well be conservative and, if this seems surprising, we must remember that items common in our culture, such as blankets and rugs, were virtually unknown. Past and present evidence indicates that many people slept in their clothes and had little other than mats for their beds. Perhaps next in number were the outer wrappings for the dead and these, like other fabrics for miscellaneous purposes, were virtually devoid of decorative techniques.

A final comment on the method of designing may be of interest. Lacking paper or any other simple medium for plotting and recording designs, the weaver depended mainly on memory. The artisan visualizing a new design had to formulate and remember all the details of construction as the work progressed. As an alternative, at times the process and details of design were worked out on a sampler. Only a small number of these have been collected and, like so many other aspects of Peruvian weaving, they remain undescribed.

RADIOCARBON DATING

The purpose of these comments is not to review all Carbon 14 dates for South America, but simply to point out what has been and is being done and to offer some suggestions which may prevent misunderstanding. The possibility of using the radiocarbon 14 isotope for age determination rests on the premise that the amount of C 14 in the atmosphere of the earth and in living matter has remained nearly constant for some time. To be constant the rate of production of C 14 in the upper atmosphere must balance off against its rate of disappearance by decomposition and dispersal; and, if age figures are to be accurate, the period of constant or static condition should exceed the age.

Certain unduplicated tests suggest some fluctuation in the C 14 pattern, but most indicate a rather long stable situation. However, the fact that mankind has altered the balance within a hundred years by burning fossil carbon fuels in which the C 14 has completely decomposed is proof that the natural balance can be disturbed.

Theoretically all the C 14 present in all living matter should match in radiation activity, as it derives directly or indirectly from the C 14 of the atmosphere. With death and the cessation of carbon intake and exchange, if the formerly living matter is not dispersed, the radiation count of its C 14 will gradually decrease, while that of the atmosphere is maintained by the constant production of new C 14. By measuring the difference of these two factors, and by knowing the decomposition rate of C 14, the date of death can be computed.

Since this method of age determination was proposed and developed by Libby, Anderson, and Arnold there have been refinements in the laboratory equipment and procedures. These have minimized the possibility of errors and have reduced the plus or minus figures of each measurement, figures based mainly on sampling errors calculated to one standard deviation or sigma. As there is one chance in three that the true age will fall outside the stated plus or minus and one chance in twenty that it will fall outside the span of two sigmas or twice the announced plus or minus, it is statistically inevitable that some of the computed results will be larger or smaller than the actual age. As long as one deals with a small number of tested samples it is difficult to recognize the deviant figures and to judge the magnitude of their deviation.

Further studies of the C 14 in modern and recently living matter have modified the earlier figures for what is called the modern value of C 14. As this newer figure is now used in calculating the age measurements, those made previously must be corrected or re-computed. As such correction does not exceed a few hundred years (for one laboratory it was announced as the addition of 240 to their published mean figures) it has a minimum effect on the larger age measurements and a maximum on the smaller ones.

Another result of the newer techniques and equipment is a reduction in the size of the sample needed. In certain counters three grams of refined carbon are now sufficient. However, the size of the raw sample naturally depends on its yield of refined carbon and this will vary greatly with the substance used and the admixture of impurities or inert matter. In one case ten grams of charcoal may be adequate; in another, fifty or more may be required. In all cases more than the minimum amount is desirable that tests can be repeated if necessary.

At present there are at least thirteen laboratories in which C 14 measurements are being made. Most are run by non-profit organizations and the results are published. Up to the present, most laboratories have issued the lists of their measurements in *Science,* and by common agreement will in the future publish in the American Journal of Science, Radiocarbon Supplement. Commercial laboratories are under no obligations to do more than process samples and return the results to the person who submitted them. The figures may appear in print anywhere, with or without adequate data. Thus when one wishes to gather all the measurements pertinent to the archaeology of any one region, it is necessary to cull through an ever-mounting mass of data, sometimes inadequately annotated, and with need in some cases of the recalculation mentioned. In an attempt to simplify this problem, the Society for American Archaeology has agreed to issue a punch card index covering all archaeological measurements to date and those which will appear during the next five years. This will be very helpful, yet it cannot do more than quote the published data. Evaluation and appraisal of the published data sometimes calls for first-hand or personal knowledge of the material tested, its source, and the circumstances of recovery, all of which may be difficult to obtain.

There are also differences in final results which seem to be related to the types of material tested. An experiment conducted at the Lamont Laboratory of Columbia University in which three radically different organic substances were used, will illustrate this point. These were shell, cattail and other swamp-land plants, and llama fur and skin. They were all contemporary and came from the middle of a dry deposit of Incaic debris at Pachacamac and can with reasonable certainty be dated as 1508 A.D. ± 25 years. The ± 25 represents the maximum time range in which the true date falls.

The samples, listed as L 123 A, B, C in the laboratory records, gave the following results:

The shell, which, from adhering material derived from the organism, was without any doubt freshly collected when discarded, yielded figures more than 3300 years in excess of actual age. A similar discrepancy has been noted when other Peruvian shells have been tested; therefore, for the present, no dates based on marine shells from the Peruvian coast should be accepted. In one measurement the Pachacamac cattail and sedge gave a mean slightly more than twice the known age; in another, a figure 80 per cent over that expected. We cannot use this example as the basis for questioning all dates derived from the C 14 in plants of these species, but we should have data on the effect of environmental differences on different species. Until we have adequate data the dates derived from swamp plants should be used with caution; unless supporting data from other material are available, or if modern examples from the same environment give the expected results. Two measurements of the C 14 in the llama fur and skin gave 450 ± 150 and 500 ± 120 years. These both bracket the known age of 450 ± 25.

The results of this experiment will serve to emphasize the obvious; that more than one measurement is desirable; that materials to be tested must be selected with discretion, and that no archaeological samples should be submitted for testing unless their cultural context is unquestionable, as was the case with the shells.

As might be expected, the majority of South American C 14 dates relate to Andean material, mainly Peruvian, with others distributed from Venezuela to South Chile. In 1951 the results of twenty measurements of sixteen samples were available. By the end of 1956 the total of published samples had risen to fifty. By mid-1959 there are, published and unpublished, about 120 measurements. Among them one finds a number of perplexing problems which may require more field-work and other related measurements and possibly additional basic research on C 14, before we can understand the results.

A single instance will serve to illustrate one of the problems mentioned. Measurement of charcoal published as associated with the oldest pottery in the Viru Valley gave 3800 ± 150 years. Measurements contracted for by Frédéric Engel at the New Zealand laboratory indicate 3800 ± 80 and 3740 ± 100 as ages for material in the upper parts of the preceramic at sites on the Central Coast. These three would suggest that the close of the preceramic period was in the magnitude of 3800 years. Using charcoal which antedated the Viru sample by sufficient time to allow for the formation of a firmly compacted midden deposit of over 45 feet thickness, another Lamont measurement gave 3780 ± 100 on one count and 3860 ± 100 on a second. These figures would indicate that the preceramic period ended about as soon as it started and that the great deposits of debris marking it accumulated at an impossible rate. In contrast seven measurements by Libby imply that the preceramic period might have a total time span of nearly 1300 years. Such discrepancies must have an explanation, but if we cannot find a satisfactory one immediately there is no reason to criticize or reject the method. We simply do not yet have sufficient knowledge of all the factors involved.

In so far as it has been possible, the chronological chart (pp. 82–83) was compiled using C 14 dates. There are reasons to believe that the indicated duration of the Chavín Horizon, particularly on the Central Coast, is too short, and that the period between the Chavín and Tiahuanaco material, in the north at least, is too long.

Unfortunately, no age measurements relating to the

Nomadic Hunters are available. If the association with extinct fauna is valid, the magnitude of their age should be at least eight or ten thousand years, judging from the C 14 dates for Mylodon, horse and hunter remains in the Magellan Strait Region and from similar dates from Mexico and the Southwestern United States.

SELECTED SOURCES

This account has been based on the extensive archaeological bibliography for the Central Andes, on examination of many museum collections, and on unpublished field-work by the authors and others. Virtually no citations have been made in the résumé in view of the fact that many excellent bibliographies exist. The following list of publications is not intended to be a complete bibliography, but contains, rather, some selected suggestions for further reading on the specific topics and regions. Only a few references are given for each division, selected, where possible, because they are written in English, because they are good source material, and because they contain additional bibliography. The references for Part 1, The Setting, and Part 3, Techniques, follow the chapter order. For Part 2, The Central Andes, the sources are cited in terms of major geographical regions, and a few selected topics. Since few field reports are confined to one period or culture, a listing of sources in terms of the major time periods of this account would require considerable duplication.

PART 1

Geography

JAMES, PRESTON E. Latin America. New York, 1942.

Early Migrants

BIRD, JUNIUS B. Antiquity and Migrations of the Early Inhabitants of Patagonia. Geographical Review, vol. 38, no. 2, pp. 250–275, New York, 1938.

—— Excavations in Northern Chile. Anthropological Papers, American Museum of Natural History, vol. 38, part 4, pp. 171–318, New York, 1943.

CARDICH, M. AUGUSTO. Los Yacimientos de Lauricocha, Peru. Revista del Centro Argentino de Estudios Prehistoricos. Buenos Aires, 1959.

HRDLIČKA, ALEŠ. Early Man in South America. Bureau of American Ethnology, Bulletin 52, Washington, 1912.

SULLIVAN, LOUIS R. AND MILO HELLMAN. The Punin Calvarium. Anthropological Papers, American Museum of Natural History, vol. 23, part 7, pp. 309–337, New York, 1925.

TSCHOPIK, HARRY, JR. Some Notes on Rock Shelter Sites near Huancayo, Peru. American Antiquity, vol. 12, no. 2, pp. 73–80, Menasha, 1946.

Plant Domestication

CUTLER, HUGH C. Races of Maize in South America. Botanical Museum Leaflets, Harvard University, vol. 12, no. 8, pp. 257–291, Cambridge, 1946.

HUTCHINSON, J. B., R. A. SILOW AND S. G. STEPHENS. The Evolution of Gossypium and the Differentiation of the Cultivated Cottons. Oxford University Press, London, 1947.

MANGELSDORF, P. C., AND C. EARLE SMITH, JR. New Archaeological Evidence of Evolution in Maize. Botanical Museum Leaflets, Harvard University, vol. 13, no. 8, pp. 213–247, Cambridge, 1949.

MANGELSDORF, PAUL C., AND R. G. REEVES. The Origin of Corn. Botanical Museum Leaflets, Harvard University, vol. 18, no. 7, pp. 329–356, Cambridge, 1959.

SAUER, CARL. American Agricultural Origins: A Consideration of Nature and Culture. *In* Essays in Anthropology, presented to A. L. Kroeber, pp. 279–297, Berkeley, 1936.

TOWLE, MARGARET ASHLEY. Description and Identification of Plant Remains from Certain Sites in the Virú Valley. *In* Cultural Stratigraphy in the Virú Valley, W. D. Strong and Clifford Evans, Jr. Columbia Studies in

Archaeology and Ethnology, vol. 4, Columbia University, New York, 1952.

—— Plant Remains from a Peruvian Mummy Bundle. Botanical Museum Leaflets, Harvard University, vol. 15, no. 9, pp. 223–246, Cambridge, 1952.

WHITAKER, THOMAS W., AND JUNIUS B. BIRD. Identification and Significance of the Cucurbit Materials from Huaca Prieta, Peru. American Museum Novitates, no. 1426, New York, 1949.

Southern Hunters

STEWARD, JULIAN (Editor). Handbook of South American Indians, Volume 1, The Marginal Tribes. Bureau of American Ethnology, Bulletin 143, Washington, 1946.

Tropical Agriculture

RADIN, PAUL. Indians of South America. New York, 1942.

STEWARD, JULIAN (Editor). Handbook of South American Indians, Volume 3, The Tropical Forest Tribes. Bureau of American Ethnology, Bulletin 143, Washington, 1948.

—— Handbook of South American Indians, Volume 4, The Circum-Caribbean Tribes. Bureau of American Ethnology, Bulletin 143, Washington, 1948.

Lowland Archaeology

EVANS, CLIFFORD, JR., AND BETTY J. MEGGERS. Preliminary Results of Archaeological Investigations at the Mouth of the Amazon. American Antiquity, vol. 16, no. 1, pp. 1–9, Menasha, 1950.

CRUXENT, J. M., AND IRVING ROUSE. An Archeological Chronology of Venezuela. Vol. 1. Social Science Monographs 6, Pan American Union, Washington, D.C., 1958. Vol. 2, Illustrations, 1959.

HOWARD, GEORGE D. Prehistoric Ceramic Styles in Lowland South America, their Distribution and History.

Yale University Publications in Anthropology, no. 37, New Haven, 1947.

KIDDER, ALFRED, 2ND. Archaeology of Northwestern Venezuela. Papers, Peabody Museum of American Archaeology and Ethnology, vol. 26, no. 1, Cambridge, 1944.

LATHRAP, DONALD W. The Cultural Sequence at Yarinacocha, Eastern Peru. American Antiquity, vol. 23, no. 4, pp. 379–388, Menasha, 1958.

MEGGERS, BETTY J., AND CLIFFORD EVANS. Archaeological Evidence of a Prehistoric Migration from the Rio Napo to the Mouth of Amazon. Social Science Bulletin, University of Arizona, no. 27, pp. 9–19, Tucson, 1958.

NORDENSKIÖLD, ERLAND. L'Archéologie du Bassin de l'Amazone. Ars Americana, vol. 1, pp. 1–67, Paris, 1930.

OSGOOD, CORNELIUS AND GEORGE D. HOWARD. An Archeological Survey of Venezuela. Yale University Publications in Anthropology, no. 27, New Haven, 1943.

PALMATARY, HELEN. Tapajó Pottery. Ethnologiska Studier, no. 8, pp. 1–136, Göteborg, 1939.

Andean Farmers

STEWARD, JULIAN (Editor). Handbook of South American Indians, Volume 2, The Andean Civilizations. Bureau of American Ethnology, Bulletin 143, Washington, 1946.

Northern Andes

BENNETT, WENDELL C. Archeological Regions of Colombia: A Ceramic Survey. Yale University Publications in Anthropology, no. 30, New Haven, 1944.

COLLIER, DONALD AND JOHN MURRA. Survey and Excavations in Southern Ecuador. Anthropological Series, Field Museum of Natural History, vol. 35, pp. 9–103, Chicago, 1943.

ESTRADA, EMILIO. Ultimas Civilizaciones Pre-Históricas de la Cuenca del Rio Guayas. Publicacion del Museo Víctor Emilio Estrada, no. 2, Ecuador, 1957.

—— Los Huancavilcas, Ultimas Civilizaciones Pre-Históricas de la Costa del Guayas. Publicacion del Museo Víctor Emilio Estrada, no. 3, Guayaquil, 1957.

—— Prehistoria de Manabi. Publicacion del Museo Víctor Emilio Estrada, no. 4, Guayaquil, 1957.

EVANS, CLIFFORD, JR. AND BETTY J. MEGGERS. Preliminary Report on Archaeological Investigation in the Guayas Basin, Ecuador. Cuadernos de Historia y Arqueología, año 4, vol. 4, no. 12, pp. 308–336, Ecuador, 1954.

EVANS, CLIFFORD, BETTY MEGGERS AND EMILIO ESTRADA. Cultura Valdivia. Publicacion del Museo Víctor Emilio Estrada, no. 6, Guayaquil, 1959.

REICHEL-DOLMATOFF, GERARDO. Investigaciones Arqueológicas en la Sierra Nevada de Santà Marta. Revista Colombiana de Antropologia, vol. 2, pp. 147–205, Bogotá, 1954.

REICHEL-DOLMATOFF, GERARDO, AND ALICIA. Momíl, Excavaciones en el Sinú. Revista Colombiana de Antropologia, vol. 5, pp. 109–333, Bogotá, 1956.

Southern Andes

BENNETT, WENDELL C., E. F. BLEILER AND F. H. SOMMER. Northwest Argentine Archeology. Yale University Publications in Anthropology, no. 38, New Haven, 1948.

BIRD, JUNIUS B. Excavations in Northern Chile. Anthropological Papers, American Museum of Natural History, vol. 38, part 4, pp. 171–318, New York, 1943.

BOMAN, ERIC. Antiquités de la Région Andine de la République Argentine et du Désert d'Atacama. 2 vols., Paris, 1908.

GONZALEZ, ALBERTO REX. Contextos culturales y cronología relativa en el área Central del N. O. Argentino. Anales de Arqueología y Etnología, vol. 11, pp. 7–32, Mendoza, 1955.

—— La cultura Condorhuasi del Noroeste Argentino. Runa, vol. 7, pt. 1, pp. 37–86, Buenos Aires, 1956.

MONTELL, GÖSTA. An Archaeological Collection from the Río Loa Valley, Atacama. Oslo Etnografiske Museums, Skrifter, vol. 5, hefte 1, pp. 1–46, Oslo, 1926.

PART 2

Central Andes General

BENNETT, WENDELL C. The Archeology of the Central Andes. *In* Handbook of South American Indians, vol. 2, pp. 61–147, Bureau of American Ethnology, Bulletin 143, Washington, 1946.

BENNETT, WENDELL C. (Editor). A Reappraisal of Peruvian Archaeology. Society for American Archaeology, Memoir No. 4, Menasha, 1948.

BUSHNELL, G. H. S. Peru. London, 1956.

ENGEL, FREDÉRIC. Sites et Etablissements sans Céramique de la Côte Péruvienne. Journal de la Société des Américanistes, Nouvelle Série, tome 46, pp. 67–155, Paris, 1957.

—— Algunos Datos con Referencia a los Sitios Preceramicos de la Costa Peruana. Arqueologicas, 3. Publicaciones del Instituto de Investigaciones Antropologicas. Museo Nacional de Antropologia y Arqueologia, Lima, 1958.

KROEBER, A. L. Peruvian Archeology in 1942. Viking Fund Publications in Anthropology, no. 4, New York, 1944.

MEAD, CHARLES W. Old Civilizations of Inca Land. Handbook Series, American Museum of Natural History, no. 11, New York, 1924.

MEANS, PHILIP A. Ancient Civilizations of the Andes. New York, 1931.

Dating

BIRD, JUNIUS. Preceramic Cultures in Chicama and Virú. Society for American Archaeology, Memoir No. 4, pp. 21–28, Menasha, 1948.

—— South American Radiocarbon Dates. *In* Radio Carbon Dating, Memoirs, Society for American Archaeology, no. 8, pp. 37–49, Salt Lake City, 1951.

KUBLER, GEORGE. Towards Absolute Time: Guano Archaeology. Society for American Archaeology, Memoir No. 4, pp. 29–50, Menasha, 1948.

LIBBY, WILLARD F. Radiocarbon Dating. Chicago, 1952.

ROWE, JOHN H. Absolute Chronology in the Andean Area. American Antiquity, vol. 10, no. 3, pp. 265–284, Menasha, 1945.

WILLEY, GORDON R. Horizon Styles and Pottery Traditions in Peruvian Archaeology. American Antiquity, vol. 11, no. 1, pp. 49–56, Menasha, 1945.

General and Illustrative Sources

BAESSLER, ARTHUR. Ancient Peruvian Art. 4 vols., Berlin and New York, 1902–3.

BENNETT, WENDELL C. Ancient Arts of the Andes. Museum of Modern Art, New York, 1954.

DOERING, HEINRICH U. The Art of Ancient Peru. New York, 1952.

KELEMEN, PÁL. Medieval American Art. 2 vols., New York, 1943.

LEHMANN, WALTER AND HEINRICH DOERING. The Art of Old Peru. New York, 1924.

MASON, J. ALDEN. The Ancient Civilizations of Peru. Pelican Books, A395, Edinburgh, 1957.

MUELLE, JORGE C. AND CAMILIO BLAS. Muestrario de Arte Peruano Precolombino. Revista del Museo Nacional, vol. 7, pp. 163–280, Lima, 1938.

SCHMIDT, MAX. Kunst und Kultur von Peru. Berlin, 1929.

North Coast of Peru

BENNETT, WENDELL C. Archaeology of the North Coast of Peru. Anthropological Papers, American Museum of Natural History, vol. 37, part 1, pp. 1–153, New York, 1939.

BIRD, JUNIUS. Preceramic Cultures in Chicoma and Virú. In A Reappraisal of Peruvian Archaeology. Memoir, Society for American Archaeology, no. 4, pp. 21–29, 1948.

COLLIER, DONALD. Cultural Chronology and Change, as Reflected in the Ceramics of the Virú Valley, Peru. Fieldiana: Anthropology, Chicago Natural History Museum, vol. 43, Chicago, 1955.

FORD, JAMES A., AND GORDON R. WILLEY. Surface Survey of the Virú Valley, Peru. Anthropological Papers, American Museum of Natural History, vol. 43, pt. 1, New York, 1949.

KROEBER, A. L. The Uhle Pottery Collections from Moche. University of California Publications in American Archaeology and Ethnology, vol. 21, pp. 191–234, Berkeley, 1925.

—— Archaeological Explorations in Peru. Part I: Ancient Pottery from Trujillo. Anthropology, Memoirs, Field Museum of Natural History, vol. 2, no. 1, pp. 1–43, Chicago, 1926.

—— Archaeological Explorations in Peru. Part II: The Northern Coast. Anthropology, Memoirs, Field Museum of Natural History, vol. 2, no. 2, pp. 47–116, Chicago, 1930.

LARCO HOYLE, RAFAEL. Los Mochicas. 2 vols., Lima, 1938–1939.

—— Los Cupisniques. Lima, 1941.

—— A Culture Sequence for the North Coast of Peru. *In* Handbook of South American Indians, vol. 2, pp. 149–176, Bureau of American Ethnology, Bulletin 143, Washington, 1946.

—— Cronología Arqueológica del Norte del Perú. Buenos Aires, 1948.

STRONG, WILLIAM DUNCAN, AND CLIFFORD EVANS, JR. Cultural Stratigraphy in the Virú Valley, Northern Peru. Columbia Studies in Archaeology and Ethnology, Columbia University, vol. 4, New York, 1952.

TELLO, JULIO C. Arte Antiguo Peruano. Inca, vol. 2, Lima, 1938.

WILLEY, GORDON R. Prehistoric Settlement Patterns in the Virú Valley, Peru. Bulletin, Bureau of American Ethnology, no. 155, Washington, 1953.

Central Coast of Peru

GAYTON, A. H. The Uhle Collections from Nievería. University of California Publications in American Archaeology and Ethnology, vol. 21, no. 8, pp. 305–329, Berkeley, 1927.

KROEBER, A. L. The Uhle Pottery Collections from Supe. University of California Publications in American Archaeology and Ethnology, vol. 21, no. 6, pp. 235–264, Berkeley, 1925.

——— The Uhle Pottery Collections from Chancay. University of California Publications in American Archaeology and Ethnology, vol. 21, no. 7, pp. 265–304, Berkeley, 1926.

STRONG, WILLIAM DUNCAN. The Uhle Pottery Collections from Ancon. University of California Publications in American Archaeology and Ethnology, vol. 21, no. 4, pp. 135–190, Berkeley, 1925.

STRONG, WILLIAM DUNCAN, GORDON R. WILLEY AND JOHN M. CORBETT. Archeological Studies in Peru, 1941–1942. Columbia Studies in Archaeology and Ethnology, vol. 1, New York, 1943.

UHLE, MAX. Pachacamac. Philadelphia, 1903.

South Coast of Peru

CARRIONÓ CACHOT, REBECA. Paracas Cultural Elements. Lima, 1949.

ENGEL, FRÉDÉRIC. Early Sites in the Pisco Valley of Peru: Tambo Colorado. American Antiquity, vol. 23, pp. 34–45, Menasha, 1957.

GAYTON, A. H. AND A. L. KROEBER. The Uhle Pottery Collections from Nazca. University of California Publications in American Archaeology and Ethnology, vol. 24, no. 1, pp. 1–46, Berkeley, 1927.

KROEBER, A. L. Archaeological Explorations in Peru. Part IV: Cañete Valley. Anthropology, Memoirs, Field Museum of Natural History, vol. 2, part 4, pp. 221–273, Chicago, 1937.

——— Paracas Cavernas and Chavín. University of California Publications in American Archaeology and Ethnology, vol. 40, no. 8, pp. 313–348, Berkeley, 1953.

KROEBER, A. L. AND WILLIAM DUNCAN STRONG. The Uhle Collections from Chincha. University of California Publications in American Archaeology and Ethnology, vol. 21, no. 1, pp. 1–54, Berkeley, 1924.

—— The Uhle Pottery Collections from Ica. University of California Publications in American Archaeology and Ethnology, vol. 21, no. 3, pp. 95–133, Berkeley, 1924.

STRONG, WILLIAM DUNCAN. Paracas, Nazca, and Tiahuanacoid Cultural Relationships in South Coastal Peru. Memoir 13, Society for American Archaeology, Salt Lake City, Utah.

North Highlands of Peru

BENNETT, WENDELL C. Chavín Stone Carving. Yale Anthropological Studies, vol. 3, pp. 1–9, New Haven, 1942.

—— The North Highlands of Peru. Anthropological Papers, American Museum of Natural History, vol. 39, part 1, New York, 1944.

McCOWN, THEODORE D. Pre-Incaic Huamachuco: Survey and Excavations in the Region of Huamachuco and Cajabamba. University of California Publications in American Archaeology and Ethnology, vol. 39, no. 4, pp. 223–400, Berkeley, 1945.

TELLO, JULIO C. Andean Civilization: Some Problems of Peruvian Archaeology. Proceedings, 23d International Congress of Americanists, New York, 1928, pp. 259–290, New York, 1930.

—— Discovery of the Chavín Culture in Peru. American Antiquity, vol. 9, no. 1, pp. 135–160, Menasha, 1943.

—— Arqueologia del Valle de Casma Culturas: Chavín, Santa o Huaylas Yunga y Sub-Chimú informe de los trabajas de la Expedicíon Arqueológica al Marañon de 1937. Editorial San Marco, Lima, Peru, 1956.

Central Highlands of Peru

BENNETT, WENDELL C. Excavations at Wari, Ayacucho, Peru. Yale University Publications in Anthropology, no. 49, New Haven, 1953.

BINGHAM, HIRAM. Machu Picchu, a Citadel of the Incas. New Haven, 1930.

FEJOS, PAUL. Archeological Explorations in the Cordillera,

Vilcabamba, Southeastern Peru. Viking Fund Publications in Anthropology, no. 3, New York, 1944.

Rowe, John H. An Introduction to the Archaeology of Cuzco. Papers, Peabody Museum of American Archaeology and Ethnology, vol. 27, no. 2, pp. 3–69, Cambridge, 1944.

South Highlands of Peru and Bolivia

Bandelier, Adolph F. The Islands of Titicaca and Koati. New York, 1910.

Bennett, Wendell C. Excavations at Tiahuanaco. Anthropological Papers, American Museum of Natural History, vol. 34, part 3, pp. 359–494, New York, 1934.

—— Excavations in Bolivia. Anthropological Papers, American Museum of Natural History, vol. 35, part 4, pp. 329–507, New York, 1936.

Kidder, Alfred, 2nd. Some Early Sites in the Northern Lake Titicaca Basin. Papers, Peabody Museum of American Archaeology and Ethnology, vol. 27, no. 1, pp. 3–48, Cambridge, 1943.

Posnansky, Arthur. Tihuanacu. The Cradle of American Man. 2 vols., New York, 1946.

Rydén, Stig. Archaeological Researches in the Highlands of Bolivia. Göteborg, 1947.

—— Andean Excavations I. The Tiahuanaco Era East of Lake Titicaca. The Ethnographical Museum of Sweden, Monograph Series, Publication no. 4, Stockholm, 1957.

—— Andean Excavations II. Tupuraya and Cayhuasi: Two Tiahuanaco Sites. The Ethnographical Museum of Sweden, Monograph Series, Publication no. 6, Stockholm, 1959.

Tschopik, Marion H. Some Notes on the Archaeology of the Department of Puno, Peru. Papers, Peabody Museum of American Archaeology and Ethnology, vol. 27, no. 3, pp. 3–57, Cambridge, 1946.

Quipu and Calculation

Locke, L. Leland. The Ancient Quipu or Peruvian Knot-Record. New York, 1923.

NORDENSKIÖLD, ERLAND. Calculations with Years and Months in the Peruvian Quipus. Comparative Ethnographical Studies, vol. 6, part 2, Göteborg, 1925.

—— The Secret of the Peruvian Quipus. Comparative Ethnographical Studies, vol. 6, part 1, Göteborg, 1925.

WASSÉN, HENRY. The Ancient Peruvian Abacus. Comparative Ethnographical Studies, vol. 9, pp. 189–205, Göteborg, 1931.

Historic Period

KUBLER, GEORGE. The Quechua in the Colonial World. *In* Handbook of South American Indians, vol. 2, pp. 331–410, Bureau of American Ethnology, Bulletin 143, Washington, 1946.

MEANS, PHILIP AINSWORTH. Fall of the Inca Empire. New York, 1932.

MISHKIN, BERNARD. The Contemporary Quechua. *In* Handbook of South American Indians, vol. 2, pp. 411–476, Bureau of American Ethnology, Bulletin 143, Washington, 1946.

ROWE, JOHN HOWLAND. Inca Culture at the Time of the Spanish Conquest. *In* Handbook of South American Indians, vol. 2, pp. 183–330, Bureau of American Ethnology, Bulletin 143, Washington, 1946.

—— The Kingdom of Chimor. Acta Americana, vol. 6, no. 1, pp. 26–59, Mexico, 1948.

TSCHOPIK, HARRY, JR. The Aymara. *In* Handbook of South American Indians, vol. 2, pp. 501–574, Bureau of American Ethnology, Bulletin 143, Washington, 1946.

PART 3: TECHNIQUES

Ceramics

HARCOURT, RAOUL D' AND MARIE D' HARCOURT. La Céramique Ancienne du Pérou. Paris, 1924.

LINNÉ, S. The Technique of South American Ceramics. Göteborg, 1925.

TELLO, JULIO C. Arte Antiguo Peruano. Inca, vol. 2, Lima, 1938.

TSCHOPIK, HARRY, JR. An Andean Ceramic Tradition in Historical Perspective. American Antiquity, vol. 15, no. 3, pp. 196–218, Menasha, 1950.

Metalwork

ANTZE, GUSTAVE. Metallarbeiten aus dem Nördischen Peru. *In* Mitteilungen aus dem Museum für Volkerkunde, 15, Hamburg, 1930.

BERGSØE, PAUL. The Metallurgy and Technology of Gold and Platinum among the Pre-Colombian Indians. Ingeniørvidenskabelige Skrifter, Nr. A 44, Copenhagen, 1937.

—— The Gilding Process and the Metallurgy of Copper and Lead among the Pre-Colombian Indians. Ingeniørvidenskabelige Skrifter, Nr. A 46, Copenhagen, 1938.

CALEY, EARLE R. AND DUDLEY T. EASBY, JR. The Smelting of Sulfide Ores of Copper in Pre-Conquest Peru. American Antiquity, vol. 25, no. 1, pp. 59–65. Menasha, 1959.

EASBY, DUDLEY T., JR. Los Vasos Retratos de Metal del Peru: ¿Cómo fueron elaborados? Revista del Museo Nacional, tom. 24, pp. 137–153, Lima, 1955.

—— Sahagún y los Orfebres Precolombinos de México. Sobretiro de los Anales del Instituto de Antropología y Historia, vol. 9, pp. 85–117, Mexico, 1957.

—— Ancient American Goldsmiths. Natural History, vol. 65, no. 8, pp. 401–409, New York, 1956.

—— Orfebrería y Orfebres Precolombinos. Anales del Instituto de Arte Americano, vol. 9, pp. 9–26, Buenos Aires, 1956.

LOTHROP, SAMUEL K. Gold and Silver from Southern Peru and Bolivia. Journal, Royal Anthropological Institute of Great Britain and Ireland, vol. 67, pp. 305–325, London, 1937.

—— Coclé, An Archaeological Study of Central Panama. Part I, Historical Background. Excavations at the Sitio Conte. Artifacts and Ornaments. Memoirs, Peabody

Museum of Archaeology and Ethnology, Harvard University, vol. 7, Cambridge, 1937.

—— Inca Treasure as Depicted by Spanish Historians. Southwest Museum, Los Angeles, 1938.

—— Gold Ornaments of Chavín Style from Chongoyape, Peru. American Antiquity, vol. 6, no. 3, pp. 250–262, Menasha, 1941.

MATHEWSON, C. H. A Metallographic Description of Some Ancient Peruvian Bronzes from Machu Picchu. American Journal of Science, vol. 40, no. 240, 1915.

MEAD, CHARLES W. Prehistoric Bronze in South America. Anthropological Papers, American Museum of Natural History, vol. 12, pp. 15–52, New York, 1915.

NORDENSKIÖLD, ERLAND. The Copper and Bronze Ages in South America. Comparative Ethnographical Studies, vol. 4, pp. 1–196, Göteborg, 1921.

PEREZ DE BARRADAS, José. Orfebrería Prehispánica de Colombia; Estilo Calima. 2 vols., Text and Plates, Madrid, 1954.

—— Orfebrería Prehispánica de Colombia; Estilos Tolima y Muisca. 2 vols., Text and Plates, Madrid, 1958.

RIVET, P. AND H. ARSANDAUX. La Métallurgie en Amérique Précolombienne. Travaux et Mémoires de l'Institut d'Ethnologie, vol. 39, Paris, 1946.

ROOT, WILLIAM C. Metallurgy. Handbook of South American Indians, Vol. 5. Bulletin 143, Bureau of American Ethnology, pp. 205–225, Washington, 1949.

—— The Metallurgy of the Southern Coast of Peru. American Antiquity, vol. 15, no. 1, pp. 10–37, Menasha, 1949.

—— The Metallurgy of the Southern Coast of Peru. Ms.

Textiles

BAILEY, TRUMAN. Native Arts Shape the Native Future. Natural History, American Museum of Natural History, vol. 53, no. 6, New York, June, 1944.

—— The Manual Industries of Peru. The Museum of Modern Art, New York [no date].

BIRD, JUNIUS B. A Pre-Spanish Peruvian Ikat. Bulletin,

Needle and Bobbin Club, vol. 31, nos. 1 and 2, pp. 73–77, New York, 1947.

BIRD, JUNIUS, AND LOUISA BELLINGER. Paracas Fabrics and Nazca Needlework. Textile Museum, Washington, 1954.

CARRIÓN CACHOT, REBECA. La indumentaria en la antigua cultura de Paracas. Wira Kocha, vol. 1, no. 1, pp. 37–86, 1931.

CRAWFORD, M. D. C. Peruvian Textiles. Anthropological Papers, American Museum of Natural History, vol. 12, part 3, pp. 53–104, New York, 1915.

—— Peruvian Fabrics. Anthropological Papers, American Museum of Natural History, vol. 12, part 4, pp. 105–191, New York, 1916.

FESTER, G. A. Einige Farbstoffe Süd Amerikanischer Kulturvolker. Isis, vol. 44, nos. 1 and 2, pp. 13–16, 1952. (English translation: Some Dyes of the Ancient South American Civilizations. Dyestuffs, Bulletin National Aniline Division Allied Chemical and Dye Corporation, vol. 4, no. 9, New York, 1954.

HARCOURT, RAOUL D'. Les Textiles Anciens du Pérou et leurs Techniques. Paris, 1934.

LEVILLIER, JEAN. Paracas, a Contribution to the Study of Pre-Incaic Textiles in Ancient Peru. Paris, 1928.

MEANS, PHILIP A. Peruvian Textiles, Examples of the Pre-Incaic Period. New York, 1930.

MONTELL, GÖSTA. Dress and Ornaments in Ancient Peru. Göteborg, 1929.

O'NEALE, LILA M. Tejidos del Período Primitivo de Paracas. Revista del Museo Nacional, vol. 1, no. 2, pp. 60–80, Lima, 1932.

—— Peruvian "Needleknitting." American Anthropologist, new series, vol. 35, pp. 405–430, 1933.

—— A Peruvian Multicolored Patchwork. American Anthropologist, new series, vol. 35, pp. 87–94, 1933.

—— Peruvian Needle Knitting. American Anthropologist, n. s., vol. 36, no. 3, pp. 405–430, 1934.

—— Pequeñas Prendas Ceremoniales de Paracas. Revista del Museo Nacional, vol. 4, no. 2, pp. 245–266, Lima, 1935.

—— Wide-loom Fabrics of the Early Nazca Period. *In* Essays in Anthropology, presented to A. L. Kroeber, pp. 215–228, Berkeley, 1936.

—— Archaeological Explorations in Peru. Part III: Textiles of the Early Nazca Period. Anthropology, Memoirs, Field Museum of Natural History, vol. 2, no. 3, pp. 119–218, Chicago, 1937.

—— Textile Periods in Ancient Peru. II: Paracas Caverns and the Grand Necropolis. University of California Publications in American Archaeology and Ethnology, vol. 39, no. 2, pp. 143–202, Berkeley, 1942.

—— Mochica (Early Chimu) and other Peruvian Twill Fabrics. Southwestern Journal of Anthropology, University of New Mexico, vol. 2, no. 3, Albuquerque, 1946.

—— Weaving. *In* Handbook of South American Indians. Vol. 5. Bureau of American Ethnology, pp. 97–138, Washington, 1949.

—— Textiles. *In* Early Ancón and Early Supe Culture, G. R. Willey and J. M. Corbett, pp. 84–130, New York, 1954.

O'Neale, Lila M. and Bonnie Jean Clark. Textile Periods in Ancient Peru. III: The Gauze Weaves. University of California, Publications in American Archaeology and Ethnology, vol. 40, no. 4, pp. 143–222, Berkeley, 1948.

O'Neale, Lila M. and A. L. Kroeber. Textile Periods in Ancient Peru. I. University of California, Publications in American Archaeology and Ethnology, vol. 28, no. 2, pp. 23–56, Berkeley, 1930.

O'Neale, Lila M., and others. Chincha Plain-Weave Cloths. Anthropological Records, University of California, vol. 9, no. 2, Berkeley and Los Angeles, 1949.

Osborne, Carolyn M. Shaped Breechcloths from Peru. Anthropological Records, University of California, vol. 13, no. 2, Berkeley and Los Angeles, 1950.

Stafford, Cora Elder. Paracas Embroideries. New York, 1941.

Tello, Julio C. Paracas. Lima, 1959.

VanStan, Ina. Peruvian Domestic Fabrics from Supe: a Study of the Uhle Collection of Painted Cloths. Notes in Anthropology, Florida State University, vol. 1, no. 3, Tallahassee, 1955.

—— Problems in Pre-Columbian Textile Classification. Florida State University Studies, no. 29, Tallahassee, 1958.

YACOVLEFF, E. AND J. G. MUELLE. Un Fardo Funerario de Paracas. Revista del Museo Nacional, vol. 3, nos. 1 and 2, pp. 63–163, Lima, 1934.

ZIMMERN, NATHALIE HERMAN. The Tapestries of Colonial Peru. Brooklyn Museum Journal, 1943–1944, pp. 25–52, New York, 1944.

INDEX

American Museum Science Books are a series of paperback books in the life and earth sciences published for The American Museum of Natural History by the Natural History Press, a division of Doubleday & Company, Inc.

*Asimov, Isaac *A Short History of Biology* B6
*Bennett, Wendell and Junius Bird *Andean Culture History* B9
*Bohannan, Paul *Africa and Africans* B8
*Branley, Franklyn M. *Exploration of the Moon* B1
 Drucker, Philip *Indians of the Northwest Coast* B3
 Hartley, W. G. *How to Use a Microscope* B10
*Lanyon, Wesley E. *Biology of Birds* B2
 Linton, David *Photographing Nature* B7
 Lowie, Robert *Indians of the Plains* B4
 Oliver, Douglas *Invitation to Anthropology* B5

*Also available in a Natural History Press hardcover edition.